PARADOX FOR WINDOWS MADE EASY

Ed Jones

Osborne **McGraw-Hill**

Berkeley New York St. Louis San Francisco
Auckland Bogotá Hamburg London Madrid
Mexico City Milan Montreal New Delhi Panama City
Paris São Paulo Singapore Sydney
Tokyo Toronto

Osborne **McGraw-Hill**
2600 Tenth Street
Berkeley, California 94710
U.S.A.

For information on translations or book distributors outside of the
U.S.A., please write to Osborne **McGraw-Hill** at the above address.

Paradox for Windows Made Easy

1234567890 DOC 99876543

ISBN 0-07-881767-6

Publisher Kenna S. Wood	**Proofreader** Jeff Barash
Acquisitions Editor Elizabeth Fisher	**Indexer** Phil Roberts
Associate Editor Scott Rogers	**Computer Designer** Marcela V. Hancik
Technical Editor David Nesbitt	**Illustrator** Susie C. Kim
Project Editor Wendy Rinaldi	**Cover Designer** Compass Marketing
Copy Editor Debra Craig	

CONTENTS

ACKNOWLEDGMENTS

Any technical book represents the combined efforts of a number of people, and this one is no different. At Osborne/McGraw-Hill, thanks to Liz Fisher, Acquisitions Editor, who artfully guided this project around a maze of other projects, schedule conflicts, and the assorted roadblocks that have a way of appearing during book production. Thanks to Scott Rogers, Associate Editor, for his tireless coordination efforts. Thanks also to Project Editor Wendy Rinaldi for all her help (particularly in pulling together a book with such a 'visual' design), and to Copy Editor Debra Craig and Designer Marcela Hancik. Thanks to Dave Nesbitt of the Nesbitt Group for technical editing (and for sympathy with the trials of beta software). And I would like to thank Nan Borreson and Karen Giles at Borland International, for keeping me supplied with the latest beta software, getting questions answered, and sometimes just providing a listening ear.

INTRODUCTION

In a relatively short period of time, Paradox has established itself as the number-two player among database managers for IBM-compatible PCs. Considering the intense competition in the software industry, that says a lot about the nature of Paradox. It is this nature, the ability to provide true database power without complicated programming, which this book is designed to imitate from the ground up.

Since the beginning of the PC software industry, database managers have earned a reputation for being difficult to use. Paradox for Windows, with its highly visual interface and its Query-by-Example technology, is very different. Previous versions of Paradox have gained a strong following among corporate users because you do not need to be a "programming guru" to decipher its use. And even though it is easy to use, Paradox for Windows offers a great deal of relational database management power. This book is designed to help you utilize that power.

How This Book Is Organized

What is in this book? Chapter 1 offers an introduction to Paradox for Windows by showing ways in which the product can be used and by describing the features and capabilities of the product. In Chapter 2, important tips are offered on the subject of database design, and you are introduced to some basic database concepts.

You will begin putting Paradox to use quickly in Chapter 3, which details how to get started with the program, how to create a database, how to add records, perform simple queries, and print simple reports. Chapter 4 explains the concepts of table views in Paradox for Windows, and shows how you can change the nature of how you view your data within a Paradox table. Chapter 5 further explores the concepts of managing your data by showing how you can edit records, find and delete records, sort tables, and view multiple tables simultaneously.

In Chapter 6, you are introduced to the significant power of Paradox' Query-by-Example technology. Using queries in Paradox, you can quickly find the data you are looking for. Chapter 7 covers the use of custom forms, a flexible design tool offered by Paradox for Windows for the display of your data in any conceivable format. Chapter 8 details the use of graphic and OLE fields in tables, a significant feature of Paradox for Windows. Chapter 9 covers in detail the design of reports, and Chapter 10 covers the use of presentation graphics. Chapter 11 shows you how you can work with relational information while using Paradox for Windows.

Chapter 12 examines a number of advanced topics that you will want to consider once you are comfortable with the basics of Paradox for Windows. Chapter 13 provides users with important tips and techniques that will help them make optimum use of Paradox on a network. Finally, Chapter 14 provides tips on customizing Paradox for Windows to better meet your specific needs. Appendix A contains instructions for installing the program, and Appendix B contains a Windows primer, for those readers who may also be new to the Microsoft Windows environment.

The style of this book encourages *learning by doing.* You will get the best results if you have your PC and your copy of Paradox for Windows at hand and if you follow along with the hands-on practice sessions outlined in most chapters. However, ample illustrations have been provided, so even if you do not have a PC and Paradox for Windows, you can still become familiar with the program by reading the book.

CHAPTER

INTRODUCING PARADOX FOR WINDOWS

Welcome to Paradox for Windows, a true high-performance database manager for the IBM PC and compatible machines running under the Windows environment. If you have never used a relational database manager for a personal computer, you will quickly realize the many benefits of this excellent database management tool. If you have used other relational database managers for personal computers prior to Paradox for Windows, you are in for a major change in expectations. For the first decade of personal computer use, relational database managers all shared a very common trait of "no pain, no gain." These powerful programs were universally difficult to use. And while some of these programs were simplified gradually, it was still widely acknowledged that if you wanted real power in a database manager, you had to sacrifice ease of use.

The menu structure and Query-by-Example feature of Paradox make the program easy to use.

Those traits have changed with Paradox for DOS, and also with its successor, Paradox for Windows. The very word "paradox" is defined as "something that cannot be, but is," and Paradox for Windows lives up to its name. High-powered database managers are not supposed to be simple to use, but Paradox for Windows is just that. Paradox for Windows uses a series of well-designed menus and a Query-by-Example feature that makes it easy to ask for specific data. At the same time, Paradox for Windows takes advantage of the Windows environment to offer significant capabilities that are not present in Paradox for DOS, such as direct links to data in other Windows programs, and the ability to store and display graphic images.

Paradox for Windows also differs from much of its competition (and even from its DOS-based predecessor) in that it is an *object-oriented* product. Many earlier databases were command-oriented, meaning you typed commands to tell the program what you wanted to do. Menus alone did not make a database program object-oriented; often, you chose a command (such as to sort a file) from a menu. Hence, the program was still command-oriented. Paradox, however, makes extensive use of objects. This means that you work with data in Paradox by using objects, manipulating objects in different ways to provide the results you need. As an example, in many command-oriented databases, you can widen a column of data by choosing a menu command. In Paradox, you widen a column by dragging the object you want to widen (in this case, the column border) to the desired location with the mouse. Here is a list of common objects in Paradox:

Throughout this book, the term "Paradox" refers to Paradox for Windows, and not Paradox for DOS.

✦ **Tables** store your data.

✦ **Forms** provide a way to view your data.

♦ **Reports** control how your data is printed.

♦ **Queries** are used to select specific data from your tables.

What Is a Database?

Although database management is a computer term, it can also apply to the ways in which information is catalogued, stored, and used. At the center of any information management system is a database. Any collection of related information grouped together as a single item, like Figure 1-1, is a *database*. Metal filing cabinets containing customer records, a card file of names and phone numbers, and a notebook with a penciled list of a store's inventory are all databases. The file cabinet or a notebook is not what makes these collections databases, however. Rather, the way pieces of information are organized makes the difference between random data and a database. Items, like cabinets, notebooks, and computer programs such as Paradox, are only aids in organizing information.

Databases organize data into categories of information having something in common.

Information in a database is usually organized and stored in the form of tables, with rows and columns in each table. One or more tables containing information arranged in an organized manner, with data divided into common categories, is a database.

For example, in the mailing list shown in Figure 1-1, each row contains a name, an address, a phone number, and a customer number. Each row is related to the others because they all contain the same types of information. Because the mailing list is a collection of information arranged in a specific order—a column of names, a column of addresses, a column of customer numbers—it is a table. Rows in a table are called *records*, and columns are called *fields*.

A simple database

Figure 1-1

Name	Address	City	State	ZIP	Phone No.	Cust. No.
J. Billings	2323 State St.	Bertram	CA	91113	234-8980	0005
R. Foster	Rt. 1 Box 52	Frink	CA	93336	245-4312	0001
L. Miller	P.O. Box 345	Dagget	CA	94567	484-9966	0002
B. O'Neill	21 Way St. #C	Hotlum	CA	92346	555-1032	0004

Figure 1-2 illustrates this idea by comparing a simple one-table database to an address filing system kept on 3×5 file cards. Each card in the box is a single record, and each category of information on a card is a field. Fields can contain any type of information that can be categorized. In the card box, each record contains six fields: a name, address, city, state, ZIP code, and phone number. Since every card in the box has the same type of information, the card box is a database. Figure 1-3 identifies a record and a field in the mailing list database.

Computerized databases save time by making the access of the data a faster process.

Using a Database

A database, or computerized filing system, can make information storage and retrieval more efficient than a traditional filing system. Tasks that would be time-consuming to accomplish manually are more practical with the aid of a computer. In principle, a database in a computer is not different from a database recorded on paper and filed in cabinets. But the computer does the tedious work of maintaining and accessing a database, and it does so quickly. A computerized database that can do all of this is known as a *database management system,* or DBMS, for short.

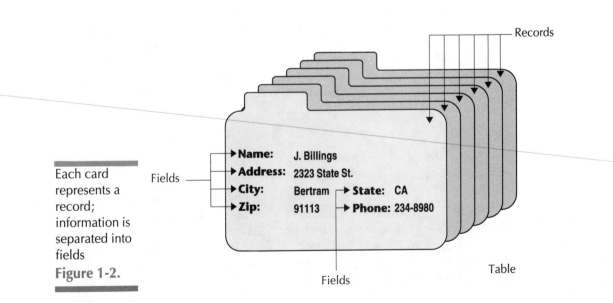

Each card represents a record; information is separated into fields
Figure 1-2.

┌─ Field

Name	Address	City	State	ZIP	Phone No.	Cust. No.
J. Billings	2323 State St.	Bertram	CA	91113	234-8980	0005
R. Foster	Rt. 1 Box 52	Frink	CA	93336	245-4312	0001
L. Miller	P.O. Box 345	Dagget	CA	94567	484-9966	0002
B. O'Neill	21 Way St. #C	Hotlum	CA	92346	555-1032	0004
C. Roberts	1914 19th St.	Bodie	CA	97665	525-4494	0006
A. Wilson	27 Haven Way	Weed	CA	90004	566-7823	0003

└─ Record

A record and a field of a database
Figure 1-3.

Several shortcomings are associated with manual database systems. A telephone book, for example, is fine for finding telephone numbers; but, if all you have is the address and not the name of the person who lives there, the telephone directory becomes fairly useless for finding the desired telephone number. A similar problem plagues conventional office filing systems: if the information is organized by name and you want to find all the clients located in a particular area, you could be in for a tedious search. In addition, organizing massive amounts of information into written directories and filing cabinets can consume a great deal of space.

Computerized databases let you search for data using different methods, or criteria.

A manual database can also be difficult to modify. For example, adding a new phone number may mean rearranging the list. If the phone company assigns a new area code, someone has to search for all phone numbers with the old area code and substitute the new one.

When a database is teamed up with a computer, many of these problems are eliminated. A computerized database provides speed: finding a phone number from among a thousand entries, or putting the file in alphabetical order takes just seconds with a computerized database. A computerized database is also compact: a database with thousands of records can be stored on a single floppy disk. A computerized database is flexible: it can examine information from a number of angles, so you, for example, could search for a phone number by name or by address.

Relational Databases

There are a number of ways to store information in a computer, but not all of these are relational database management systems like Paradox. A database manager that draws information from different tables linked by a common field is known as a *relational database manager*.

Consider an example of two tables; one contains a record of auto parts, and the other contains purchasers who have ordered certain parts. These tables are typical examples of tables that benefit from the use of a relational database. The parts table contains part numbers, descriptions, and the cost of each part. The orders table, on the other hand, contains the names of customers who have ordered certain parts, as well as the part numbers and the quantities of the parts that have been ordered.

Relational databases can access two or more tables simultaneously.

If you used a single table to track all of this information, each time a customer ordered a part that had been ordered previously you would have to duplicate the part description and the part cost. To avoid such unnecessary duplication, a relational database manager lets you link the two tables together based on a common field (in this example, the field containing the part number).

A word processing program can be used to organize data in the form of a list; however, it offers only limited flexibility to manipulate that data once you've entered it. A level above word processors are simple file managers and spreadsheets with simple database management capabilities. Such programs can also perform sorting and other data management tasks.

Relational database managers like Paradox can also store information in database files. However, in addition to being more sophisticated than file managers, relational database managers can access two or more tables simultaneously. By comparison, file managers can access only one table at a time, which is a severe constraint. If the file manager is accessing information from one table but needs three pieces of information from a second table, it can't continue unless the second table is available. Only after the file manager is finished with the first table can it proceed to the second table. But what good is this when the file manager needs information from both tables simultaneously? The only solution is to duplicate the three fields from the second table into the first table. Fortunately, this is not a problem with a relational database manager like Paradox, which can access both tables at once.

Features of Paradox

From the very start, Paradox will prove its ease of use. Thanks to an automatic installation procedure, the program installs itself on your hard disk, creating the needed subdirectory. Once you load the program and display a table of data, Paradox presents a Main menu on the screen, along with a group of icons known as the *SpeedBar* (you'll learn more about the SpeedBar in Chapter 3). Paradox provides access to all of its powerful features through the menu, and you can use the SpeedBar icons to quickly perform many common tasks in Paradox.

A significant feature of Paradox is its SpeedBar, which lets you quickly perform common tasks.

If you have used other Windows programs, Paradox's menu design should be familiar. As with other Windows programs, you can select menu choices by holding the [Alt] key while pressing the first letter of the command, or by clicking the desired menu choice with the mouse and dragging down to the desired menu option.

Creating Tables

With Paradox for Windows, creating a table to store your data is a simple task. Using the File menu, you select the table type (you can create tables in either Paradox or dBASE file formats), enter a name for the table, and define the names and types of fields you will use. You can use many different data types in Paradox, including *alphanumeric* data (combinations of alpha and numeric characters) and *memo fields* (which can contain large amounts of text).

Once you create a table, you can use the various menus or the SpeedBar to open tables and forms that let you enter data into the table. Paradox lets you enter data into a table-based view (see Figure 1-4) or into a form-based view (see Figure 1-5). You can quickly create a standard form for any table or design custom forms which contain fields at locations you desire, along with borders or descriptive text. Table views will be discussed in detail in Chapter 4, while forms will be covered in Chapter 7

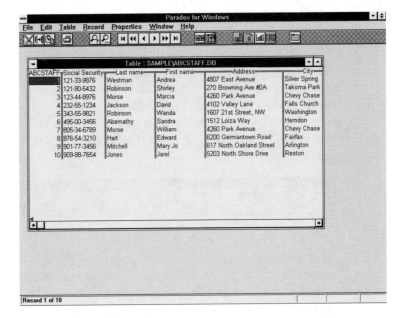

Table-based
view
Figure 1-4.

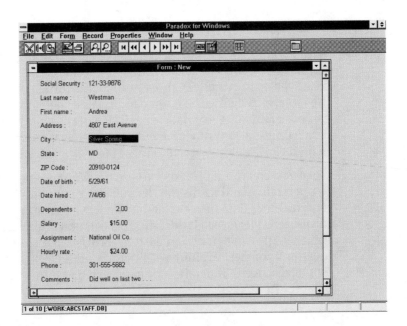

Form-based
view
Figure 1-5.

To perform queries that will extract data from your table, you can use Paradox's Query-by-Example feature. You can display a Query Form and add desired tables to it, and then check off the fields you want to see in an answer to the query. Finally, you can enter matching data in any desired fields of the Query Form to isolate the subset of records. Figure 1-6 shows a Query Form and the resultant answer to the query. Chapter 6 covers queries in further detail.

Queries provide a fast way to obtain selective data from your database.

To get more detailed information from your Paradox tables, you will want to build detailed reports. The QuickReport icon in the Paradox SpeedBar lets you create quick tabular-style reports. If you need additional flexibility, you can use Paradox's powerful Report Design window to design custom reports, in either a tabular or a free-form format. These topics are discussed in Chapter 9.

Paradox also offers excellent presentation graphics. Numeric data contained in a Paradox table can be visually represented in the form of a graph, as detailed in Chapter 10. Paradox offers a wide variety of graphs, including bar, pie, and line graphs. The graphs you create can be displayed or printed, and you can customize many parts of a graph,

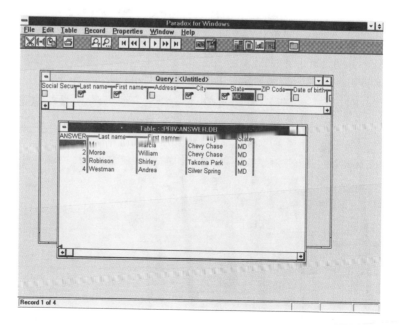

An example query

Figure 1-6.

such as the colors of various objects and the fonts used as labels within the graphs. Figure 1-7 shows a sample graph created with Paradox.

Finally, advanced users will find no shortage of available power in Paradox. You can make use of scripts, which are automated actions stored in a file which Paradox carries out as if individual commands had been entered at the keyboard (similar to "macros" in other software). Paradox scripts are stored as Object PAL, the Paradox Application Language. You can use Object PAL to build complete, menu-driven custom applications that novices can use without any special training.

How Paradox Compares to the Competition

Paradox is one of a number of competing products in a market built on the popularity of the IBM-PC and its descendants, and on the usefulness of relational database managers for microcomputers. There

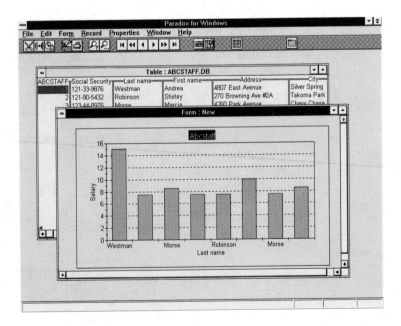

A sample
Paradox graph
Figure 1-7.

1

are many excellent products on the market comparable in power to Paradox, including Paradox for DOS, dBASE IV, FoxPro, and others. All of these products offer relational database management, integral programming languages for applications development, and similar top-of-the-line features. However, Paradox for Windows excels at providing the features and the power of Windows while maintaining a simple, friendly, user interface.

See Appendix A for details on installing Paradox.

A major difference between Paradox and its earlier, DOS-based competition is the highly visual nature of the program. Other database managers force you to build strings of commands to carry out operations, and these commands must follow a precise syntax. Some products offer menu systems that help you build parts of these commands, but you must nevertheless supply the commands correctly to carry out your desired tasks. By comparison, Paradox lets you perform much of your work by manipulating objects on the desktop.

System Requirements

To use Paradox, you will need an IBM PC or other 100% IBM-compatible computer. Your PC must also have Windows installed, which means that your PC must meet the minimum hardware requirements for Windows (80286 or better processor, hard disk, and EGA or VGA monitor). While Windows will technically run with one megabyte of RAM, Paradox for Windows requires a minimum of 4 megabytes of installed RAM. Also, note that a mouse is required for some operations within Paradox for Windows. If you are using Paradox on a local-area network, refer to your Network Administrator's Guide (packed with your Paradox documentation) for additional requirements regarding network use.

Specifications

Specifications for Paradox include the following. Note that these capabilities are theoretical maximums, and they may be lower on your system if your system is limited in terms of installed memory.

Maximum characters per table: 262 million

Maximum fields per table: 255

Maximum characters per field: 255 (excluding memo fields, which can store an unlimited number of characters per field)

Maximum characters per record: 4,000 for nonindexed tables; 1,350 for indexed tables

Maximum number of tables that can be joined in a query: 24

Quick Summary

A *database* is a collection of information grouped together, with data organized based on common categories.

In Paradox, databases can be displayed as *tables*, containing rows of data called *records*, and columns of data called *fields*.

CHAPTER

2 DATABASE DESIGN

At this point, you may be anxious to load Paradox into your computer and begin using the program. Resist this temptation to use Paradox for a new task you've never done by computer before; there's an excellent reason to approach the job of designing a database with patience. Planning is vital to effective database management. Many buyers of database management software have gotten started with the software, created a database, and stored data within that database, only to discover to their disappointment that the database does not provide all of the needed information. Although powerful databases like Paradox let you make up for the mistakes committed during the design process, correcting such errors can be a tedious job. This chapter will focus on database design to help you avoid such time-consuming mistakes.

TIP: Creating a database without proper planning often results in a database with too few or too many fields.

Plan your database on paper before attempting to store it in a computer.

Just as you would not haphazardly toss a bunch of files into a filing cabinet without designing some type of filing system, you cannot place information into a database file without first designing the database. Database design requires that you think about how the data should be stored and how you and others will ask for data from the database file. During this process, you should outline your needs on paper. As you do so, you must define the kinds of information that should be stored in the database.

About Data and Fields

Data and fields are two important terms in database design. *Data* is the information that goes into your database. An individual's last name—Smith, for example—is data. *Fields* are the types of data that make up the database. A field is another name for a category, so an entire category of data, such as a group of names, is considered to be a field. Names, phone numbers, customer numbers, descriptions, locations, and stock numbers are common fields that your database might contain.

Information is extracted from a database in the form of reports.

Besides determining what kinds of information will go into your database, you must give careful consideration to the ways in which information will come out of your database. You extract information from a database in the form of *reports*. When you ask the computer for a list of all homes in the area priced between $100,000 and $150,000, or for a list of employees earning less than $15.00 per hour, you are asking for a report. When you request John Smith's address, you are also asking for a report. A report is a summary of information. Whether the computer displays a few lines on the screen or hundreds of lines on a

2

stack of paper, it is providing a report based on the data contained within the database file.

The hands-on practice sessions in this book use a hypothetical example to demonstrate how you can design and use a database. The particular scenario faced by ABC Temporaries is employed throughout this book to illustrate how to use Paradox effectively for database management. ABC Temporaries is a temporary services firm that must keep track of the number of employees working for the firm, and must also track the client companies to which those temporary employees are currently assigned. For some time, ABC Temporaries handled this task with ordinary 3×5 file cards, but the paperwork load finally grew too large to be efficiently handled in this manner. A major task at ABC Temporaries is to effectively track just how much time each temporary employee spends at a particular client, so accurate bills can be generated. The relational capabilities of Paradox will make such tracking a relatively simple matter.

This book makes significant use of learn-by-example techniques, using a hypothetical temporary services company.

Successive chapters of this book will show how the staff at ABC Temporaries successfully used Paradox to manage information. By following along with these examples, you will learn how to put Paradox to work within your particular application.

Three Phases of Database Design

Designing a database file, whether it is for ABC Temporaries or for your own purposes, involves three major steps:

1. Data definition (an analysis of existing data)
2. Data refinement (refining necessary data)
3. Establishing relationships between the fields

These three phases in the process of putting together a database will be described in detail in the following sections.

Data Definition

During the first phase, data definition, you must make a list, on a piece of paper, of all the important fields involved in your application. To do

During the data definition phase, it is better to have too many fields than to have too few fields. You can always consolidate or eliminate unneeded fields during the data refinement phase.

this, you must examine your application in detail to determine exactly which fields, or categories of data, you want stored in the database.

In discussing the database design, the staff at ABC Temporaries determined that they need to know certain items about each temporary worker: the employee's name, his or her address, the date of birth, the date of hire, the salary, and the name of the client firm to which the employee is assigned. The staff also included a comment field in which they can record textual descriptions of an employee's performance. The resulting list of fields is shown in Figure 2-1.

During the database design phase, it's important to list all possible fields you may need in your database. Although you may list more fields than are actually needed by your particular application, you can eliminate unnecessary fields during the data refinement stage.

Data Refinement

During the data refinement phase, you will perfect the fields on your initial list so that they form an accurate description of the types of data that are needed in the database. Carefully examine your list of fields, making any necessary additions or deletions. At this stage, it is vital to incorporate suggestions from as many other users of the database as possible.

TIP: The people who will use the database are likely to know what kinds of information they will want to get from the database.

Initial list of fields
Figure 2-1.

```
                        Fields


                 1. Employee Name
                 2. Employee Address
                 3. Employee Salary
                 4. Assigned To (Firm)
                 5. Date of Birth
                 6. Date Hired
                 7. Comments
```

2

It's important to establish relationships when planning a database. This helps determine which fields are important.

When the staff of ABC Temporaries took a close look at their initial list of fields, they realized that most of the refinements were obvious. For example, they determined that the address field should be divided into street address, city, state, and ZIP code. When they further examined the initial field list, they realized that the index card system of employees contained multiple occurrences of employees with the same last name. To avoid confusion, they further divided the name field into last name and first name. The staff also followed suggestions to add the phone number, salary, number of dependents, and hourly billing rate charged to the client. Figure 2-2 shows the refined list of fields that ABC came up with. Similarly, in your own case, some refinements may quickly become evident while others may be less apparent. Carefully going over your written list of fields will help make any necessary refinements more obvious.

Establishing the Relationships Between Fields

During the third phase of database design, drawing relationships between the fields can help determine which fields are important and which are not so important. One way to determine such relationships is to ask yourself the same questions that you will ask your database. If a manager wishes to know how many different employees worked on

```
              Fields


        1.  Employee Last Name
        2.  Employee First Name
        3.  Street Address
        4.  City
        5.  State
        6.  ZIP Code
        7.  Phone
        8.  Salary
        9.  No. of Dependents
       10.  Assigned to Firm
       11.  Rate Charged to Firm
       12.  Date of Birth
       13.  Date Hired
       14.  Comments
```

Refined list of fields

Figure 2-2.

temporary assignments for Mammoth Telephone & Telegraph, the database must draw a relationship between an employee identifier (such as the social security number) and the names of the clients for whom that employee worked.

Relationships can be more complex. The company president might want to know how many employees who are data entry operators worked for Mammoth Telephone & Telegraph between July and October. The database management system must compare fields for that particular client with fields for the type of job and the time the job was performed. Asking these types of questions can help reveal which fields are unimportant so that you can eliminate them from the database; if there are fields containing information that is never needed in a query or in a report, those fields likely don't belong in the database.

Chapter 11 provides further details on why and how fully relational databases can be created in Paradox.

During this third phase, it is particularly important that you determine which, if any, relationships between data will call for the use of multiple tables, keeping in mind the fact that Paradox is a relational database. In a nutshell, *relational capability* means that the data within one table can be related to the data in another. Such links between tables are established using a common field, or a field that contains the same data in two tables. As an example, a Social Security field could be used to link a table of employee salaries with a table of employee addresses. When designing a database, it is important not to lose sight of that fact. Too many users take relational database management software and proceed to create bulky, nonrelational databases, an approach that drastically increases the amount of work involved.

As an example, the proposed staff table to be used by ABC Temporaries has fields that will be used to describe each employee. A major goal of computerizing the firm's personnel records is to provide automated billing. If ABC Temporaries creates another table showing which employees worked at a given assignment during a certain week, they can prepare bills for the services that they provide to their clients. If they took the nonrelational approach of adding fields for a week ending date and for the number of hours worked, they could store all of the information needed in each record. However, they would also have to fill in the name, address, and other information for each employee, week after week. A better solution would be to create two tables, one containing the fields that include the details about each employee, and the other containing the number of hours worked, the week ending

2

date, the client for whom the work was performed, and a way of identifying the employee, as shown in Figure 2-3.

When establishing relationships between different tables, you may determine that an additional field is necessary. For example, ABC Temporaries decided to identify employees by social security number, so this field was added to the proposed list of fields, resulting in the finalized list of fields shown in Figure 2-4. The table created in the next chapter is based on this list. Later, the Social Security field will be used in a different table that records the hours worked by each employee, and the tables will be linked (a relationship established between them) on the basis of the Social Security field.

When designing a database, ask users for suggestions.

During this aspect of the design phase—as during the other phases—it is critical to consult potential users to determine what kinds of information they will expect the database to supply. Just what kinds of reports do they want from the database? What kinds of queries will they make of the database? By continually asking these types of questions, you'll think in terms of what you will need to get from your database, and this should help you determine what is important and what is unimportant.

You may have noticed that throughout the entire process, the specific data, such as employees' names, addresses, and so forth, has not been

Common field used to establish relationship between two tables
Figure 2-3.

```
Social Security
Last Name
First Name
Address
City
State
ZIP Code
Phone
Salary
Dependents
Assigned To
Hourly Rate
Date of Birth
Date Hired
Comments
```

```
Social Security
Hours Worked
Week Ending Date
Client Name
```

```
                 Fields

         1.  Employee Social Security Number
         2.  Employee Last Name
         3.  Employee First Name
         4.  Street Address
         5.  City
         6.  State
         7.  ZIP Code
         8.  Phone
         9.  Salary
        10.  No. of Dependents
        11.  Assigned to Firm
        12.  Rate Charged to Firm
        13.  Date of Birth
        14.  Date Hired
        15.  Comments
```

Final list of
fields
Figure 2-4.

discussed. You needn't identify any specific data at this point; you just need to define the fields. Once you have finalized a given design, you should test that design using samples of existing data. Testing with real data can reveal problems with the database design, such as foreign postal codes (when a field was designed for U.S. ZIP codes) or name titles such as M.D. that were not originally planned for.

TIP: Look at examples of your data before finalizing your list of fields. This should help you to track down variations that may not have been allowed for, fields that may have been omitted, and other potential problems.

Keep in mind that even after the database design stage, the design of your database file is not set in stone. You can change the design of a database file later if necessary. However, if you follow the systematic approach of database design for your specific application, it's more likely that your database will provide you with all the information that you need and will not require extensive redesigning later.

Paradox lets you change the design of a table at any time, although such changes are often inconvenient to make once the database is

2

designed. For example, if you used Paradox to create a database file that handles a customer mailing list, you might include fields for names, addresses, cities, states, and ZIP codes. At first glance this might seem sufficient. You could then begin entering customer information into the database and gradually build a sizeable mailing list. But if your company later decides to begin telemarketing using the same mailing list, you may realize that you have not included a field for telephone numbers. Using Paradox, you could easily change the design to include such a field. But then you would still face the possibly mammoth task of adding a telephone number for every name currently in the mailing list. If this information had been added as you developed the mailing list, you would not face this inconvenience. Careful planning during the database design process can help you to avoid such minor or catastrophic pitfalls.

Quick Summary

Effective database management begins with proper planning.

In planning your database, include the three phases of database design—data definition, data refinement, and establishing relationships.

During the planning process, consider common fields that will serve to establish relationships between multiple tables.

CHAPTER

3

GETTING STARTED WITH PARADOX FOR WINDOWS

In this chapter, you will learn many of the basics involving the use of Paradox for Windows. You will learn how to create and open tables, how to enter and edit data in a table, and how to generate quick reports. This chapter assumes that you have already installed Paradox on your system and that a Paradox program group appears on your Windows desktop. If you have not yet installed Paradox, refer to

Appendix A, and install Paradox on your system before proceeding.

Starting Paradox

Paradox for
Windows

To start Paradox, double-click the Windows program group containing Paradox to open it, if it is not already open. (If you accepted the default choices during installation of the program, this program group will be called Paradox for Windows.) With the program group open, double-click the Paradox for Windows icon contained within the Program Group to start Paradox.

After the program starts, you will briefly see an introductory screen and a copyright message. A moment later the Paradox desktop will appear, as shown in Figure 3-1.

About the Desktop

The Paradox desktop is where you will perform work in Paradox. The desktop itself is a powerful tool of Paradox. You will work with Paradox

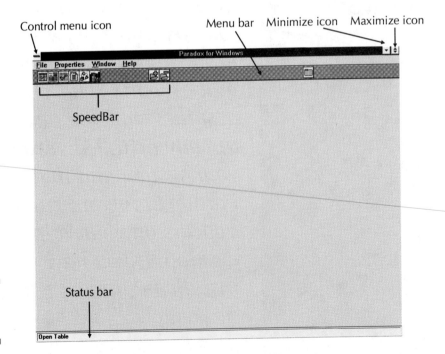

Paradox
desktop
Figure 3-1.

objects (like tables, forms, or reports) from the desktop. You'll also use the desktop for file management tasks, such as opening and closing various files, and copying, deleting, or renaming tables. And you'll set the working environment—choosing the default directory you'll want to work with—from the desktop. You can think of the desktop as your 'working space' when you are using Paradox.

As you work with objects, your desktop will take on an arrangement that suits your style of work, just as a real desk does. The placement of objects on your desktop—the directory you are using, and the size and appearance of tables, forms, and reports, for example—is collectively referred to as _preferences._ From the time you start Paradox until you exit the program is called a _session_. When you end a session, Paradox remembers your preferences, and those preferences are restored automatically the next time you start Paradox.

Profile

3

If you have worked with other Windows applications, you may already be familiar with the concept of parent and child windows. Most applications under Microsoft Windows normally appear in a main window, or *parent* window, and you can then create files (such as different documents if you're using a word processor) in various *child* windows. Sometimes the parent window is referred to by the term *application window*; and child windows are called *document windows*. The child windows are dependent on the parent window; you cannot close the parent window (containing, for example, your word processor) and still have child windows (containing documents from the word processor) open on the screen. Paradox is no different; the desktop is the parent window, and the objects that you create (such as tables, forms, or reports) appear in child windows, as shown in Figure 3-2.

Each kind of object in Paradox (such as a table, form, or report) appears within its own kind of window. As an example, forms appear in Form windows, and queries appear in Query windows.

The Desktop Menus

In Paradox, the highest-level menu is the Desktop menu. From the Desktop menu, you can open and close files, establish preferences such

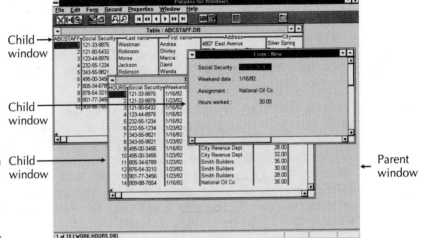

Child window →

Child window →

Child window →

Parent window containing child windows
Figure 3-2.

Parent window ←

as printer setup and network settings, get help, and work with other Windows applications. When you first load Paradox, assuming no child windows have been left open on the desktop, only the File, Properties, Window, and Help menus will be visible, as shown earlier in Figure 3-1. Once you open an object under Paradox (such as a table, a form, or a report), additional menu options appear on the menu bar. Figure 3-3 shows the desktop with a table visible in a child window.

Note that three additional menu choices appear on the menu bar: Edit, Table, and Record. The additional choices that appear on the menu bar will vary, depending on the type of object that has been opened in the child window. You will learn more about the various menu choices when you create different types of objects throughout this text. For now, the following is an overview of the common menus found on the menu bar.

File   The File menu contains various commands that relate to the different files you will use under Paradox. You can use these commands to open files, to create new files of various types, and to save files. You can also use certain File menu commands to print and to exit from Paradox.

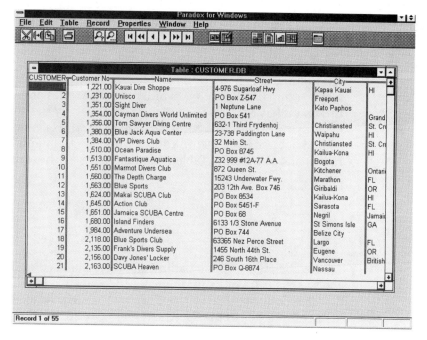

3

Desktop
containing a
table within a
child window
Figure 3-3.

Edit   The Edit menu contains various commands that relate to
the editing of different objects under Paradox. You can use
commands on the Edit menu to cut, copy, and paste selected text
between different objects, or to link objects in other Windows
applications (such as documents in a word processor or graphic
images in a paint program) to fields in a Paradox table.

Properties   The Properties menu provides various commands
that let you change the appearance and function of an object. For
example, you can change the style of gridlines (the lines used
between columns of a table) or the style of column headings with
this menu.

Window   The Window menu contains various commands that
relate to the manipulation and arrangement of windows on the
Paradox desktop. For example, you can tile (arrange all open
windows in a tiled fashion) all windows, or close all open
windows, using this menu.

Help   The Help menu provides one way of accessing the help system under Paradox. (You can also gain access to the help system by pressing the `F1` key.)

Throughout this book, you will often be asked to choose one or more menu commands. When you must choose a series of menu commands, this text refers to them in sequence, separated by slashes. For example, if an instruction in this book asks you to choose File/New/Table, you should open the File menu, choose the New command from that menu, and choose the Table command from the next menu that appears.

The SpeedBar

Located below the menu bar in Paradox is a collection of buttons and tools in the form of icons; these are collectively referred to as the *SpeedBar*. You can use the icons on the SpeedBar to speed up various tasks. Most icons in the SpeedBar offer fast equivalents to commands that can be found on various menus; some icons also provide useful ways for you to navigate through data in a table or form.

The SpeedBar provides a handy way to choose commonly-used commands in Paradox.

When you are just starting out with Paradox, you may not be able to remember the purpose of each SpeedBar icon. However, there is an easy way to determine each icon's purpose. Just point to any icon, and its name will appear at the left side of the status bar in the bottom of the window. Table 3-1 lists each tool and its function in the Paradox SpeedBar that appears when a table is open.

It is important to remember that the SpeedBar will change as you work with various types of objects in Paradox. For example, the SpeedBar that appears when a table is in the active window is different than the SpeedBar that appears when a form or report is in the active window. As you begin to work with different objects (such as tables, forms, and reports) throughout this book, the icons in the SpeedBar will be explained in further detail.

Tool	Description	Function
	Cut to Clipboard	Cuts selected data and moves it to the Windows Clipboard.
	Copy to Clipboard	Copies selected data to the Windows Clipboard.
	Paste from Clipboard	Pastes the contents of the Windows Clipboard into the active window, at the cursor location.
	Print	Prints the contents of the active window at the default printer.
	Locate Field Value	Displays Locate dialog box which can be used to search for a specific value in a field.
	Locate Next	Repeats the previous search, to find the next record containing the same search value.
	First Record	Moves cursor to first record.
	Previous Set of Records	Moves cursor backwards by one window full of records
	Previous Record	Moves cursor backwards by one record.
	Next Record	Moves cursor forward by one record.
	Next Set of Records	Moves cursor forward by one window full of records.
	Last Record	Moves cursor to last record.
	Field View	Enters Field view.

SpeedBar Icons
Table 3-1.

Tool	Description	Function
	Edit Data	Enters edit mode; allows changes to records.
	Quick Form	Creates a standard form based on the active table.
	Quick Report	Generates a standard report based on the active table.
	Quick Graph	Displays Define Graph dialog box which can be used to create a graph.
	Quick Crosstab	Displays Define Crosstab dialog box which can be used to create a crosstab.
	Open Folder	Opens the folder for the current (or working) directory

SpeedBar Icons
(*continued*)
Table 3-1.

TIP: The SpeedBar changes according to the object that appears in the active window.

Other Aspects of Windows

Both Paradox and Microsoft Windows use windows, or discrete rectangular areas of your screen, as work areas. Because Paradox is a Windows application, some aspects of how Paradox behaves are common to Windows applications. The following summarizes common Windows techniques; you can refer to Appendix B or to your Windows documentation for more details regarding Windows operation.

✦ Menus can be opened by clicking the menu. Or you can hold the Alt key depressed, and press the underlined letter on the menu bar. As an example, you could open the Edit menu by pressing Alt+E.

♦ To move a window, point at its title bar, and click and drag the window to the desired location. You can also move a window by opening its control menu (press `Alt`+`-` or use the mouse), choosing Move, and using the cursor keys to move the window.

♦ To resize a window, point at any border of the window, and click and drag the window to the desired size. You can also resize a window by opening its control menu (press `Alt`+`-` or use the mouse), choosing Size, and using the cursor keys to resize the window.

See Appendix B for an overview of Microsoft Windows.

♦ To close a window, press `Ctrl`+`F4`.

♦ To tile all open windows (arrange them into adjacent tiles), choose Tile from the Window menu.

♦ To cascade all open windows (arrange them in layered fashion), choose Cascade from the Window menu.

♦ To switch to another window, choose the desired window by name from the Window menu.

♦ To close all open windows, choose Close All from the Window menu.

About the Folder Window

Paradox provides a way of managing objects from the desktop, using *folders*. Paradox does not require the use of folders; they are simply an aid in managing your work. You can liken folders to conventional file folders, in that you can place things that you regularly use within them, for fast and easy access. You can open a folder window, either by choosing File/Open/Folder from the menus, or by clicking the Open Folder on the SpeedBar. When you do so, you see the Folder window for the current, or working, directory, as shown in Figure 3-4.

Each subdirectory has its own folder.

By default, Paradox displays icons representing all major objects—tables, forms, reports, scripts, and queries—in the Folder window. You can quickly open any of the objects in the folder by double-clicking the desired object. You can organize a folder in whatever way suits you; you can add objects to a folder, or you can remove objects from a folder. Note that a new menu option, titled Folder, is added to the menu bar when a folder is open.

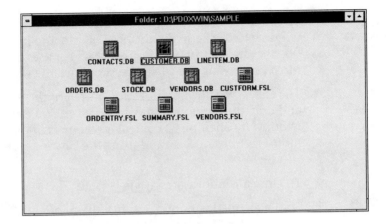

Adding and Removing Objects

To add an object to the folder, choose Folder/Add item from the menu
bar, or click the Add item icon on the SpeedBar. The Select File dialog
box will open, and you can choose the desired file to add to the folder,
then click OK to add the file.

TIP: To add several objects to the folder at once, click all the desired
files in the Select File dialog box, then click OK to add them all to
the folder window.

To remove an object, choose Folder/Remove Item, or click the Remove
Item icon in the SpeedBar. A Remove Item dialog box will appear,
similar to the example shown in Figure 3-5.

All objects in the folder appear in the dialog box. Click the desired file
(or files) you want to remove, then click OK to remove the file or files.

NOTE: Removing a file from a folder does not delete the file; it
simply removes it from view in the folder.

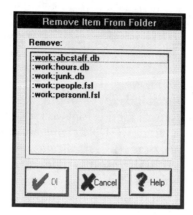

Remove Item
dialog box
Figure 3-5.

Arranging Objects

You can arrange the objects in a folder manually, by dragging them to the desired locations in the window. Or, you can let Paradox arrange them automatically; to do so, choose Folder/Tidy icons from the menu bar, and Paradox will rearrange the objects.

Showing All Files

You can tell Paradox to display all files that are in the current directory. To show all files, choose Folder/Show All Files from the menu bar; all files in the working directory will appear in the folder. This will include objects that would not normally appear because they are not major objects, such as index files, program files, or files containing text or graphics.

As mentioned earlier, whenever a folder is open, the SpeedBar contains two additional icons; an Add Item icon, and a Remove Item icon. If the folder for the working directory is closed, you can open it by clicking on the Open Folder icon.

The Maximize/Minimize icons and the Control Menu icon, also shown in Figure 3-1, are universal to Windows applications. Because Paradox runs under Windows, you need to be familiar with how you can manipulate windows as you work in Paradox. Each window will contain the following components, which were shown in Figure 3-1.

Control Menu Icon   This icon represents a pull-down menu that contains commands for changing the size or location of a window. There are control menus for two types of windows: object windows and application windows. *Object windows* contain objects, like Paradox tables, forms, or reports. *Application windows* contain applications, like Paradox. (With Microsoft Windows, you can have more than one application window open on the screen at once; you can have Paradox running in one application window, and a word processor like Windows Write running in another application window.)

You can open the Control menu for an application window by pressing Alt + Spacebar, by clicking the Control menu icon with the mouse, or by pointing to the icon with the mouse and clicking the left mouse button. To open the Control menu for a document window, you use the Alt + - key combination.

Maximize Icon   You use this icon to bring the window currently in use, or *active window*, to full-screen size. You can maximize a window by opening the Control menu and selecting the Maximize command, by pressing Alt + F10, or by clicking the Maximize icon with your mouse.

Minimize Icon   You use this icon to reduce the active window to a small icon that appears at the bottom of the screen. You can minimize a window by opening the Control menu and selecting the Minimize command, by pressing Alt + F9, or by clicking the Minimize icon with your mouse.

When you minimize a window, you reduce it to the size of an icon, but the object represented by the window remains in memory. You can later quickly restore the object to view by clicking the icon. On the other hand, if you close the window (rather than minimize it), you are closing any file associated with the object. If you later want to open the same object, it will take longer for your computer to open the file.

Scroll Bars   You can use the scroll bars at the bottom and right edges of a window to move to other areas of the window. If the window contains a table, the arrows located within the scroll bar will move you by one row or a column at a time. Clicking the up or down arrow in the right (or vertical) scroll bar moves you up or down a row at a time. In a similar fashion, clicking the left or right arrow in the scroll bar at the bottom of the window (the horizontal scroll bar) moves you left or right by a column at a time. You can also drag the boxes located in the scroll bars to move by a relative amount; for example, if you drag the box in the vertical scroll bar halfway down the bar, you will move halfway down the window's contents.

If the name of an option (within the menu) is followed by three periods, choosing that menu option will always reveal some type of dialog box.

Dialog Boxes   In Paradox, some menu options, when chosen, will result in the appearance of a dialog box asking for additional information. Figure 3-6 shows an example of a dialog box that appears when File/Open/Form is chosen from the menu bar.

Other dialog boxes may contain some or all of the options shown in this example. A dialog box may contain a number of different options,

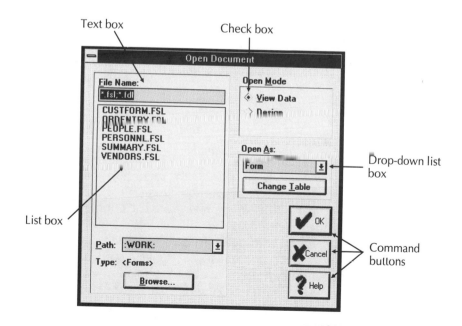

Open Document dialog box

Figure 3-6.

such as check boxes, list boxes, command buttons, and text boxes. Here is a description of these items, which are illustrated in Figure 3-6.

A *check box* is a small diamond-shaped box that you use to turn an option on or off. To select a check box, just click it.

A *list box* is a rectangular area used to display a list of available names, such as filenames. List boxes may have scroll bars, to aid you in viewing the contents of the list box.

A *drop-down list box* shows the currently selected item only. To display more items, click the arrow and drag down the list until you have highlighted the option you want.

A *command button* is a rectangular button with rounded edges to implement a command or some other action. Nearly all dialog boxes contain at least three command buttons; an OK or Save button, a Cancel button, and a Help button. The OK button, when present, is used to accept the options chosen within the dialog box, and the Save button, when present, is used to save a file. The Cancel button is used to cancel the operation and remove the dialog box from the screen. Some dialog boxes may contain other buttons (such as Save As or Sort) for performing various operations. Select the desired command button by clicking it.

A *text box* is a rectangular area in which text that is needed for a command can be entered. (As an example, when saving files you enter desired filenames into text boxes.) Within the text box, you can type text, and you can edit or delete text with the [Backspace] and/or [Del] keys.

About the Keyboard

If you're already familiar with the PC keyboard, you should skip this section and begin reading the section "About the Mouse." Paradox uses a number of special-purpose keys for various functions. On some keyboards, the function keys are the double row of keys at the left side of the keyboard, as shown in Figure 3-7. On other keyboards (including those used with newer IBM-compatible PCs), the function keys are in a horizontal row at the top of the keyboard, as shown in Figure 3-8. The function keys on most older keyboards are labeled [F1] through [F10], for Function 1 through Function 10. Most newer keyboards have 12 function keys. Usually grouped on the left side of the keyboard are five

The IBM PC
keyboard
Figure 3-7.

Laptop and notebook computers often place multiple key functions on a single key.

frequently used keys: the (Esc) key, the (Tab) key (it may have the double arrows on it), the (Shift) key (it may have the hollow upwards-pointing arrow), the (Ctrl) (Control) key, and the (Alt) (Alternate) key. The (Shift), (Ctrl), and (Alt) keys are used in combination with other keys. For example, pressing (Alt)+(E) opens the Edit menu in Paradox. Some keyboards have the (Esc) key in a different location. Find these keys before going further, as they will prove helpful for various operations.

You should locate the template supplied with your package of Paradox, and place it where you can refer to it for the uses of the function keys. The uses for the various function keys will be described in detail in later chapters, as they become relevant.

Towards the right side of the keyboard is another (Shift) key. Usually located below the right (Shift) key is a key labeled (Caps Lock) which is used to change all typed letters to uppercase. Some keyboards will have the (Caps Lock) key located near the left (Shift) key. (The (Caps Lock) key does not change the format of the numbers in the top row of the keyboard.) Just above the right (Shift) key is the (Enter) key; it performs a function that is

The enhanced
IBM PC
keyboard
Figure 3-8.

similar to the return key of a typewriter. Above the [Enter] key is the [Backspace] key, which may be marked with a leftward-pointing arrow.

NOTE: [Caps Lock] and [Num Lock] are *toggles*, meaning you press them once to turn them on and press them again to turn them off.

On the right side of the keyboard, in the numeric keypad area, is a key labeled [Del]. You can use this key to delete characters or other objects when you are using Paradox. Finally, the far right side of your keyboard may include two gray keys with plus ([+]) and minus ([-]) labels. Normally, these keys will produce the plus and minus symbols.

On the far right side of the keyboard is the numeric keypad. On some computers, this area can serve a dual purpose. You can use the keys on this keypad that contain [↑], [↓], [←], and [→] to move around in a worksheet. In addition, you can press the [Num Lock] key and then use these same keys to enter numbers. Some keyboards will have a separate area with arrow keys.

TIP: When you press the [Num Lock] key, the arrow keys on many keyboards create numbers instead of moving the cursor. If you press an arrow key and get an unwanted number, check the status of the [Num Lock] key.

TIP: The [Esc] key is your most useful key whenever you are somewhere you don't want to be. In many cases, pressing [Esc] will get you out of an operation. However, [Esc] won't undo or cancel edits that you have already made to a record.

About the Mouse

If you are already familiar with the use of the mouse, you can skip this section and move on to the section "Getting Help."

There are three basic operations you perform with the mouse: pointing, clicking, and selecting (also called dragging in Paradox). The mouse controls the location of a special cursor, called the *mouse pointer*.

Pointing refers to positioning the mouse pointer directly on an object. To do this, simply move the mouse in the direction of the object. As you do so, the mouse pointer will move in the same direction on the screen.

3

Clicking refers to pressing and releasing the left mouse button once. By pointing to different objects and clicking them, you can select many of the objects while in Paradox. Note that you can examine properties of many objects in Paradox by clicking the right mouse button once; to differentiate this procedure from clicking with the left mouse button, it will be referred to as right-clicking. *Double-clicking* refers to pressing the left mouse button twice in rapid succession.

Dragging refers to pressing and holding down the left mouse button while moving the mouse. This is commonly done to choose menu options within Paradox.

If you have just purchased your mouse for use with Windows and Paradox, here are a few helpful tips to keep in mind:

Throughout this book, "click" refers to using the left mouse button, and "right-click" refers to using the right mouse button.

◆ **Software drivers** Most mice require software drivers to be installed before they will work properly. The Windows installation process automatically installs drivers for different brands of mice; if your mouse works with Windows, it will work with Paradox. If your mouse is not working properly within Windows, refer to your Windows documentation and correct the problem (you may have to reinstall Windows) before trying to use your mouse with Paradox.

◆ **Mouse surface** When manipulating a mouse, a surface with a small amount of friction seems to work better than very smooth desks. Commercial pads are available if your desktop is too smooth to obtain good results.

◆ **Cleaning the mouse** If you turn the mouse upside down, you will probably see instructions which indicate how the ball can be removed for cleaning. A cotton swab dipped in alcohol works well for cleaning the ball. If your mouse uses an optical sensor design instead of a large ball underneath, you should refer to the manual which accompanied the mouse for any cleaning instructions. Some mice do not require regular cleaning, so check your manual to be sure.

Getting Help

Should you need help, Paradox provides detailed information on subjects ranging from basic Paradox concepts to programming in Object PAL, the Paradox Application Language, all of which is stored on a Help file and accessible to Paradox. A series of menus will assist you in finding the information you are searching for. You can get to the help menus either by pressing the Help function key, F1, or by choosing Index from the Help menu.

The help system in Paradox is context-sensitive. What this means is that if you are in a particular area—for example, if you are in the process of creating a table—and you ask for help, you are provided with help regarding that particular topic. If you are not in any particular area when you ask for help, Paradox displays the contents page of the help system, as shown in Figure 3-9. From anywhere in the help system, you can click the Contents command button in the upper-left corner of the screen to display this contents page. Once the contents page is visible, you can click any of the headings in that page to move to the named topic. You can also click the Search button and then enter a search term, or scroll through the list box of topics that appears.

To gain a familiarity with the help system, you may wish to take a few minutes to browse through the help screens. When you are done viewing the screens, choose Exit from the File menu to get back to the program.

TIP: At any point in Paradox, pressing F1 reveals a help screen.

Changing Directories

As you work with files in Paradox, you will probably need to change the working directory used by the program. The *working directory* is the default directory, or the directory you happen to be using at a given

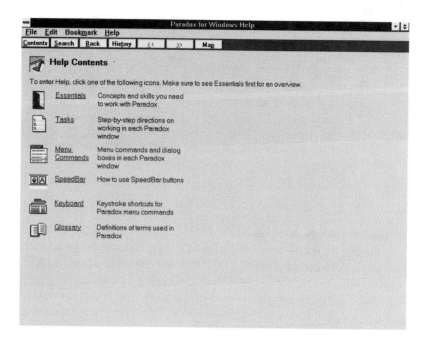

Help screen
Figure 3-9.

point in time. It is a good idea to create one or more directories in which to store your data files; this will keep your data files separate from the program files that come with Paradox. If you used the default single-user installation of Paradox, the program has already created one subdirectory called SAMPLE. You can store the additional tables you create in this subdirectory, or you can create other directories by using DOS commands or by using the File/Create Directory option from the Windows File Manager. (See your DOS or Windows documentation for more details on creating subdirectories.)

You can transform an existing directory into the working directory in Paradox by choosing the File/Working Directory option. When you do so, a dialog box appears, prompting you for the name of the desired directory.

You can enter the directory name (using normal DOS file naming conventions), or you can click the Browse button, and then choose the directory by name from the list of directories that appears. Once you have done this, click the OK button, and Paradox will use the directory that you have named as the working directory; all tables and other files that you create will be stored in this directory.

If you have not yet changed to a directory other than the one containing the Paradox program files, do so now. Choose the File/Working Directory option and enter **C:\PDOXWIN\SAMPLE** (assuming your hard disk is C and the SAMPLE subdirectory exists on your hard disk). If the drive letter for your hard disk is something other than C, substitute that letter. If you are using a subdirectory other than the SAMPLE subdirectory, enter that directory name, along with the appropriate drive letter. Finally, click OK to set the working directory.

Creating a Table

As mentioned in Chapter 1, Paradox stores data in the form of tables. To create a table, you must choose New from the File menu, and then choose Table from the next menu to appear. (Remember, you can choose menu options by clicking them with the mouse. Alternatively, you can press Alt followed by the underlined menu letter to open a menu, and then use the cursor keys and the Enter key to choose various options. For example, pressing Alt+F opens the File menu. Generally, using the mouse is easier.)

Open the File menu now, and choose New. A second menu appears, asking you what kind of object you want to create.

```
Form...
Library
Query...
Report...
Script
Table...
```

From this menu, choose Table. The dialog box shown in Figure 3-10 appears, asking you to choose the desired table type.

Paradox for Windows lets you create tables under Paradox or dBASE file formats.

If you have used earlier versions of Paradox for DOS, this feature will be new to you. Paradox for Windows lets you save tables under Paradox or dBASE file formats. The default is Paradox for Windows, but if you open the list box (by clicking the arrow on its right side), you will see additional choices offered for Paradox 3.5, dBASE III PLUS, and dBASE IV. Users of Paradox 4.0 for DOS can use existing Paradox for Windows files as-is in Paradox 4.0 for DOS. (The programs are file-compatible; however, if your Paradox for Windows files contain graphic or OLE-type files, Paradox 4.0 for DOS will not be able to display or edit contents of these files. See Chapter 12 for additional information.) Throughout this book, you'll use the default Paradox for Windows file type for your tables. But if you use Paradox for DOS or dBASE for DOS in your work, you may find it convenient to create your tables using

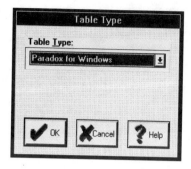

Table Type
dialog box
Figure 3-10.

one of these formats, so you can easily make use of the same tables while in Paradox for DOS or dBASE for DOS. Also note that other table types may be available to you, depending on what types of servers are available (if your PC is connected to a local area network).

TIP: If you save tables using the Paradox 3.5 or dBASE file format, this will limit the available field types when you design your tables. This is because DOS versions of Paradox and dBASE do not, at the time of this writing, support as many field types as does Paradox for Windows. For example, Paradox 3.5 for DOS and dBASE for DOS do not allow formatted memo fields, nor do they allow the use of graphic fields. Paradox 4.0 can directly load Paradox for Windows files, but it cannot display graphic fields. See Chapter 12 for more details about the restrictions involved when working with Paradox for DOS and dBASE-type tables.

Leave the Table Type set to the default of Paradox for Windows, and click OK. In a moment, you'll see a child window containing the Create Paradox for Windows Table dialog box shown in Figure 3-11.

The left side of the window contains the *field roster area.* In this area, you tell Paradox how the database should be structured by naming the fields you want and indicating their sizes and types. On the right side of the window are various options for specifying validity checks. *Validity checks* are rules that govern what kinds of values you can enter in a field. You can ignore this portion of the window for now; the subject of validity checks for fields will be covered in Chapter 5. The Borrow button in the lower-left corner of the window lets you create a new

3

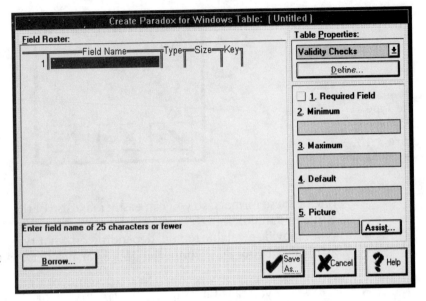

Create Paradox
for Windows
Table dialog box
Figure 3-11.

table based on the design of an existing table. This feature can be useful once you are working with many tables; for now, you can ignore this option also.

The cursor appears under the Field Name column, since Paradox is waiting for you to assign a name to the first field of the table. When naming a field, use a name that best describes the contents of that field. Field names can be composed of letters and numbers, and can be up to 25 characters in length. Field names can contain spaces (although they cannot start with a space). Field names can include any printable character except for double quotes, square brackets, left and right parentheses, curly braces, or the -> character combination.

TIP: While Paradox lets you create long field names, it is a good idea to keep your field names relatively short. Doing so will keep the headings in your simpler reports from occupying too much space.

You may remember the list of suggested fields for the employees table outlined in Chapter 2. In that list, the first attribute is the employee's social security number, so enter **Social Security** for the first field name, then press [Tab] to move over to the Type column. Press the [Spacebar] and a Type menu will appear.

Paradox allows a choice of ten types of fields. They are:

✦ **Alphanumeric fields**   These are used to store any characters, including letters, numbers, any special symbols, or blank spaces. An alphanumeric field has a maximum size of 255 characters. You define a field as alphanumeric by entering the letter "A" in the Field Type column of the structure table, next to the name of the field.

✦ **Number fields**   These fields use numbers with or without decimal places. You can enter numbers of up to 15 significant digits, so unless you are performing scientific calculations, you should not have a problem with numerical accuracy. (If you enter numbers with more than 15 digits, Paradox automatically rounds them and stores them in scientific notation.)

✦ **Currency fields**   These are special types of number fields designed to handle currency. Paradox automatically formats values that you store as currency with two decimal places, making this format ideal for storing amounts describing most types of currency. The values stored in currency fields are automatically displayed using whatever currency symbol you have chosen through the Windows Control Panel.

In currency fields, the formatting affects how the data is displayed, but does not change the value of the data itself. For example, if you entered a value of 553.4572 into a currency field, it would be displayed as $553.46. However, Paradox would internally store the value you originally entered (553.4572), and would use this internal value in any calculations you performed based on that field.

✦ **Date fields**   These fields are used to store dates. While Paradox accepts dates between 1/1/100 and 12/31/9999, amateur genealogists and others concerned with dates should note that date tracking in Paradox is based on the Gregorian calendar in present

You can change the currency symbol throughout the Windows Control Panel. See Chapter 12 for details.

3

use, so dates earlier than the 16th century may vary when compared to the calendar you decide to use.

Paradox lets you enter the dates in any of four formats: *mm/dd/yy, dd-mon-yy, dd.mm.yy,* or *yy.mm.dd.* Paradox defaults to dates in the twentieth century. For other dates, you can enter all four numbers of the year as part of the date. Paradox automatically checks the validity of a date as you enter it. If you attempt to enter a date that cannot exist (such as 63/85/1993) into a date field, Paradox will beep and display an error message.

TIP: You can perform arithmetic on a date field (such as adding or subtracting a number of days to a date to come up with another date), and you can perform queries (select subsets of tables) based on a date or a range of dates.

✦ **Short number fields**   These are fields used for storing *short numbers*, or numbers within the range of -32,767 and +32,767. You should not use the Short Number field unless you are an advanced Paradox user or developer. While this type of field takes less space in a database, there are serious limitations on how short number fields can be displayed in Paradox forms.

✦ **Memo fields**   These are fields containing large amounts of text (typically too large to be stored in an alphanumeric field). The amount of text you can store in a memo field is limited only by available hard disk space. Memo fields are typically used to store comments that vary greatly in length, such as descriptions of a product, or written evaluations of an employee.

✦ **Formatted memo fields**   These are memo fields that let you store formatted text, including various fonts, point sizes, and type styles.

✦ **Binary fields**   These fields contain binary data such as sound. Binary fields should be used only by advanced Paradox users or application developers. You cannot display or access a binary field

3

through Paradox; you can only access a binary field through Object PAL, the underlying programming language used by Paradox.

✦ **Graphic fields** These fields contain graphic images. You can create graphic images using paint programs or a scanner. See Chapter 8 for more information on working with graphics in a Paradox table.

✦ **OLE fields** These fields contain objects from other Windows applications that support OLE (Object Linking and Embedding). See Chapter 8 for more information on working with OLE objects in a Paradox table.

Most fields in a table will be of the alphanumeric or the number type, although there will be times when you need most of the different field types that Paradox offers.

TIP: Use number fields for numbers that must be calculated. Numbers on which you never need to perform calculations (like phone numbers) should be stored in alphanumeric fields, as Paradox uses slightly less space to store alphanumeric data than numeric data.

Along with the type of field, in some cases you'll also need to specify a desired size for the field. The field types and corresponding limits for field sizes are shown in Table 3-2.

With the Type menu still open, choose Alphanumeric from the list of field types. (You will never need to perform calculations on the basis of social security numbers, so there is no need to store these entries in a numeric field.)

Next, press (Tab) to move over to the Size column. With the cursor in this column, enter **11**. This width will be sufficient to store the nine digits and two hyphens in a social security number.

Press (Tab) again to move the cursor to the Key column. Type an asterisk (or press the (Spacebar) once to add an asterisk) to designate this field as a key field (key fields are discussed in the next section). Then press (Tab) to move to the Field Name column for the next field.

Field Type	Symbol	Size Values Allowed
Alphanumeric	A	1-255
Number	N	none needed
Short number	S	none needed
Currency	$ (default symbol)*	none needed *
Date	D	none needed
Memo	M	0-255 **
Formatted memo	F	0-255 **
Graphic	G	none needed
OLE object	O	none needed
Binary	B	none needed

* You can use the Windows Control Panel to change the default currency symbol to something other than the dollar sign.

** Memo fields and formatted memo fields can contain any amount of text. The size values that you enter when designing the table will refer to the amount of text of the memo field that is stored as part of the table; the rest of the memo field is stored elsewhere. As an example, if you assign a size of 30 to a memo field, the first 30 characters of the memo field get stored with the Paradox table. The remainder of the memo field gets stored elsewhere, and is retrieved as you scroll through the records of the table.

Paradox Field
Types and Sizes
Table 3-2.

About the Key Field Concept

Paradox lets you define any field as a key field. A key field is a field that you specify as a primary index for the table. When you do so, Paradox treats that field differently. Probably the most important thing to remember is that key fields will contain unique information; Paradox will not let you put the same entry into the key field of two records. Also, when designing the structure of the table, you must place all key fields in sequential order, beginning at the first field in the table's structure. (You cannot place key fields in a random order all over the structure of a table.) Also note that when you save the file, records are arranged by key field. Because key fields are unique, you should be careful when deciding what should be a key field. If the first two fields of a table were Last Name and First Name, making both fields key fields would mean you could never enter two records with an identical last and first name. In such a case, you might want to use a combination of Last Name, First Name, and Address as key fields. Also, note that you don't have to make any field a key field; doing so will often boost performance but is not required.

In addition to preventing duplications, designating a field as a key field causes Paradox to keep an internal index that will help speed sorts and queries based upon the contents of that field. Since social security numbers are unique, the asterisk is placed after the field type to designate that field as a key field.

3

Making a field a key field often improves performance especially when sorting tables or searching for data.

Enter **Last Name** as the second field name. Press [Tab] to move over to the Type column, press the [Spacebar], and choose Alphanumeric from the list. Press [Tab] to move to the Size column, and enter **15**. Continue pressing [Tab] until you are back at the Field Name column, where you can enter the third field name.

Enter **First Name** as the third field name. Press [Tab] to move over to the Type column, press the [Spacebar], and choose Alphanumeric from the list. Press [Tab] to move to the Size column, and enter **15**. Then press [Tab] to get back at the Field Name column, where you can enter the fourth field name.

Enter **Address** as the fourth field name. Press [Tab] to move to the Type column, press the [Spacebar], and choose Alphanumeric from the list. Press [Tab] to move over to the Size column, and enter **25**. Then press [Tab] to get back at the Field Name column.

Moving down the list, enter **City**, choose a field type of Alphanumeric, and enter a width of **15** for the field. For the next field enter **State**, choose a field type of Alphanumeric, and enter a width of **2** for the field.

The next field will be ZIP Code. Before proceeding, what do you think the field type for ZIP codes would be? ZIP codes consist of numbers, so at first it might make sense to use a number field. However, this is not really practical. If you make use of the nine-digit business ZIP codes, Paradox will not allow the entry of the hyphen; if you try it, Paradox displays an "invalid entry" message. It will also delete beginning zeroes in ZIP codes such as 00123.

You will never use a ZIP code in a numerical calculation, so it makes more sense to store the ZIP code as an alphanumeric field rather than a numeric field. A number stored in an alphanumeric field cannot be directly used in a numerical calculation, although you could convert the value to a number with a Paradox function. Now enter **ZIP Code** as the field name, choose Alphanumeric as the field type, and enter **10** for the field width.

You may recall from Chapter 2 that the next two fields in the personnel database are dates, which you should assign a field type of Date. Enter **Date of Birth** for the next field name. Press [Tab] to move to the Type column, press the [Spacebar], and choose Date from the list of field types. Continue pressing [Tab] until you are back in the Field Name column. Enter **Date Hired** for the name of the next field. Press [Tab] to move over to the Type column, press the [Spacebar], and choose Date from the list of field types. Continue pressing [Tab] until you are back in the Field Name column.

Enter **Dependents** for the next field name. Press [Tab] to move to the Type column, press the [Spacebar], and choose Number from the list of field types. You need not specify a size for number fields, so continue pressing [Tab] until you are back in the Field Name column.

Enter **Salary** for the next field name. Press [Tab] to go to the Type column, press the [Spacebar], and choose Currency from the list of field types. You need not specify a size for currency fields, so continue pressing [Tab] until you are back in the Field Name column.

Enter **Assignment**, choose Alphanumeric, and enter a width of **20** for the field. For the next field enter **Hourly Rate** and choose Currency as the field type. For the following field, enter **Phone** as the field name, choose Alphanumeric, and enter a width of **12** for the field.

Enter **Comments** as the next field name. Press [Tab] to move to the Type column, press the [Spacebar], and choose Memo from the list of field types. Press [Tab] to go to the size column and enter **20**. Be sure to press [Tab] or Enter to complete the entry. This completes the entry of the new table's definition.

Correcting Mistakes

If you make any mistakes while defining the structure of the table, you can correct them before completing the table definition process. To correct mistakes, use the mouse or the cursor keys to move to the field name or field type containing the offending characters, and use [Backspace], along with the character keys, to make any desired corrections. If you start on a correction and then you want to cancel the edit, press [Esc] before leaving the field, and the original entry will be restored. More specifics on data entry and editing can be found in Chapter 5.

Saving the Table Definition

At this point, you are ready to save the table's definition. Click the Save As button at the lower-right corner of the window. Paradox will display a Save Table As dialog box, similar to the example shown in Figure 3-12. Yours will differ; if you haven't saved any tables, there may not be any other names in the dialog box.

Table names cannot contain spaces.

You must name tables using eight or fewer characters, and you cannot use spaces. Table names should be unique; if you specify a name that is already in use, Paradox warns you and asks for confirmation. If you go ahead with the confirmation, Paradox overwrites the existing table. There is no need to add an extension to your table names, as Paradox will automatically assign file extensions as needed.

Enter **ABCSTAFF** as a name for the table; then click OK. Paradox will save the new table, and the Create Table dialog box will vanish, leaving the desktop visible.

WARNING: Paradox uses temporary tables named ANSWER, STRUCT, and KEYVIOL at various times. You should not try to assign these names to any tables that you create, as they may be overwritten by Paradox.

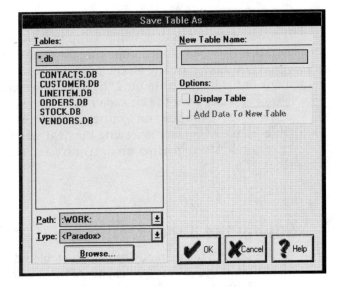

Save Table As
dialog box
Figure 3-12.

The Save Table As dialog box contains a Browse button and the two list boxes Path and Type near the bottom of the dialog box. The Type list box indicates the type of object you are working with; because you are saving a Paradox table, <Paradox> appears in the Type list box. You can use the Path list box to choose a different path. In Paradox, a path is an alias, or different name, that you give a directory. (You can assign paths by choosing the File/Alias option.) For example, you could assign an alias of myfiles to a directory named C:\PDOXWIN\ACCTS. You could then refer to the directory by choosing the alias of myfiles in the Path list box, rather than having to type the entire directory name of C:\PDOXWIN\ACCTS. The Browse button brings up a file browser that lets you examine the files available in the current directory or any other directory. Chapter 12 provides more details on using aliases and on using the File Browser. For now, you can leave the objects you will create in the default directory.

Opening a Table

Once you've created a table, you can add records to it and edit the contents of those records. Before you can work with the data in a table, you must open it, just as you would open a word processing document or a spreadsheet file before working with it. To open a table in Paradox, you use the File/Open/Table option and choose the desired table by name from a dialog box that appears.

Form...
Library...
Query...
Report...
Script...
Table...
Folder

Choose the File/Open option now; this brings up another menu, asking which type of object you want to open.

Select Table from this menu; when you do so, the Open a Table dialog box appears, similar to the example shown in Figure 3-13 (your list of table names may be different).

3

Existing tables must be opened before you can add or edit data in them.

Click ABCSTAFF.DB as the desired table name and then click OK. (Alternatively, you can simply double-click ABCSTAFF.DB.) In a moment, the table opens, and additional options appear on the menu bar, as shown in Figure 3-14. (With wide tables like this one, you may not be able to see all the fields at once.) Let's take a moment to consider the appearance of the tables and the new menu options in Paradox, since you'll probably be spending considerable time working with tables in their respective windows.

When you open a table, it appears in its own window. You can move or resize the window as desired, using the same techniques that you use to move or resize any window under Microsoft Windows.

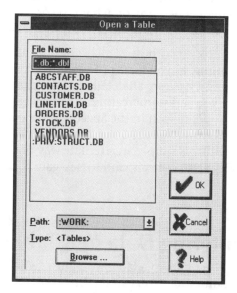

Open a Table dialog box
Figure 3-13.

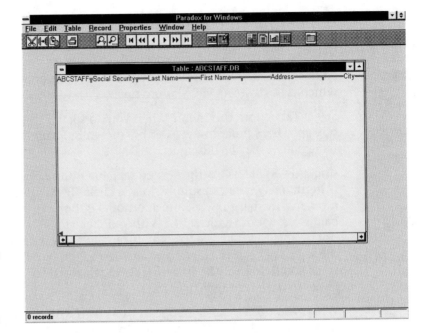

New table open
in a view
window
Figure 3-14.

Three new options appear on the menu bar when you open a table: Edit, Table, and Record. As mentioned, the appearance of the SpeedBar changes depending on what type of window is active. The SpeedBar you currently see is the Desktop SpeedBar shown in Figure 3-15.

The precise purpose of all of the SpeedBar icons may not be apparent at this time, as you have not yet worked with forms, queries, reports, or scripts. These are all detailed in the chapters that follow; for now, note that you can start creating any of these objects by clicking the appropriate icon in the SpeedBar. For example, you can click the Quick Form icon to create a standard form based on the table in use. The SpeedBar is simply an alternate way of choosing the most commonly used menu options, and to navigate within a table.

Entering Data in a Table

To enter data in a table, you must switch from the default View mode to Edit mode. You can do this in any of three ways:

3

✦ You can press F9.

✦ You can click the Edit Data icon in the SpeedBar.

✦ You can choose the Table/Edit Data option from the menu bar.

Once you perform any of these steps, the word "Edit" appears at the right side of the status bar, indicating that you are in Edit mode. Once you are in Edit mode, you can place the cursor in any of the table's fields and begin typing to add data. If you haven't already done so, perform any of the suggested steps shown above to switch to Edit mode. Add the following data to the table. (You can press Tab to move between the fields of the table.)

Social Security:	123-44-8976
Last Name:	Morse
First Name:	Marcia
Address:	4260 Park Avenue
City:	Chevy Chase
State:	MD
ZIP Code:	20815-0988
Date of Birth:	3/1/54
Date Hired:	7/25/85
Dependents:	2
Salary:	8.50
Assignment:	National Oil Co.
Hourly Rate:	15.00
Phone:	301-555-9802

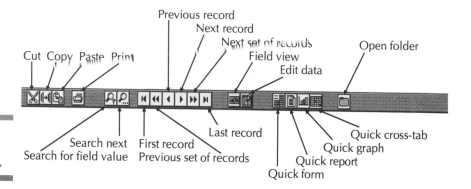

Desktop SpeedBar Figure 3-15.

Once you have entered these items, the cursor will be at the memo field named Comments. If you try to enter data directly, you'll hear a beep and Paradox will display the message "Press F2 for Field View to edit this field" in the status bar. The next section covers how to enter data into memo fields.

Entering Data into a Memo Field

Use F2 to enter data in a memo field.

Entering data into a memo field is different than entering data into alphanumeric, currency, date, or number fields. When the cursor is in a memo field (as it is now), you are at the entry point for a memo window that can store a theoretically unlimited amount of text. (In practice, you are limited only by your available hard disk space.) To enter data into memo fields, you must be in Field View mode, rather than in Edit mode. You can quickly switch to Field View mode by pressing F2.

With the cursor in the Comments field, press F2 to switch to Field View mode. You can now enter the text of the desired memo. For this example, type **Experienced in accounting, tax preparation, has MBA in business management**. When you are finished, press F2 again to switch back to Edit mode. After the cursor moves off the memo field, you may notice that the memo field contains the words "BLOB memo." This is simply a reference to the type of data stored in the field. In Paradox lingo, BLOB stands for *binary linked object*. Whenever the cursor is in another field, you will see the partial text of the memo field, and you can always see all of the text by placing the cursor in the memo field and pressing F2 to switch to Field View mode.

Press Tab to move to the next record, and proceed to add the remaining records for the ABCSTAFF table, which are listed here. Remember to switch to Field View mode using the F2 key when you need to enter data in the memo fields.

Social Security:	121-33-9876
Last Name:	Westman
First Name:	Andrea
Address:	4807 East Avenue

3

City:	Silver Spring
State:	MD
ZIP Code:	20910-0124
Date of Birth:	5/29/61
Date Hired:	7/4/86
Dependents:	2
Salary:	15.00
Assignment:	National Oil Co.
Hourly Rate:	24.00
Phone:	301-555-5682
Comments:	Did well on last two assignments.

Social Security:	232-55-1234
Last Name:	Jackson
First Name:	David
Address:	4102 Valley Lane
City:	Falls Church
State:	VA
ZIP Code:	22044
Date of Birth:	12/22/55
Date Hired:	9/5/85
Dependents:	1
Salary:	7.50
Assignment:	City Revenue Dept.
Hourly Rate:	12.00
Phone:	703-555-2345
Comments:	Absentee rate high.

Social Security:	901-77-3456
Last Name:	Mitchell
First Name:	Mary Jo
Address:	617 North Oakland Street
City:	Arlington
State:	VA
ZIP Code:	22203
Date of Birth:	8/17/58
Date Hired:	12/1/87

Dependents:	1
Salary:	7.50
Assignment:	Smith Builders
Hourly Rate:	12.00
Phone:	703-555-7654
Comments:	Too new to evaluate, but has excellent references from temporary agency in Chicago, IL, where she lived previously.

Once you are done entering the records, you can end the data entry process by pressing F9, by clicking the Edit Data icon in the SpeedBar, or by choosing End DataEntry from the Table menu. Press F9 now to complete the data entry process.

Table Mode Versus Form Mode

Viewing and entering records in this manner gets the job done, but as you can see, it is impossible to view all of the fields in the table at the same time, because they will not all fit on the screen. Paradox normally displays information in table form, because most users find it easier to grasp the concept of a database when it is shown in this fashion. It is easy to see a number of records, and the records and fields are clearly distinguished. However, not being able to see all of the fields also presents a clear drawback. For example, when you are viewing the name of an employee, the Date of Birth, Date Hired, and remaining fields are hidden. To view these fields, you could scroll the window contents to the right using the mouse, but then the name fields disappear off to the left. This makes it hard to recall which line containing the Date Hired, Date of Birth, and Salary fields matches a particular employee name.

To avoid this problem, some database managers display information as an on-screen form rather than as a table. Paradox lets you use either method, and you can quickly move between the two with the Quick Form (F7) key. (You can also click the Quick Form icon on the SpeedBar, or you can choose Quick Form from the Table menu.) Press F7 now, and in a moment Paradox will display a database record within a new form window, as shown in Figure 3-16. Like all windows under Microsoft Windows, you can resize or maximize this window to better view the data contained in the record.

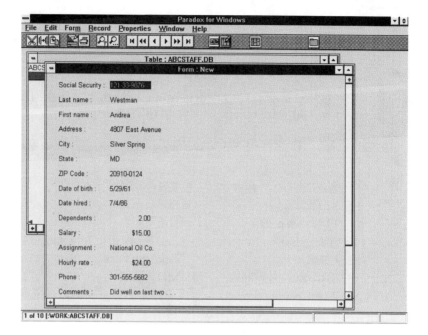

Form View of a
record
Figure 3-16.

You use different techniques to move around the table when in Form mode rather than Table mode. Try Pg Up and Pg Dn, and then try using the ↑ and ↓ keys. Where previously (in Table mode), Pg Up and Pg Dn would have moved you up and down by a screenful of records, they now move you up and down by one record at a time. And the ↑ and ↓ keys now move the cursor between fields instead of between records. In addition, when you are using Form mode, the name of the Table menu changes to Form in the menu bar.

You can use the F7 key to switch back and forth between Table and Form mode.

A significant advantage of forms is evident when you are working with tables that contain memo fields. You do not need to press F2 (Field View) to edit an entry in a memo field when you are working in a form, which you must do when working with tables.

As said earlier, you can use the F7 key to switch back and forth between Table and Form mode. Use the mode of your choice to add the remaining records for the ABCSTAFF employees to the table now. (Remember, you can begin editing by pressing F9 or by choosing Edit Data from the Table or Form menu.) If you are in Form mode, use the

Pg Dn key to get to a new, blank record. If you are in Table mode, use the mouse to click in a new, blank record at the bottom of the table.

TIP: If you are in Form mode, you must use the Pg Dn key each time you want to add a new, blank record.

Social Security:	121-90-5432
Last Name:	Robinson
First Name:	Shirley
Address:	270 Browning Ave #3C
City:	Takoma Park
State:	MD
ZIP Code:	20912
Date of Birth:	11/02/64
Date Hired:	11/17/91
Dependents:	1
Salary:	7.50
Assignment:	National Oil Co.
Hourly Rate:	12.00
Phone:	301-555-4582
Comments:	Too new to evaluate.
Social Security:	343-55-9821
Last Name:	Robinson
First Name:	Wanda
Address:	1607 21st Street, NW
City:	Washington
State:	DC
ZIP Code:	20009
Date of Birth:	6/22/66
Date Hired:	9/17/87
Dependents:	0
Salary:	7.50
Assignment:	City Revenue Dept.

Hourly Rate:	12.00
Phone:	202-555-9876
Comments:	Absentee rate has been excessive.
Social Security:	876-54-3210
Last Name:	Hart
First Name:	Edward
Address:	6200 Germantown Road
City:	Fairfax
State:	VA
ZIP Code:	22025
Date of Birth:	12/20/55
Date Hired:	10/19/90
Dependents:	3
Salary:	8.50
Assignment:	Smith Builders
Hourly Rate:	14.00
Phone:	703-555-7834
Comments:	Performed well on last four assignments.
Social Security:	909-88-7654
Last Name:	Jones
First Name:	Jarel
Address:	5203 North Shore Drive
City:	Reston
State:	VA
ZIP Code:	22090
Date of Birth:	9/18/61
Date Hired:	5/12/92
Dependents:	1
Salary:	12.00
Assignment:	National Oil Co.
Hourly Rate:	17.50
Phone:	703-555-2638
Comments:	Too new to evaluate.

3

If you are adding records in Table mode, remember to use F2 to add data to memo fields.

Once you are done entering the records, end the data entry process by pressing F9, by clicking the Edit Data icon on the SpeedBar, or by choosing End DataEntry from the Table (or Form) menu. If you are still using a form, press Ctrl+F4 to close the Form window (answer No to the Save prompt) to return to viewing your data in table format.

An Introduction to Queries

Your data is now stored in Paradox, ready for use. Successive chapters will describe in detail how you can make use of data once you have entered it into a table. So you can get started, however, this section briefly introduces how you will ask Paradox for information and produce simple reports.

In Paradox, you'll use queries to obtain specific information from a table.

One regular task for any database user takes the form of inquiries; you'll often need to obtain a particular set of facts, such as a list of all employees living in Maryland. In Paradox, it's easy to request such information, since you can build *queries* that ask Paradox to extract specific information from a table. To try a quick example, do the following:

1. Choose the File/New option.
2. From the next menu that opens, choose Query.
3. In the Select File dialog box that appears, highlight the ABCSTAFF file, and then click OK.

In a moment, an empty window titled Query:<Untitled> appears, and a new set of icons appears on the SpeedBar, as shown in Figure 3-17. (These icons will be explained in further detail in Chapter 5.)

To use the Query Form, you select the fields that you want to see included in the answer that Paradox will provide. To do this, you click in the check box in each desired field. In addition, you type a matching criteria to select the desired records in the field of your choice.

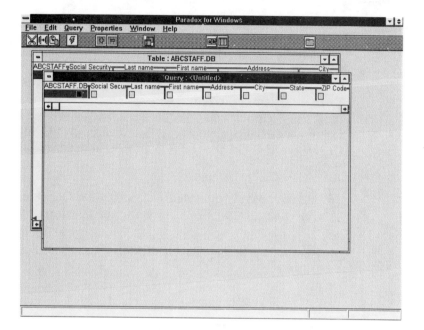

Query Form
Figure 3-17.

4. Click the check box at the left of the Last Name field. When you do this, a check mark will appear in the field. Do the same for the First Name, City, and State fields.

This action tells Paradox that you will want to see the Last Name, First Name, City, and State fields included in the list Paradox provides in response to your query. Once you finish checking the boxes, the query form resembles the one shown here:

5. With the cursor still in the State field, enter **MD** to tell Paradox that you want the query to select only records containing the letters "MD" in the State field.

You have just provided Paradox with a query using the Query-by-Example system. There are no arcane commands or strange syntax to decipher; you just check the fields you need to see, fill in an example of what data you want in any desired field, and choose Query/Run (or click the Run Query icon in the SpeedBar) to perform the query.

6. If you haven't yet done so, click the Run Query icon in the SpeedBar (it's the one containing the lightning bolt).

Paradox will perform the query, and display the results in a temporary table named ANSWER.DB, as shown in Figure 3-18. If

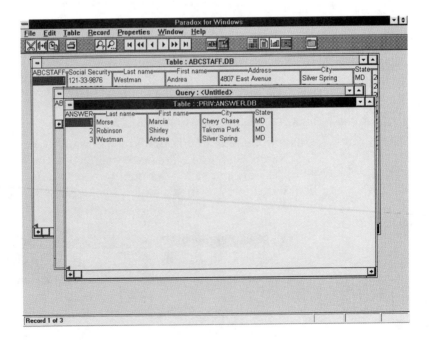

Results of a query

Figure 3-18.

3

your results do not match the ones shown, check that the entry in the State field of the Query Form matches the way you originally entered "MD" in the table. Make any corrections needed, and click the Run Query icon in the SpeedBar to run the query again.

The use of the Query Form is covered in more detail in Chapter 6.

Generating a Quick Report

You can generate a quick printed report of the results of a query (or of any table) with a single key combination. Paradox uses the [Shift]+[F7] key as the Quick Report key. Alternatively, you can click the Quick Report icon in the SpeedBar (it's the one that looks like a page of a report with a corner folded over), or you can choose Quick Report from the Table menu. If you have a printer, make sure that it is turned on and that paper is loaded. Then click the Quick Report icon in the SpeedBar or press [Shift]+[F7]. When a report appears on the screen, click the Print icon in the SpeedBar. In a moment, the Print the File dialog box appears as shown here:

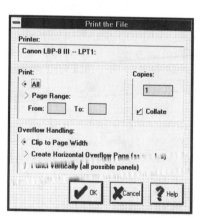

The options in this dialog box will be detailed in Chapter 9. Choose OK from the dialog box to begin printing. You should get a printed report based on the temporary table created by the query; the report will resemble the example shown here.

```
Thursday, April 9, 1992      ANSWER            Page 1
Last Name      First Name    City              State
Morse          Marcia        Chevy Chase       MD
Robinson       Shirley       Takoma Park       MD
Westman        Andrea        Silver Spring     MD
```

You can use the same techniques to get a report of your entire database. The Quick Report key (or icon) will produce a report based on whatever table is in the active window. Since the ANSWER table was the active window when you printed the report, its contents were printed. Close the window containing the ANSWER table now; you can quickly do so by pressing Ctrl+F4. (Experienced users of Windows should recall that Ctrl+F4 is the Close Document Window key in any Windows program.) Press Ctrl+F4 again to close the query window. A dialog box asks if you want to save this query. Since you won't need this query later, click the No button in the dialog box.

Quick reports let you obtain printouts of your data without needing to design any reports beforehand.

At this point, the window containing the ABCSTAFF table is the active window. Click the Quick Report icon in the SpeedBar (or press Shift+F7). In a moment, the Print File dialog box again appears. Choose OK from the dialog box to begin printing. This time, you should get a printed report based on the entire table. Note that all the fields will not be included, as they cannot all fit on the width of a single sheet of paper. In Chapter 9, you will learn how to design reports that contain all of the data you need.

You can produce far more detailed reports in Paradox. Such reports can include customized headers and footers, customized placement of fields, inclusion of graphic images, word-wrapped text, and numeric results based on calculations of fields. Such reports are covered in detail in Chapter 9.

Producing a Quick Graph

You can also use Paradox to produce presentation graphs. You will learn more about this subject in Chapter 10, but for now, you'll generate a quick graph so you can glimpse the presentation capabilities of Paradox. To display a quick graph, make sure the desired table is visible in the active window and press the Graph key (Ctrl+F7), or click the Quick Graph icon in the SpeedBar. The Define Graph dialog box will appear, as shown in Figure 3-19.

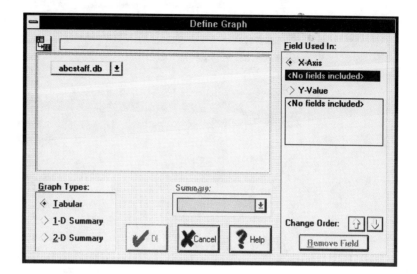

Define Graph
dialog box
Figure 3-19.

This dialog box will also be explained in detail in Chapter 10. For now, click the ABCSTAFF drop-down list box in the upper-left corner of the dialog box; this will display a list of fields. Choose Last Name from the list; this causes Last Name to appear as the X-Axis field at the right side of the dialog box. Next, click the Y-Value button at the right side of the dialog box. Again, click the ABCSTAFF drop-down list box, but this time choose Salary from the list of fields. This causes Salary to appear as the Y-Value field at the right side of the dialog box. Finally, click the OK button. In a moment, you should see a graph similar to the one shown in Figure 3-20.

Never exit Paradox by turning off your computer. You could damage or lose files if you do so.

Press Ctrl+F4 to close the window containing the graph (answer No to the prompt that asks if you want to save the graph).

If this is a good time for a break, choose Exit from the File menu to exit from Paradox. Remember, never exit from Paradox by turning off the computer. Always use the Exit option from the File menu, and then exit Windows in the normal manner before turning off the computer.

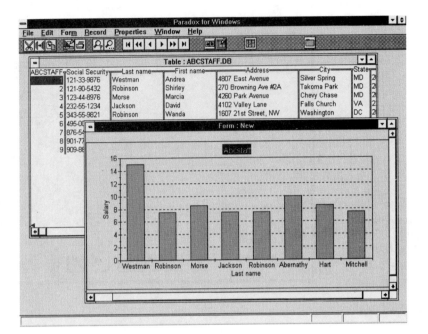

Quick Graph
Figure 3-20.

Quick Summary

Starting Paradox

To start Paradox, double-click the Windows program group containing Paradox to open it, if it is not already open. With the program group open, double-click the Paradox for Windows icon.

Creating a Table

Choose File/New/Table. From the dialog box that appears, choose the desired table type (Paradox or dBASE) and then click OK. Fill in the Create Table dialog box with the structure of the desired table (field names, types, and widths where necessary). Then choose OK and provide a table name when prompted.

Quick Summary (*continued*)

Adding Data to a Table

Choose File/Open/Table and choose the desired table from the list box that appears. Change from View to Edit mode by pressing `F9` or by clicking the Edit Data icon in the SpeedBar. Add a new, blank record by moving the cursor down past the last record (if you are in Table mode) or by using the `Pg Dn` key (if you are in Form mode). When you are done, press `F9` or click the Edit icon in the SpeedBar to accept the additions.

Editing a Table

Choose File/Open/Table and choose the desired table from the list box that appears. Change from View to Edit mode by pressing `F9` or by clicking the Edit Data icon in the SpeedBar. Move to the desired records and/or fields using the mouse or the various icons in the SpeedBar, and then make the desired changes. When you are done, press `F9` or click the Edit Data icon in the SpeedBar to accept the changes.

Getting a Quick Report

Make the window containing the desired data the active window (click anywhere in the desired window to make it active). Then click the Quick Report icon in the SpeedBar or press `Shift`+`F7`.

3

CHAPTER

4

VIEWING YOUR DATA

Paradox for Windows provides you with several ways to view your data. Chapter 3 introduced the concept of views; remember, you learned that Paradox can display tables in a view window. A view window can be thought of as containing two distinct items: the table itself, which contains the data, and the view properties of the table, which determine how that data is displayed. Throughout this chapter you will learn how to change these properties to govern the appearance of your data.

Chapter 5 provides additional details on changing the data itself.

Opening a Table in a View Window

You may recall from the previous chapter how to open a table. Follow these steps to open the ABCSTAFF table that you created earlier:

1. Choose Open from the File menu.
2. Choose Table from the next menu that appears.
3. From the Open a Table dialog box that appears, choose ABCSTAFF and then click OK. Paradox displays your table in a view window, as shown in Figure 4-1.

Moving Around in a Table

You can move around in a table in a number of ways. As in other windows, you can use the scroll bars to view various portions of the table. If the table contains more records than will fit in the window, a

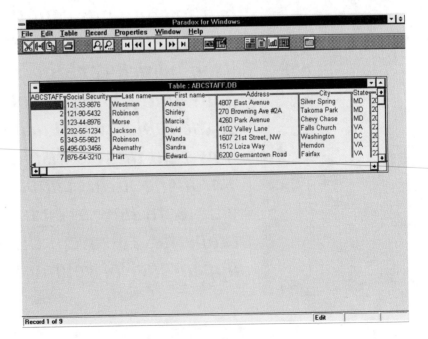

ABCSTAFF
table in a view
window
Figure 4-1.

vertical scroll bar appears at the right edge of the window, as you can see in Figure 4-1. You can click the up and down arrows in the vertical scroll bar to scroll the database vertically. You can also move through your data by dragging the scroll box. For example, if you drag the scroll box three-fourths of the way down the scroll bar and release it, you will be positioned about three-fourths of the way down the database.

If you want to edit a table, press F9 *. For more on editing, see Chapter 5.*

If the table contains more fields than will fit in a window, a horizontal scroll bar appears at the bottom edge of the window. (You can see such a scroll bar in Figure 4-1.) Clicking the left and right arrows moves the table columns horizontally, and dragging the scroll moves you more quickly through the table columns.

You can also use various keys or key combinations to move through a table. You can press ← or → to move the cursor to the left or right through the fields of a record, and you can use ↑ or ↓ to move the cursor up and down between records of a table. You can also use the Tab and Shift+Tab keys to move the cursor between fields; Tab moves the cursor to the right, while Shift+Tab moves the cursor to the left. The Pg Up key scrolls the table upwards by a window full of records, while the Pg Dn key scrolls the cursor downwards by a window full of records. The Ctrl+Home key combination moves the cursor to the first field of the current record, while the Ctrl+End key combination moves the cursor to the last field of the bottom record in the table.

Navigating with the Record Menu

The Record menu, shown here, provides a number of commands that you can use to navigate through a table. Choose First or Last from the menu to move the cursor to the first or last record in a table. Choose Next or Previous to move the cursor to the next record or to the prior record. Next Set moves you down by a window full of records, while Previous Set moves you up by a window full of records. Note that there are function key equivalents for these menu options: Ctrl+F11 for First, Ctrl+F12 for Last, F12 for Next, F11 for Previous, Shift+F12 for Next Set, and Shift+F11 for Previous Set. (As you can see, these shortcuts are displayed to the right of the option names in the Record menu.)

Record	
First	Ctrl+F11
Last	Ctrl+F12
Next	F12
Previous	F11
Ne**x**t Set	Shift+F12
Pre**v**ious Set	Shift+F11
Lo**c**ate	▶
Locate Ne**x**t	Ctrl+A
Insert	Ins
Delete	Ctrl+Del
Lo**c**k	F5
Cancel Changes	Alt+Bksp
Post/**K**eep Locked	Ctrl+F5
Lookup **H**elp	Ctrl+Space
Move Help	Ctrl+Shift+Space

The Insert, Delete, Lock/Unlock, Cancel Changes, and Post/Keep Locked commands are available when you are in

4

Edit mode. While in Edit mode, Insert lets you insert a record; Delete deletes the current record; Lock lets you lock a record you are editing (this applies to users of Paradox on a network), and Post/Keep Locked lets you maintain a lock in a record (on a network) even after you have finished changing its value. (Chapter 5 contains more details on changing records.)

Navigating with the SpeedBar

You can also move through your database by using the SpeedBar. Whenever a table is in the active window, the table version of the SpeedBar appears, as shown here:

As with all mouse operations, you can click the appropriate icon to perform the desired operation. The First Record, Previous Record, Next Record, and Last Record buttons behave the same as their counterparts in the Record menu. You can click any of these icons to move the cursor to the specified location. The Previous Set and Next Set buttons move the cursor by a set, or window full of records. (This is the same as pressing the `Pg Up` or `Pg Dn` keys, or using Record/Previous Set or Record/Next Set.)

`Ctrl`+`Z` is a shortcut for searching for a field value.

You can use the Locate Field Value and Locate Next buttons to quickly find a record based upon the contents of a particular field. (These options are covered in more detail in the next chapter.) When you click the Locate Field Value button, a Locate Value dialog box appears, as shown here:

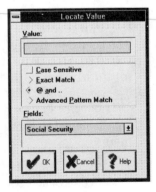

You can accept the field that appears or select a different field from the list box. Type the desired search term in the Value text box, and then click OK to begin the search. Use the Search Next button on the SpeedBar to search for additional occurrences of the same value. For more details on searching for specific data, see Chapter 5.

Changing a Table's Properties

Aspects of a table that govern its appearance, such as column widths and styles of gridlines, are known as table properties.

While working with your data, you may find that you frequently need to see particular kinds of information at a glance. For example, the ABC Temporaries table contains a number of fields, not all of which can be viewed in tabular form at the same time. However, for most day-to-day needs, the staff can get the needed data from four fields: Last Name, Social Security, Phone, and Assignment. If these fields could be viewed at once, most requests for information could be satisfied with one quick glance at the screen.

4

To meet such needs, Paradox lets you change the appearance of a table on the screen. You can move columns, or shrink or expand column widths, to present an optimal viewing area. You can change the alignment of data in fields, or of headings. You can change the fonts used to display data, the number and currency formats, and the colors used. The underlying data in your table does not change when you do this; only the appearance of the table on the screen is affected.

Using Direct Manipulation

Many of the properties of a table in Paradox are most easily changed using direct manipulation. *Direct manipulation* simply means that you can change something by using the mouse to work directly with the desired object. For example, you can move columns by clicking the desired column headings and dragging the heading to a new location; you can resize columns by dragging their right border; and you can change the height of a row by dragging the *record marker* (the line underneath the first field at the upper left of the table) up or down. As you move the mouse pointer over various parts of the table, it changes shape. The areas where the pointer changes shape are known as *hot zones*, and you can use the mouse to directly manipulate various properties of a table when in these hot zones. Figure 4-2 shows the different hot zones of a table.

Column grid line

Heading

Record marker

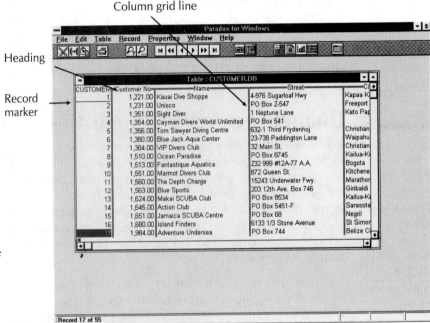

Direct manipulation of a table with hot zones
Figure 4-2.

Manipulating Columns

To move a column, click and drag its column heading. Notice that when you click the heading, the mouse pointer changes into a double-headed arrow. Drag the arrow to the left or right to the desired location for the column and release the mouse button. Paradox will move the column to the new location.

You can also use the keyboard to change the order of the columns in a table by using the Rotate key (Ctrl+R). Select the desired column by clicking anywhere within it or by moving the cursor to the column; then press Ctrl+R. Paradox will move the selected column to the end of the table, and will shift to the left all other columns.

Changing Column Widths

You can expand or reduce the width of a column to display more information per column or to provide additional room for the display of other columns. To change a column's width, you click the column's right grid line while the pointer is in the heading area. You'll know that you have the pointer in the correct area when it changes into a double-headed arrow, as shown here.

$$\Longleftrightarrow$$

Drag the grid line to the left to decrease the column width, or to the right to increase the column width.

4

Changing Properties by Inspection

Throughout Paradox, you right-click things to inspect their properties.

Paradox lets you change many properties of a table by *inspecting* it. You inspect parts of a table (or any other object in Paradox) by pointing at it and clicking the right mouse button. With a table, you can inspect the fields (columns) of the table, the column headings, or the grid. For example, if you right-click the mouse while the mouse cursor is located in any field of a table, a properties menu appears that lets you inspect the properties of that field. Figure 4-3 shows the properties menu for the Dependents field. As you would expect, this menu appears whenever you right-click within the Dependents field. You can use these menu options to change the alignment, colors, or fonts used for this particular field. And in the case of numeric, currency, or date fields, you'll use the properties menu to change the format used by the values. Changing number and currency formats will be covered in a later section.

Changing Alignment

Right-click in any field to open that field's properties menu and change the various properties for the field.

You can change the alignment of a field or of a column heading. Paradox lets you align the text both horizontally (at the left, center, or right of the column), and vertically (at the top, bottom, or center of the row). In Figure 4-4, the first column of data is left-aligned, the second column is centered, and the third column is right-aligned. The change takes effect for the entire field; you cannot change the alignment of a single record of data.

To change the alignment of a field, right-click any field in the desired column to open the properties menu for that field. (If you wish to

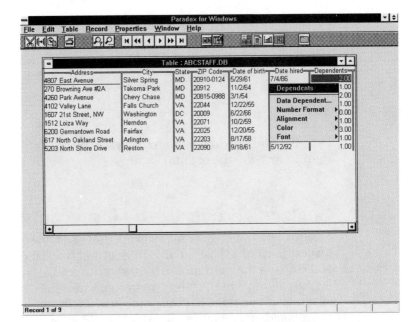

Properties
menu
associated with
Dependents
field
Figure 4-3.

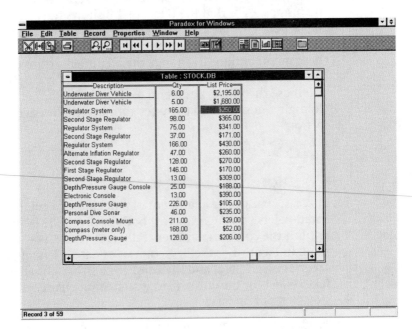

Possibilities for
column
alignment
Figure 4-4.

change the alignment for a column heading, right-click the heading itself.)

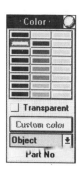

From the properties menu, choose Alignment. From the next menu to appear, choose Left, Center, or Right as desired for the horizontal alignment; and choose Top, Center, or Bottom as desired, for the vertical alignment.

Changing Colors

Your monitor and/or printer must support color in order for colors to be displayed or printed.

To change colors for the contents of a field or for a column heading, first right-click the desired field (or the heading) to open the properties menu for that field or heading. Then choose Color to display the Color Palette, which is shown here:

4

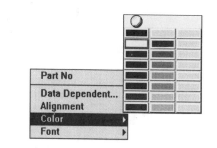

You can apply the desired color by clicking it. When you click a color, Paradox applies that color to the contents of the chosen field or column heading and the Color Palette disappears.

Note that you can experiment with different colors, or use the same Color Palette to make changes to a number of parts of a table, by clicking the *snap*, the circular button located at the upper-left side of the Color Palette. If you click the snap, the appearance of the Color Palette changes, and you can now drag the Color Palette around on the screen. The snap simply "snaps," or attaches the palette, so it does not disappear when you make color changes; you must put it away by clicking the snap again.

You can now apply a color and the Color Palette will remain open. You can click other fields or column headings, and make additional changes using the Color Palette. When you are done making changes, click the snap to put the Color Palette away.

Changing Fonts

To change the font used for the contents of a field or for a column heading, first right-click the desired field (or the heading) to open the properties menu for that field or heading. Then choose Font. The next menu to appear provides a choice of typeface, size, style, or color.

When you choose the Typeface option, Paradox displays a menu of available typefaces. (Your available typefaces will vary depending on the fonts that are installed on your system under Windows. Most systems will have Arial or Helvetica, Times New Roman or Times Roman, Courier, and System as available fonts.) Click the desired typeface to apply it to the selected field or column heading.

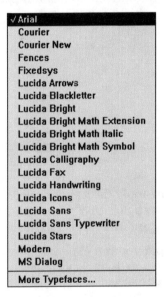

When you choose the Size option, Paradox displays a menu of available point sizes. Click the desired size to apply it to the selected field or column heading.

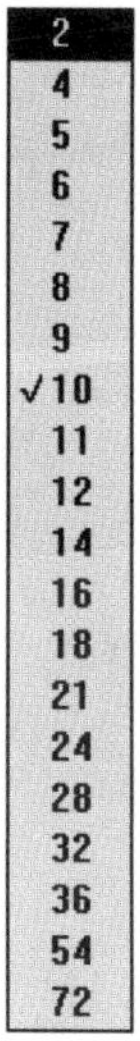

4

```
  2
  4
  5
  6
  7
  8
  9
√ 10
 11
 12
 14
 16
 18
 21
 24
 28
 32
 36
 54
 72
```

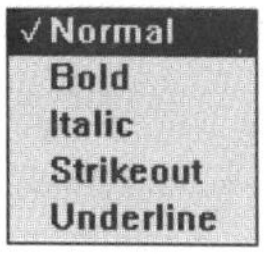

```
√ Normal
  Bold
  Italic
  Strikeout
  Underline
```

You can use the Style option to select from among various styles of text: Normal, Bold, Italic, Strikeout, and Underline. Choose Normal to remove any of the other style attributes that you set previously, returning the text to normal. Choose Bold to display the text in a heavier style; choose Italic to display the text using italics; choose Strikeout to display the text with a line running through it; and choose Underline to display the text with underlining.

The Color option lets you change the colors used by the text, using the same Color Palette as was described earlier.

You can change font properties for more than one field or heading at a time by using the snap button located at the top of the Font menu. When you click the snap, the appearance of the Font menu changes, as shown here, and you can now drag the Font menu around on the screen.

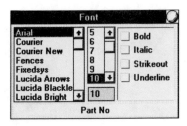

You can now apply a font, and the Font menu will remain open. You can then click other fields or column headings and modify them using the Font menu. When you are done making changes, click the snap to close the Font menu.

Changing Number and Currency Formats

You can change the formats used to display numbers by inspecting the field and choosing Number Format. When you inspect (right-click) a number field and choose Number Format from the properties menu, several options appear. Choose the desired format to apply it to the contents of the chosen field. As an example, you could choose Integer as a format if you wanted numbers displayed with no decimal places.

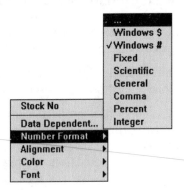

✦ The Windows $ format uses the default currency symbol and currency format, as set by the International setting option in the Windows Control Panel.

✦ The Windows # format is the default Windows format for numeric display. You define this format with the International setting

See Chapter 14 for details on changing the default number and currency symbols used by Windows.

option in the Windows Control Panel. (See Chapter 14 for details on using the Windows Control Panel to change currency settings.)

✦ The Fixed format displays the numbers with two decimal places. Thousands separators are not used, and negative numbers are preceded by a minus sign.

✦ The Scientific format displays numeric values using scientific, or exponential, notation. Values appear as numbers from one to ten, with two decimal places, multiplied by a power of ten. For example, the number 14,000,000 would be represented as 1.4E+07 in scientific notation. Scientific notation is useful for representing very large or very small numbers.

✦ The General format displays values with two decimal places if the number includes a decimal value, and omits trailing zeroes. Thousands separators are not used, and negative numbers are preceded by a minus sign.

✦ The Comma format displays values with two decimal places if the number includes a decimal value. Trailing zeroes are included, and commas appear as thousands separators. Negative numbers are displayed within parenthesis.

✦ The Percent format displays values as a percentage, and the Integer format displays numbers as integers, or whole numbers.

Changing Date Formats

If you inspect any date field in a table, Paradox includes a Date Format option in the menu that appears. Choosing the Date Format option

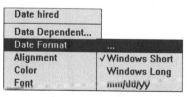

reveals another menu with three choices: Windows Short, Windows Long, and mm/dd/yy. Select Windows Short, and Paradox displays the dates using the short date format defined in the International setting of the Windows Control Panel dialog box. Select Windows Long, and Paradox displays the dates using the long date format defined in the International setting of the Windows Control Panel dialog box. Select mm/dd/yy, and Paradox displays dates with two-digit numbers separated by slashes for the month, followed by the day, followed by the year.

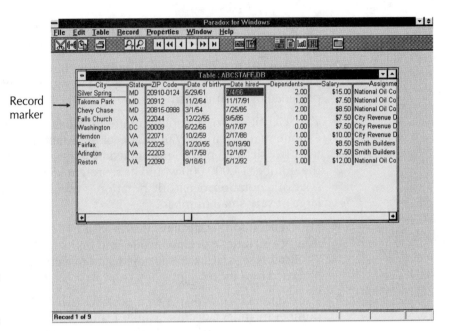

Record marker →

Record marker
Figure 4-5.

Changing the Spacing Between Records

You can change the spacing between records by dragging the record marker. As Figure 4-5 shows, the record marker is the line that appears in the leftmost field of the uppermost record. When you change the spacing between records, you are in effect changing the depth of a row. Use less spacing between rows to fit more rows in a given area; use more spacing between rows to increase readability, or to add room for graphics in graphic fields.

If you place the mouse pointer on the record marker, it changes to a double-headed arrow. Click and drag upwards or downwards as desired, and the space between records will change by a corresponding amount. Note that this changes the spacing between all records, and not just the one containing the current record. Figure 4-6 shows the ABCSTAFF table after this technique was used to drag the record marker downwards approximately one eighth of an inch.

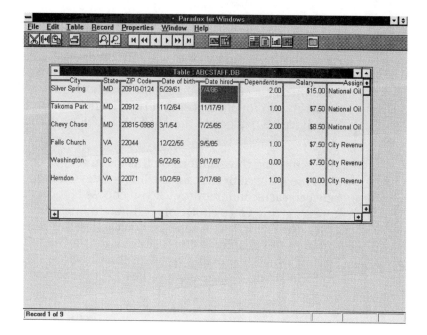

ABCSTAFF
table with
increased
spacing
between rows
Figure 4-6.

4

Changing the Grid Lines

You can also change the *grid lines*, or the pattern of lines that appears
between columns of a table. Paradox lets you change the style of lines,
their color, and also the number of lines displayed. As you can see, grid
lines appear by default between the table's columns. In addition, you
can add grid lines between the rows of records.

To change the grid lines, inspect the grid line by placing the pointer on
the line and right-clicking. When the properties menu appears, choose
Grid Lines. The next menu to appear, shown here, offers six options:
Heading Lines, Column Lines, Row Lines, Color, and Spacing.

The first three options are *toggles*; you can choose them to turn them on or off. When these options are on, a check mark appears to their left. Choosing Heading Lines will turn on or off the lines that appear in the table heading. Choosing Column Lines will turn on or off the lines that appear between columns. Choosing Row Lines will turn on or off lines between rows. (This option is off by default.) In Figure 4-7, row lines have been added to the ABCSTAFF table with the Row Lines option.

The remaining three options on this menu let you change the style of lines used, the color used for the lines or the number of lines displayed between each column or row. If you choose Line Style, another menu appears giving you a choice of six different line styles. If you choose Color, the Color Palette appears. You can use this palette as described earlier in this chapter to choose a color for the lines. If you choose Spacing, Paradox provides you with three choices: single, double, or triple. In Figure 4-8, the table at the top of the screen uses single-line

Table : ABCSTAFF.DB					
Last name	First name	Address	City	State	ZI
Westman	Andrea	4807 East Avenue	Silver Spring	MD	209
Robinson	Shirley	270 Browning Ave #3C	Takoma Park	MD	209
Morse	Marcia	4260 Park Avenue	Chevy Chase	MD	208
Jackson	David	4102 Valley Lane	Falls Church	VA	220
Robinson	Wanda	1607 21st Street, NW	Washington	DC	200
Hart	Edward	6200 Germantown Road	Fairfax	VA	220

ABCSTAFF
table with row
lines added
Figure 4-7.

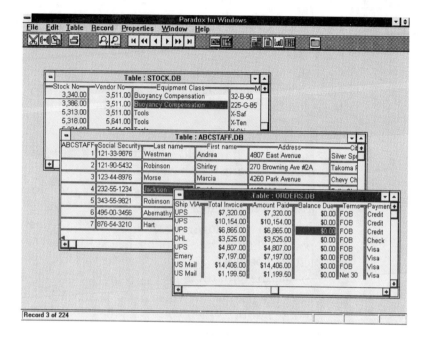

Tables using
different line
spacing
Figure 4-8.

spacing; the one in the middle of the screen uses double-line spacing;
and the one at the bottom of the screen uses triple-line spacing.

Saving Changes to a View

When you modify the view properties used by a table, these changes
are not permanent unless you tell Paradox to save them. You can save
changes made to a view's properties by choosing View Properties from
the properties menu and then choosing Save from the menu that
appears. When you save a table's properties in this way, the underlying
structure of the table does not change; the table's appearance changes
in accord with the changes you've made to the view. The next time you
load the table under Paradox, any changes to the view that you saved
will be automatically loaded. Also, if you make changes to a table's view
and then decide that you would rather restore the table to its original
view, you can choose View from the properties menu and then choose
Restore from the menu that appears.

Hands-On Practice: Changing the Table's Layout

Since the ABC Temporaries staff wants to see the Social Security, Last Name, Phone, and Assignment fields most frequently, you can move the columns containing those fields to the left side of the table. Follow these steps to do so:

1. First, if the Phone field is not already in view, use the scroll bars as needed to bring it into view.

2. Place the pointer in the heading area of the Phone field; it should assume a rectangular shape.

3. Click and hold down the left mouse button; as you do so, the pointer changes into a double-headed arrow. Drag the arrow to the left. As you reach the left side of the window, the table will scroll so that the leftmost fields of the table come into view.

4. Place the pointer anywhere in the First Name field and release the mouse button. When you do so, the Phone field will appear in its new location, between the Last Name field and the First Name field.

5. Using the same technique, click and drag the Assignment field over the existing First Name field. When you release the mouse button, the Assignment field should be placed between the Phone and First Name fields.

With this modified table, ABC Temporaries employees can now view all the desired fields at the same time, as shown in Figure 4-9.

You might want to try making other changes to the view of the table now. Try dragging down the record marker (remember, it's the horizontal line under the first record in the far left column) to increase the row spacing. Right-click the grid line between any two columns to bring up the properties menu and choose Grid Lines. From the Grid Lines menu that appears, turn on the Row Lines options to add lines between the table's rows. Figure 4-10 shows how your table might look after such changes.

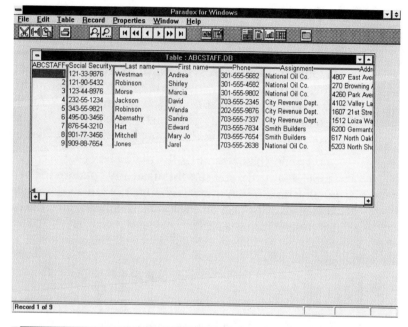

ABCSTAFF
table with
changes in field
locations
Figure 4-9.

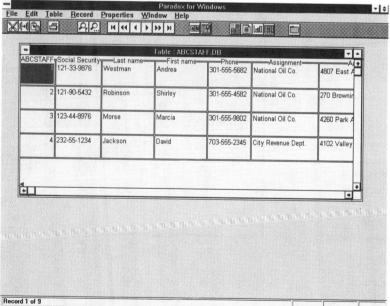

Table with row
lines and
increased row
spacing
Figure 4-10.

Listing a Table's Structure

As you work with multiple tables, on occasion you may not recall exactly what fields are present in your tables. Of course, you could open a table and scroll across its width to see the names of the fields, but there is a faster way. You can choose Info Structure from the Table menu to get information on the structure of a Paradox table. For example, if ABCSTAFF is the active table and you choose Info Structure from the Table menu, the dialog box shown in Figure 4-11 appears.

To examine the structure of a table, choose Table/Info Structure.

This dialog box resembles the dialog box that you use when creating a table. However, you cannot make any changes to the table from this dialog box. If you want to change the table's design, you must use the Restructure option on the Table menu. Chapter 12 contains the details on restructuring a table.

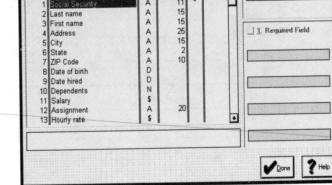

Table Info
Structure dialog
box
Figure 4-11.

Quick Summary

Moving Around in a Table

With the mouse, use the scroll bars, or use the SpeedBar icons for next record, next set, previous record, previous set, first record, and last record.

From the keyboard, you can use the cursor keys, and/or the Pg Up and Pg Dn keys. You can also use the options of the Record menu; open the Record menu, and choose next record, next set, previous record, previous set, first record, or last record.

Moving a Column

Click and drag the column heading to the desired new location.

Changing a Column's Width

Place the pointer over the column's right grid line in the heading area, where it changes to the shape of a double-headed arrow. Drag the grid line left or right as desired to widen or narrow the column.

Changing a Row's Height

Place the pointer over the record marker (the line at the leftmost column of the uppermost record), where it changes to the shape of a double-headed arrow. Drag the grid line up or down as desired to widen or narrow the row.

Changing a Field's Alignment

Right-click the field to open the properties menu, and choose Alignment; then, choose the desired alignment from the next menu to appear.

Changing a Field's Color

Right-click the field to open the properties menu, and choose Color; then, choose the desired color from the Color Palette.

4

Quick Summary *(continued)*

Changing a Field's Fonts

Right-click the field to open the properties menu, and choose Font; then, choose Typeface, Size, or Style from the next menu to appear, and select the desired typeface, style, or character font.

Changing a Field's Number, Currency, or Date Formats

Right-click the field to open the properties menu, and choose Number Format (in the case of number or currency fields) or choose Date Format (in the case of date fields). From the next menu to appear, choose the desired format.

Saving Changes to a View

Choose Properties/View Properties. From the next menu to appear, choose Save.

Listing a Table's Structure

Choose Table/Info Structure.

CHAPTER

5

ENTERING AND EDITING DATA

As you work with your data within Paradox, you will find that much of your time is spent adding new records, finding specific information, making changes, moving and copying data between different tables, rearranging records through sorting, changing the structure of tables, and performing similar tasks that keep your database current. This chapter will explain how to perform those tasks effectively.

Chapter 3 provided an introduction to editing records within Paradox. Because updating information is a major task with any database, it is worth spending the time to learn the ways you can edit with Paradox.

Of course, before you can edit records in any table, you must open and activate that table. As described in Chapter 3, you can open a table by choosing the File/Open/Table option. If multiple tables are open, you can activate any table by choosing it by name from the Window menu or by clicking anywhere within it.

More About Editing

In Paradox, you must be in Edit mode to make changes to a table.

Paradox lets you edit records in three ways: by pressing the Edit (F9) key, by choosing the Edit Data option from the Table menu, or by clicking on the Edit Data icon in the SpeedBar. Using any of these three methods places you in Edit mode. Whenever you are in Edit mode, Paradox displays the word "Edit" in the status bar, as shown in Figure 5-1. And as you learned earlier, you can press Form Toggle (F7) to move back and forth between Table mode, which displays the records in a tabular fashion, and Form mode, which displays the records one at a time in an on-screen form.

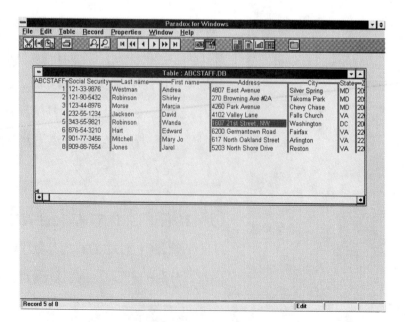

Table in Edit mode
Figure 5-1.

When you are in Edit mode, typing within a field immediately erases any previous entry in that field. You cannot move the cursor to individual characters while you are in this mode, but you can use the [Backspace] key as necessary to delete characters and then retype to correct mistakes. You can also use the [Ctrl]+[Backspace] key combination to delete an entire value in any field. Once you've made the desired changes to a field, use [Enter], [Tab], or the cursor keys to move out of the field. Once the cursor leaves a field, any changes you made are automatically saved to the record.

REMEMBER: When editing, you can use [F7] to move between Form mode and Table mode.

5

Inserting and Deleting Records

As you've just learned, you can edit existing material in your table by getting into Edit mode and modifying existing records. In addition, you can edit your database by deleting records from or adding new records to your table with the techniques outlined in this section. You can insert new records in either of two ways. While you are in Edit mode, you can press the [Ins] key or choose Insert from the Record menu to open a new, blank record at the cursor location. Then you can make the desired entries into the fields and press [F9] when you are done to leave Edit mode.

WARNING. Deletions are permanent. Make sure you want to delete a record before doing so.

To delete a record, place the cursor in any field of the desired record and press [F9] to enter Edit mode. Next, choose Delete from the Record menu or press [Ctrl]+[Del]. Note that a deleted record is gone for good; you cannot use the Undo option on the Edit menu to retrieve a deleted record. The only way to get back a deleted record is to reenter the entire record.

Using Field View Mode

With long entries, it would be time-consuming to correct errors by backspacing or deleting large amounts of text. Fortunately, Paradox provides another editing mode known as Field View mode. The normal Edit mode that Paradox uses is more ideally suited for data entry. Remember, when you place the cursor in a field and begin typing, Paradox replaces any existing entry with the newly typed text. If instead you want to move to a field containing existing text and move the cursor around in that field to add or change text without eliminating the existing entry, you must use Paradox's Field View mode.

Once you are in Edit mode, you can enter Paradox's Field View mode in any of the following ways:

◆ By choosing Field View from the Table menu. If you are using a form, you can choose Field View from the Form menu.

◆ By pressing F2.

◆ By clicking the Field View icon in the SpeedBar.

◆ By double-clicking on an unselected field.

◆ By clicking once on a field that is already selected.

Using any of these methods places you in Field View mode. Paradox displays the message, "In field view, press F2 to leave field" on the left side of the status bar and displays the word "Field" on the right side of the status bar, as shown in Figure 5-2.

When you want to make minor corrections to existing entries, Field View mode is best.

Once you are in Field View mode, a text cursor appears at the end of any existing text in the field. You can then use the cursor keys to move around within the existing entry and make the desired changes. To exit from Field View mode, press F2 or click an unselected field.

It's important to note that the editing keys behave somewhat differently in Field View mode than in Edit mode. In Edit mode, the cursor keys move you from field to field. In Field View mode, by contrast, the cursor keys move you between characters within the field. Table 5-1 describes how the editing keys work in Field View mode.

5

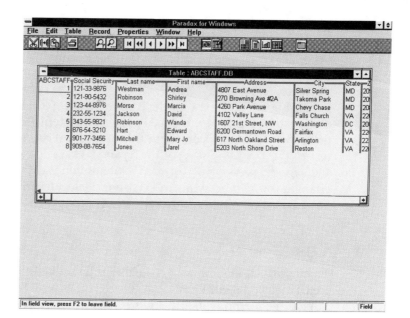

Table in Field
View mode
Figure 5-2.

Key	Results in Field View Mode
←	Moves left one character
→	Moves right one character
↑	Moves up one line within field *
↓	Moves down one line within field *
Backspace	Deletes character to left
Del	Deletes selected text
Ins	Inserts record
Home	Moves to start of field
End	Moves to end of field
Enter	Stores value and moves to next field
Tab	Stores value and moves to next field
* If field contains more than one line, as with long character fields or memo fields	

Editing Keys
Available in
Field View
Mode
Table 5-1.

About Persistent Field View

If you want to make minor corrections to a large number of records, Persistent Field View can be very useful.

Normally when you're in Field View mode, moving to another field takes you out of Field View mode and places you back in Edit mode. However, in some cases, you will want to move between fields while remaining in Field View mode. Paradox lets you do this through the use of Persistent Field View mode. To enter Persistent Field View mode, press Ctrl+F2. Once you are in this mode, you can move between fields using Tab, Enter, Shift+Tab or the ↑ and ↓ keys. To exit Persistent Field View mode, press Ctrl+F2 again. Note, if you want to make any changes to the table while in Persistent Field View mode, you must also be in Edit mode (press F9 to enter Edit mode).

Using Field View to Edit Data in Memo Fields

As mentioned in Chapter 3, you also enter and edit data within memo fields by using Field View mode. Once you enter Edit mode, place the cursor in a memo field and enter Field View mode using any of the methods mentioned previously, you'll see a memo view window containing the text of the memo. Figure 5-3 shows a record in the

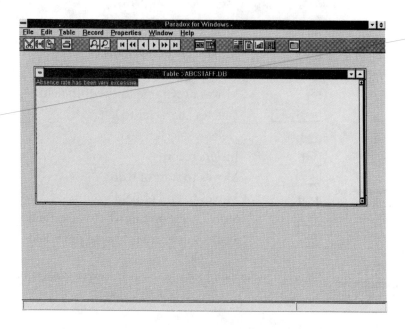

ABCSTAFF table with Comments field visible in Field View mode
Figure 5-3.

ABCSTAFF table with the Comments field visible in a memo view window.

You can enter data just as you would in any other field when you are in Field View mode. Since memo fields are typically used for large amounts of text, you may find it helpful to use Windows' cutting, copying, and pasting techniques to copy or paste information from other applications such as a Windows word processor document into a Paradox memo field. See the section "Copying and Moving Data" later in this chapter for more details.

A Note About Graphic Fields

5

Since Paradox supports graphic fields, you can insert graphic data from other programs into a graphic field. This process will be fully explained in Chapter 8. However, this section briefly describes the steps needed to place graphic data into a graphic field.

REMEMBER: Paradox supports .BMP, .TIF, .PCX, or .CGM graphic image formats.

To place graphic data into a graphic field, first enter Edit mode by pressing `F9`. Next, enter Field View mode by pressing `F2`. Then either type the filename of the graphic object into the graphic field, or cut or copy the graphic object from its source application under Windows and paste it into the graphic field of the table. (If the graphic was previously stored in the Windows Clipboard, you can choose the Edit/Paste/Paste From Clipboard option.) To cut and paste graphics from another application, perform the following steps:

1. Open the graphic in the source application.
2. Select the object and use the Cut or Copy command on the Edit menu to cut or copy it to the Windows Clipboard.
3. Activate Paradox and open the table or form into which you want to insert the graphic.
4. If necessary, press `F9` to enter Edit mode.

5. Select the graphic field where you want to insert the graphic.

6. Choose Paste from the Edit menu or click the Paste From Clipboard icon in the SpeedBar.

After the graphic has been inserted, you can adjust the size of the field to see as much of the image as you want.

TIP: See Chapter 8 for further details on this subject and for examples that make use of graphic fields.

 ## Hands-On Practice: Adding and Editing Records

To add a new record to the ABC Temporaries table, follow these instructions:

1. Place the cursor at any record in the Social Security field.

2. Press F9 to enter Edit mode and then press the Ins key to add a new, blank record.

3. Enter the following information to fill in the new record:

Social Security:	495-00-3456
Last Name:	Abernathy
First Name:	Sandra
Address:	1512 Loiza Way
City:	Herndon
State:	VA
ZIP Code:	22071
Date of Birth:	10/02/59
Date Hired:	02/17/88
Dependents:	1
Salary:	10.00
Assignment:	City Revenue Dept.
Hourly Rate:	18.00
Phone:	703-555-7337
Comments:	Too new to evaluate.

Suppose you learn that Ms. Shirley Robinson has moved to a different apartment on the same street and you wish to correct the address without retyping the entire line. Follow these steps to do so:

1. Move the cursor to the address for Shirley Robinson and press F2 to get into Field View mode.

2. Change the address to 267 Browning Ave, #2A.

3. Press F2 or Enter to leave Field View mode.

Helpful Shortcuts

While adding new records, you may find certain of Paradox's shortcut key combinations to be quite useful. One such shortcut is the Ditto key combination (Ctrl+D), which you can use to repeat a prior entry without retyping. If you press Ctrl+D from within a blank field in a new record, Paradox repeats the entry stored in the field immediately above. Another useful shortcut key that only applies to date fields is the Spacebar. If you press the Spacebar while in a date field, Paradox automatically enters the current month, day, and year (as measured by your PC's clock) into the date field.

5

Hands-On Practice: Using the Shortcut Keys

For example, suppose ABC Temporaries hired the spouse of an existing employee, Marcia Morse. Instead of manually typing all of the characters for William Morse, you can insert a new record under the one for Marcia Morse and then use the shortcut keys to duplicate much of the information and to enter today's date as the date of hire. To do so, follow these instructions:

1. If you are not in Edit mode now, press F9 and move the cursor to the record immediately following the one for Marcia Morse.

2. Press the Ins key once to create a new record, as shown in Figure 5-4.

3. Make sure the cursor is in the Social Security field and enter **805-34-6789**.

4. Move the cursor to the First Name field and enter **William**.

5. For most of the remaining fields, you can duplicate the fields in the previous record, the one for Marcia Morse. First, move the cursor to the Last Name field and press [Ctrl]+[D] to duplicate the entry for the prior record.

6. Use the same technique to duplicate the Address, City, State, and ZIP Code fields, from the previous record. Just move to each field and press [Ctrl]+[D].

7. In the Date of Birth field, enter **8/17/52**.

8. For the Date Hired field, press the [Spacebar] three times. Each time you press the [Spacebar], Paradox will insert part of the current date: the month, then the day, and finally the year.

9. Now enter **1** for Dependents, **7.50** for Salary, **Smith Builders** for Assignment, and **12.00** for Hourly rate.

10. Then move to the Phone field and again use [Ctrl]+[D] to duplicate the prior entry.

11. In the Comments field, press [F2] to begin editing in memo view and then enter the text **Too new to evaluate**.

12. Finally, press [F9] to exit from field view of the memo field, and to end the editing process.

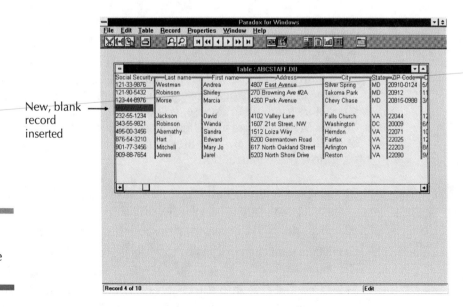

New, blank
record
inserted

New record
inserted into
existing table
Figure 5-4.

Locating Records

With a table as small as the ABCSTAFF table, you can easily find a record by looking for a specific name within the table. However, when there are hundreds or thousands of names and items in your tables, finding a record is not that simple. Paradox offers sophisticated query features for selecting one or more records; these are described in detail in Chapter 6. However, you can also use a quick method to search for the first record that contains the desired information: the Zoom key (Ctrl + Z).

Use the Zoom key (Ctrl + Z) to quickly locate a record.

When you press Ctrl + Z , the Locate Value dialog box appears, as shown here. From within this dialog box, choose the field on which to conduct the search from the Fields drop-down list box. (Click on the downward-pointing arrow on the right side of the list box to display a list of available fields from which to choose.) Then enter the value that you wish to search for and click the OK button to initiate the search.

5

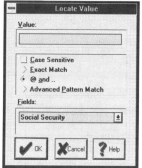

Follow these steps to try the Zoom feature on the ABCSTAFF table:

1. Make sure that the ABCSTAFF table is active and then press Ctrl + Z . Paradox will display the Locate Value dialog box that you just saw.

2. Select Social Security in the Fields list box and enter **876-54-3210** in the Value text box. Then click OK. The cursor will move to the matching Social Security number, which is for Mr. Hart

3. Now press Ctrl + Z to display the Locate Value dialog box again.

4. Select Last Name from the Fields list box and enter **Westman** in the Value text box. The cursor will move to the record for Ms. Westman.

The Zoom feature works well for simple searches, or for searches in which you are searching a unique key field such as Social Security. Note, however, that the Zoom key finds the first occurrence of the item.

See Chapter 6 for additional ways to effectively search for data.

In other words, if you search for Robinson in the Last Name field, you will find the first "Robinson" in the table, which may or may not be the one you are looking for. You can use the Ctrl+A key combination (Locate Next) to find the next occurrence of the same search value. However, this method may not be that effective in a large database with many duplicates in the field in which you are searching. For example, if you are searching for Zora Jones in a database that contains several hundred occurrences of the name Jones, this technique will not serve you well.

In addition, when you want to search for items that are dependent on more than one field (as in a combination of Last and First Name), you must resort to the more powerful query features offered by Paradox. Again, these features are covered in detail in Chapter 6.

You can also search for a specific field or for a record based on the record number. To do so, choose Locate from the Record menu. The next menu to appear offers three available choices: Field, Record Number, or Value, as shown here:

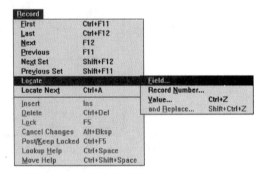

If you choose Field, a list of the table's fields appears, as shown here:

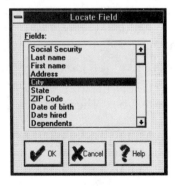

Select the desired field and the cursor will move to that field in the current row of the table. If you choose Record Number, a dialog box requests the desired record number:

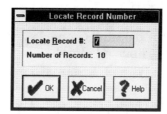

(The record numbers appear in the far left column of a table, and are automatically provided by Paradox.) Enter the record number and click OK to move the cursor to that record. The last choice, Value, brings up the Locate Value dialog box that appears when you press the Zoom (Ctrl+Z) key.

5

Copying and Moving Data

In some cases, you can save time by copying data from one place in a table to another, or by moving data within the table. You can use the Cut, Copy, and Paste options on the Edit menu to copy and move data between the fields of a table, or between fields of different tables. You can also use these menu options to move data from other Windows applications into the fields of a Paradox table.

To move data, first enter Edit mode by pressing F9. Then select the desired data with the mouse and choose Cut from the Edit menu. This removes the data from its existing location and places it on the Windows Clipboard. Next, place the cursor in the field that is to receive the data and choose Paste from the Edit menu to paste the data from the Clipboard into the new location.

NOTE: If you are cutting or copying data between fields, you can only paste the contents of one field of one row at a time. You could not, for example, copy the contents of two rows into two other rows.

You use a similar process to copy data from one location in a table to another. First get into Edit mode by pressing F9 . Then select the desired data with the mouse and choose Copy from the Edit menu to copy the selected data into the Windows Clipboard *without removing it from its original location*. Next, place the cursor in the field that is to receive the data and choose Paste from the Edit menu to paste the data from the Clipboard into the new location.

Copying Data from Other Windows Applications

You can use Windows' cut and copy techniques to copy text from word processing documents into Paradox memo fields.

These cut and copy techniques are especially useful if you have documents in other Windows applications that contain information that you want to insert into Paradox memo fields. As an example, perhaps you need to insert into a Paradox memo field some paragraphs of text from a document that you created in a Windows word processor such as Windows Write. The basic procedure is the same as for copying material within Paradox.

1. With Paradox still running, get into Windows Write or any other Windows word processor (see your Windows documentation for details) and enter the following text:

   Mr. Hart has been an excellent employee. His skills in the area of team leadership have proved quite valuable during the construction project at the Landover Farms housing development.

   If you have an existing document you want to use instead, just open that document.

2. Select the desired text and choose Copy from the Edit menu. In this case, select all of the text you just entered. However, you can also select just a portion of the text from an existing document.

3. Get into Paradox by pressing Alt + Esc or using any other Windows method for switching between applications.

4. Open the table if it is not already open. If it is open, activate the desired Paradox table by clicking anywhere within it.

5. Move to the desired record—in this case the record for Edward Hart—and place the cursor in the memo field. Then press F2 to enter memo view.

6. Finally, choose Paste from the Paradox Edit menu to paste the data copied from the word processor document into the memo field.

TIP: If you work with memo fields and you use Windows-based word processors, you may be able to save time by copying data from your word processor documents directly into Paradox memo fields.

Remember, Paradox places no limits on the amount of text you can store in a memo field.

As an example of this process, consider Figure 5-5. The top half of the screen contains a document in Windows Write, and the first paragraph of that document has been selected using normal mouse selection techniques. After choosing Copy from the Edit menu of Windows Write, the Paradox window is made active, and the cursor has been placed in the Comments field of the table. Once F2 is pressed to begin editing in memo view, Paste is chosen from the Edit menu in Paradox. The result appears in Figure 5-6; the selected text of the memo appears in the Comments field of the table.

5

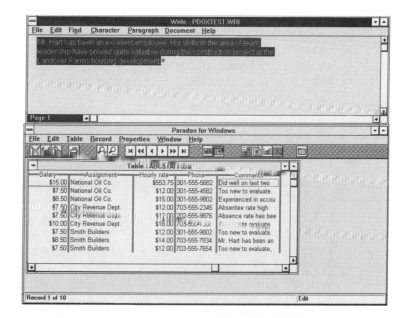

Windows Write
document with
selected text
Figure 5-5.

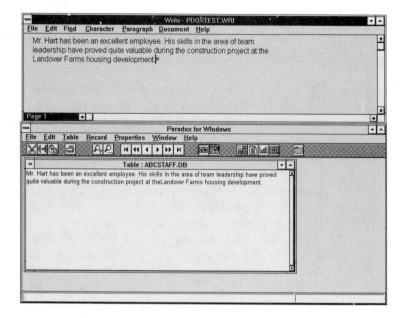

Paradox table after selected text has been copied into memo field **Figure 5-6.**

Using Validity Checks

Validity Checks is a powerful Paradox feature that lets you define the conditions that entries into fields must meet before they will be accepted. Using this feature, you could, for example, specify a minimum and a maximum salary for a salary field, or you could specify that a date field not allow any entries earlier than a certain date.

TIP: Validity checks are very useful for reducing possible data entry errors.

Validity checks apply both to records that you change and to records that you add. To set validity checks, you choose Restructure from the Table menu. This brings up the Restructure dialog box, which is shown in Figure 5-7. In the left side of the dialog box, you highlight the field you wish to set validity checks for.

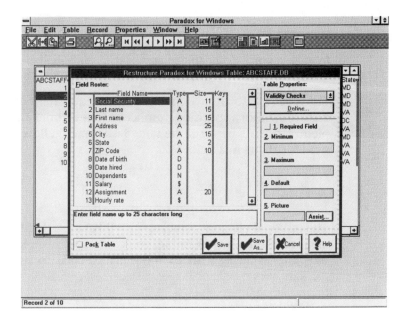

Restructure
dialog box
Figure 5-7.

The right half of this dialog box contains an area you can use to specify validity checks. You can set five types of validity checks in Paradox: Required Field, Minimum, Maximum, Default, and Picture. The Required Field option specifies that a field must have an entry. You use the Minimum and Maximum options to specify a minimum and maximum value. Such values can be numbers, dates, or even letters. For example, you could enter an "A" for a minimum value and "Mz" for a maximum value to accept only names that start with the letters "A" through "M." The Default option lets you set a default value that Paradox will automatically place in a particular field. For instance, you could place the minimum wage as a default value in a salary field if most employees were paid that amount.

The Required Field validity check can be placed on any type of field, including graphic and OLE fields.

The Picture option is a bit more complicated than the rest. It lets you specify a valid format that entries must match before they will be accepted. For example, you could limit telephone numbers to a ten-number format, with the area code surrounded by parentheses and the prefix and suffix separated by hyphens. To do so, you would use a picture format like this:

(###)###-####

Click the
Assist button
in the
Restructure
Table dialog
box to see a
help screen
for picture
format.

In this case, Paradox would supply the literal characters (the hyphen and parenthesis) automatically; the user would not need to type these in each record. You can use any of the symbols shown in Table 5-2 within a picture format.

The repetition count (*) character is the equivalent of repeating another picture symbol a specified number of times. For example, the following picture formats perform the same task, that of allowing up to ten numeric digits in a field:

    ##########
    *10#

The optional elements brackets [ ] tell Paradox that the entry in this area is optional. For example, you could specify a picture format for a telephone number with an optional area code, by using the following format:

    [###] ###-####

You can use the comma to separate alternate values. This is useful for multiple-choice applications. For example, if four different prices of

Character	Description
#	Represents any numeric digit
?	Represents any letter
@	Represents any character
&	Converts letters to uppercase
!	Accepts any characters and converts letters to uppercase
;	Takes the next character literally, not as a special picture character
*	Repetition counts (use to repeat a character)
[]	Items specified are optional
{}	Grouping operator
,	Alternate values

Picture Formats
Table 5-2.

1.99, 2.99, 5.99, and 7.99 are the only acceptable entries in a dollar field, you could use a picture format such as this:

{1.99,2.99,5.99,7.99}

Note the use of the curly braces as grouping operators. The braces surround any group of acceptable items in a picture format.

Setting a Required Field

You use the Required Field option to specify whether a field can be left blank or requires an entry. This option is useful if you want to ensure that data gets entered into a field such as a social security number or a date of birth. If you click in the check box to turn on the option, the field will require an entry. If you try to leave the field without making an entry, Paradox beeps and displays a "required entry" message in the status bar.

Setting a Maximum or Minimum Value

Maximum, minimum, and default values cannot be used with graphic, binary, OLE, or memo fields.

As mentioned, you can use the Maximum option to set a maximum value for a field. As an example, consider setting a maximum salary for employees of ABC Temporaries. Follow these steps to do so:

1. Choose Restructure from the Table menu now. The Restructure dialog box will appear.

2. On the left side of the dialog box, click the Salary field to select it.

3. Making sure that Validity Checks is selected in the list box under Table Properties, click in the Maximum text box and enter **18.00** as the maximum acceptable hourly salary.

Don't close the dialog box yet, as you will set additional validity checks in the paragraphs that follow. If you were done setting validity checks, you would click on the Save button at this point.

Setting a Default Value

At times, you may want to set a default value for a field. When you set a default value, Paradox automatically enters that value in the field when you add a new record to the table and then move the cursor into that field. If a single value is the most common entry in a field, setting a default value can save a significant amount of time during data entry. For example, if you were creating a table of customer names and addresses and most of your company's customers lived in a particular state, you could enter the name of that state as a default value. During data entry, the state name would be filled in automatically. You would only need to make an entry in that field if the state differed from the default.

TIP: Setting a default value can significantly reduce the time you spend doing data entry.

Suppose ABC Temporaries wants to set up a default value for hourly wage. Since most of the agency's employees are billed at a rate of $7.50 per hour, they want this amount to be the default value. To set up this default, follow these easy steps:

Once a default value has been set, you can always override it by typing a new value in that field.

1. If the Restructure Table dialog box is not already open, choose Restructure from the Table menu to open it now.

2. Select the Hourly Rate field on the left side of the dialog box.

3. Click within the Default text box and enter **7.50** as the default value. Again, if you were done setting validity checks, you would click on the Save button at this point.

Keep in mind that you can set default values for alphanumeric as well as number and currency fields. For instance, if most entries for a field called City were Los Angeles, you could enter a default value of Los Angeles for that field.

Using the Picture Option

As mentioned, you can use the Picture option to specify a picture, or format, that the data should match. For example, the Picture option would be useful with the Social Security field of the ABCSTAFF table. With entries in this field, you have a specific pattern of numbers separated by hyphens in specific locations. Without a pattern controlled by the use of the Picture command, you could enter a social security number using different formats. For example, you could enter the same social security number in three different ways:

121-33-5678
121 33 5678
121335678

Using a picture format can reduce accidental duplicate entries.

If you did this, Paradox would treat records with these entries in the key (Social Security) field as three different records, because the values appear different to Paradox. This could lead to accidental duplicates of the same employee. You can prevent this problem by using a picture format that not only restricts the field to precisely 11 characters, but also forces the hyphens to appear at the proper locations automatically.

While still defining the validity checks, click Social Security so you can set validity checks for that field. Then click in the Picture text box in the Restructure dialog box and enter the following:

###-##-####

This picture format tells Paradox to accept as a valid entry any three numbers, followed by a hyphen, followed by any two numbers, followed by a hyphen, followed by any four numbers. When you enter data into the field, Paradox will add the hyphens automatically because they are *literal characters*—that is, characters that are not used as picture symbols. Remember, the picture symbols were shown in Table 5-2.

Testing the Sample Validity Checks

If you want to see the effects of the validity checks you entered in the preceding examples, you can enter a new record. You can enter any data, since you will discard the new record shortly.

1. First, choose Save to close the Restructure dialog box and finish setting the validity checks.
2. Press F9 to begin editing the table, and move the cursor down to the bottom of the table to display a new, blank record.
3. With the cursor in the first field of the table, type **222334444**. Note that as you type the social security number, the picture

format you recorded earlier causes the hyphens to appear in the proper places.

4. Now try moving to the Salary field and entering a value greater than 18.00. Because of the maximum value you set for this field, Paradox does not allow values greater than 18.00 and displays a warning message in the status bar.

5. Next, move the cursor into the Hourly Rate field. Notice that when you move out of the field, Paradox automatically puts the default value of 7.50 into the field.

Since you won't need to use this record in further exercises throughout this book, choose Delete from the Record menu to get rid of the record. Then press F9 to complete the editing process without saving the new record.

Clearing Validity Checks

You can clear validity checks from a table by choosing Restructure from the Table menu, clicking on the desired field in the Restructure dialog box that appears, and turning off or deleting the validity check options, as desired.

Creating the Hours Table

Because Paradox is a relational database, you can use it to work extensively with multiple tables at the same time. Later chapters will explain how you can draw relationships between multiple tables. For now, however, being able to simply view more than one table on the screen will come in handy.

ABC Temporaries needs an additional table that will show how many hours were worked by a given employee while on assignment with a given firm. This table, called HOURS, will be used along with the ABCSTAFF table throughout the remainder of this text, so we will create it in this section.

After some analysis, the management staff at ABC Temporaries decides that the fields shown in Table 5-3 need to be tracked. Note that in this table, a key field designation will not be assigned to any field. There will be intentional duplicates in every field of this table; any record

Field Name	Field Type	Size
Assignment	Alphanumeric	20
Social Security	Alphanumeric	11
Weekend Date	Date	
Hours Worked	Number	

Fields for the
HOURS Table
Table 5-3.

may have the same social security number as other records, and the same is true for the Assignment, Weekend Date, and Hours Worked fields.

Follow these steps to create the HOURS table:

1. Choose the File/New/Table option to begin creating a table.
2. When the Table Type dialog box appears, choose OK to accept the default file type of Paradox for Windows.
3. Using Table 5-3 as a guide, create the four fields of the table. When you have finished defining the fields, the table structure should look like the example shown in Figure 5-8.
4. Click on Save As and enter **HOURS** as the new name for the table in the dialog box. Then click OK to save the new table's definition.

You will need the HOURS table for examples in other chapters of this book.

Now that you've created the new table, you are ready to add data to it. Follow these instructions to do so:

1. Choose the File/Open/Table option.
2. When the Open a Table dialog box appears, choose HOURS and then click the OK button.
3. When the new table appears, press F9 to begin editing. The cursor will appear in the first record of the new table. If you prefer to use a form for entry, press F7 to switch to a form.
4. Now add the records shown in Table 5-4 to your new table. Don't forget the helpful shortcut Ctrl+D key combination for duplicating data.

When you are done adding the records, press Edit (F9) to complete the editing process.

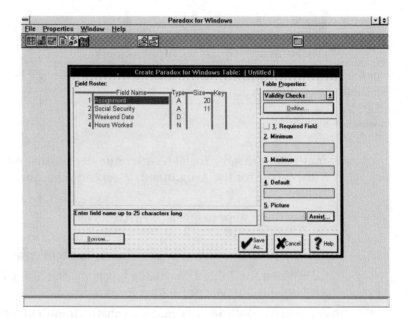

Structure for
HOURS table
Figure 5-8.

Assignment	Social Security	Weekend Date	Hours Worked
National Oil Co.	909-88-7654	7/16/92	35
National Oil Co.	121-33-9876	7/16/92	30
National Oil Co.	121-90-5432	7/16/92	27
National Oil Co.	123-44-8976	7/16/92	32
City Revenue Dept.	343-55-9821	7/16/92	35
City Revenue Dept.	495-00-3456	7/16/92	28
City Revenue Dept.	232-55-1234	7/16/92	30
Smith Builders	876-54-3210	7/23/92	30
Smith Builders	901-77-3456	7/23/92	28
Smith Builders	805-34-6789	7/23/92	35
City Revenue Dept.	232-55-1234	7/23/92	30
City Revenue Dept.	495-00-3456	7/23/92	32
City Revenue Dept.	343-55-9821	7/23/92	32
National Oil Co.	121-33-9876	7/23/92	35
National Oil Co.	909-88-7654	7/23/92	33

New Records
for the HOURS
Table
Table 5-4.

Sorting a Table

After you construct a database, you may need to arrange it in a variety of ways. As an example, consider the needs of the staff at ABC Temporaries. Judi, who does the accounting, often wants to refer to a list of employees arranged by the amount of the salary. Marge, the personnel administrator, prefers to keep a list organized in alphabetical order by name, while Bill, who mails assignments and paychecks to the staff, wants to keep a list arranged by ZIP codes. You can arrange a table by sorting, or changing the order of the table.

When Paradox *sorts* a table, it rearranges all records in the table according to the new order specified. If the table you sort contains a key field, Paradox automatically writes the sorted records to a new table. If the table is not keyed, you can either leave the sorted records in the existing table or place them in a new table. If you sorted a table of names arranged in random order, the sorted table would contain all the records that were in the old table, but they would be arranged in alphabetical order, as shown in Figure 5-9.

You must choose one or more fields on which to sort. In some cases, you will need to sort a database on more than one field. For example, if

5

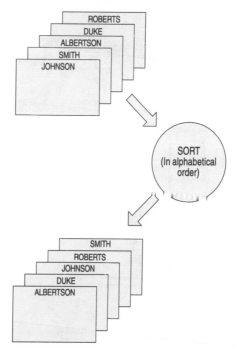

Sorting records in a database
Figure 5-9.

you sort a database using last names as the sort field, you may get groups of records with the same last names but with the first names in random order. In such a case, you can sort the database using one field (such as last name) as the primary sort field and using another field (such as first name) as the secondary sort field. To perform a sort, choose Sort from the Table menu to display the Sort Table dialog box, which is shown in Figure 5-10.

You can sort on any field types except memo, formatted memo, OLE, binary, and graphic.

The Sort Table dialog box enables you to sort a table in ascending or descending order using any field or combination of fields. First, you select the fields upon which you want to base the sort from the Fields list box. Then you add them to the Sort Order list by clicking on the right-pointing arrow to the right of the Fields list box. (The right-pointing arrow places a selected field in the Sort Order list box. The left-pointing arrow removes a selected field from the Sort Order list box; this button is only available if there are field names in the Sort Order list box. The Clear All button removes all fields from the Sort Order list box; this option too is only available when there are field names in the Sort Order list box.) Then you set the options at the top of the dialog box to the desired settings; these options are described in detail a bit later in the chapter.

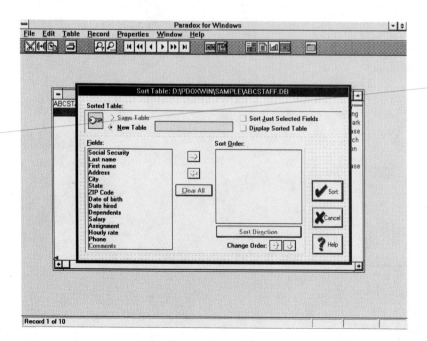

Sort Table
dialog box
Figure 5-10.

The priority of the sort is determined by the order in which you place the fields in the Sort Order list box. For example, suppose you want to sort a table by ZIP codes and—where the ZIP codes are the same—by last names. To do this, you would first move the ZIP Code field to the Sort Order list box. Then you would move the Last Name field to the Sort Order list box. Figure 5-11 shows a Sort Table dialog box filled in to perform this sort.

Indicating the Sort Order

Paradox assumes you wish to sort fields in ascending order. Ascending order means from "A" through "Z" if the sorted field is a text field, lowest to highest number for number fields, and earliest to latest date for date fields. This is indicated by the presence of the numbers, "123..." beside the field names in the Sort Order list box. In most cases, this is how you'll want the table to be sorted. When you instead want to perform a descending order, you can indicate this preference by highlighting the desired field in the Sort Order list box and clicking on the Sort Direction button in the Sort Table dialog box. When you do so, the numbers beside the field name change to "321...," indicating that Paradox will sort the table in descending order.

5

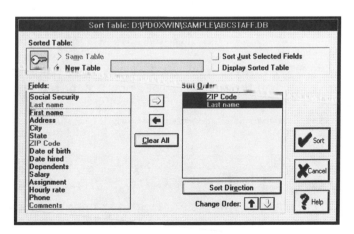

Sort Table dialog box set up to sort a table by ZIP Code and then by Last Name
Figure 5-11.

Selecting the Options

After choosing the desired fields for the sort, you can turn on any desired options at the top of the dialog box. These include the Same Table and New Table buttons, the Sort Just Selected Fields check box, and the Display Sorted Table check box. If you check Same Table, the sorted material overwrites the existing table. (Remember, you cannot sort a keyed table to itself. If the table you are sorting has an index key, the Same Table button will be dimmed, meaning that you cannot select it.) If you check New Table, Paradox displays a text box into which you can enter the table name. The results of the sort will then be stored in the new table.

If you are sorting to a new table and you want to see the data in that table, turn on the Display Sorted Table check box.

When you check the Sort Just Selected Fields check box, Paradox ignores all but the fields selected in the Sort Order list box when performing the sort. In other words, the table is sorted based only on the fields selected; if there are records with the same data in these fields, no additional sorting occurs. On the other hand, if the box is not checked and there are records with the same data in the selected fields, the records in that sorted group will be further arranged in the order of the remaining fields of the table, from left to right. If the Display Sorted Table check box is checked, the sorted table will be opened after the sort has been performed.

Performing the Sort

Once you have entered the desired designations in the Sort Table dialog box, click the Sort button in the dialog box to perform the sort.

TIP: If you want to print records in a report in a particular order, sort the table first. Then produce the report using the sorted table.

Hands-On Practice: Sorting a Table

Things are always clearer with an example. Choose Sort from the Table menu. Paradox will display the Sort Table dialog box.

To satisfy Judi's request for a list of employees arranged by order of the amount of the salary, follow these steps:

1. Click the Salary field in the Fields list box.
2. Then click the right-pointing arrow to move the Salary field into the Sort Order list box.
3. Turn on the New Table button in the upper-left corner of the dialog box. In the text box that appears, enter **SORTS** as the name for the new table. Also turn on the Display Sorted Table check box.
4. Finally, click the Sort button. The new table will appear, arranged by the size of the salary in ascending order, as shown in Figure 5-12.

 NOTE: If you add records to a table that you have already sorted, Paradox does not automatically place the new records in any sorted order. If you want those records to be arranged in a particular order, you must again sort the table after adding the records.

Sorting on Multiple Fields

Assume that you print the table and pass it along to Judi, who immediately decides that wherever the salaries are the same the names should appear in alphabetical order. If you examine the records in your

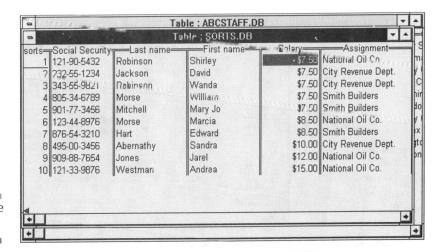

Sorted database
Figure 5-12.

sorted table, it will be clear that for each group of equal salaries, the names are not in alphabetical order. To sort first by salary and then by last name, you need to sort on more than one field, as described here:

1. First, close the SORTS table you just created from the previous sort. Answer No to the prompt that asks if you want to save the table's properties.

2. Then choose Sort from the Table menu.

3. When the Sort Table dialog box appears, click the Salary field in the Fields list box and then click the right-pointing arrow to move the Salary field into the Sort Order list box.

4. Next, click the Last Name field in the Fields list box and then click the right-pointing arrow to place this field in the Sort Order list box.

5. Finally, click the First Name field in the Fields list box and then click the right-pointing arrow. At this point, the Sort Table dialog box should resemble the one shown in Figure 5-13.

The order that you have entered indicates that the table should be sorted in three ways. First, it will be arranged by the salary amount, in

Sort Table dialog box set up to sort on multiple fields
Figure 5-13.

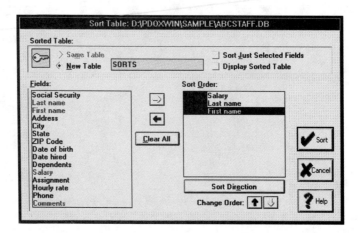

ascending numeric order. Secondly, where salaries are equal, the records will be sorted by last name in ascending alphabetical order. Finally, where last names are the same, the records will be sorted by first name in ascending alphabetical order.

6. Now click the New Table button to select it. In the text box that appears, enter **SORTS** as the name for the new table.

7. Finally, turn on the Display Sorted Table check box and then click the Sort button. The table shown in Figure 5-14 will appear, arranged by the size of the salary in ascending order, and where salaries are the same, by last and then first name. In Figure 5-14, the columns have been rearranged by pressing the Ctrl+R key to simultaneously show the name and salary fields.

5

Changing the Sort Direction

The Sort Direction button in the Sort Table dialog box can be used to change the direction of the sort.

Judi is happy with the printed table you've supplied. However, Marge would rather see a list arranged by date hired with the earliest dates at the bottom of the list. To sort in descending order, you'll need to change the direction of the sort. Follow these steps to do so:

1. Close the SORTS table you just created from the previous sort. Answer No to the prompt that asks if you want to save the table's properties.

2. Choose Sort from the Table menu.

3. When the Sort Table dialog box appears, click the Date Hired field

sorts	Social Security	Last name	First name	Salary	Assignn
1	232-55-1234	Jackson	David	$7.50	City Revenue
2	901-77-3456	Mitchell	Mary Jo	$7.50	Smith Builde
3	805-34-6789	Morse	William	$7.50	Smith Builde
4	121-90-5432	Robinson	Shirley	$7.50	National Oil
5	343-55-9821	Robinson	Wanda	$7.50	City Revenue
6	876-54-3210	Hart	Edward	$8.50	Smith Builde
7	123-44-8976	Morse	Marcia	$8.50	National Oil
8	495-00-3456	Abernathy	Sandra	$10.00	City Revenue
9	909-88-7654	Jones	Jarel	$12.00	National Oil
10	121-33-9876	Westman	Andrea	$15.00	National Oil

Table : SORTS.DB

Database sorted on multiple fields

Figure 5-14.

in the Fields list box and then click the right-pointing arrow to move the Date Hired field into the Sort Order list box.

4. Next, click the Sort Direction button while the Date Hired field is still highlighted within the Sort Order list box. Notice that when you do this, the "123..." designation beside the Date Hired field changes to "321...," indicating the descending order of the sort.

5. Click the New Table button to select it. In the text box that appears, enter **SORTS** as the name for the new table.

6. Finally, click the Display Sorted Table check box to select it and then click the Sort button. The new table will appear, arranged in order of date of hire and with the earliest dates at the bottom of the table, as illustrated in Figure 5-15.

Future chapters will demonstrate how you can use Paradox to draw relationships between the two tables you have created—ABCSTAFF and HOURS—so you can produce reports showing the fees that should be billed to each of ABC Temporaries' clients. If this is a good time for a break, be sure to use Exit from the File menu to leave Paradox.

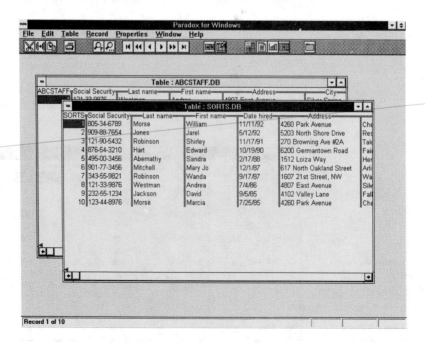

Table sorted in descending order by date hired
Figure 5-15.

Quick Summary

To Enter Edit mode

Open the desired table by choosing the File/Open/Table option. Use your preferred search methods (the cursor keys, the `Pg Up` and `Pg Dn` keys, or the Locate option on the Record menu) to place the cursor at the desired record. Then press Edit (`F9`).

To Insert Records

Enter Edit mode by pressing `F9`. Then use the `Ins` key or choose Insert from the Record menu.

To Delete a Record

Place the cursor in any field of the desired record and press `F9` to enter Edit mode. Next, choose Delete from the Record menu or press `Ctrl`+`Del`.

To Locate a Record

Press Zoom (`Ctrl`+`Z`). In the Locate Value dialog box that appears, choose the desired field to search from the list box. Then enter the value that you wish to search for in the Value box.

To Sort a Table

Choose Sort from the Table menu to display the Sort Table dialog box. Click the field that you want to be the primary sort field and then click the right-pointing arrow to place the field in the Sort Order list box. Then choose any other fields on which you want to sort and add them to the Sort Order list box in the same manner. Choose any other desired options within the dialog box. Also enter a name for the new table, if you turn on the New Table button. Then click Sort to initiate the sort.

5

C H A P T E R

PERFORMING QUERIES

Now that you have significant sets of data stored within a Paradox database, it is time to examine more complex ways to get at the precise data you will need. In the previous chapter, you used the helpful Zoom key combination ([Ctrl]+[Z]) to quickly locate a record, but this is only a simple form of query. You will often need to isolate one or more records based upon a matching condition. For example, you may need to generate a list of all employees working at a particular assignment, or all employees earning over $8.00 per hour. In Paradox, you do this by means of *queries*. The word query means "to ask," and when you use a query in Paradox, you are asking about your data.

Query-by-Example uses simple visual steps, rather than complicated commands, to get at the data you need.

This chapter explains in detail how you can use the File/New/Query option to display a query form, in which you can compose queries. This powerful feature of Paradox uses Query-by-Example design and artificial intelligence technology to make complex requests easy for the user. You won't have to think about any arcane logic behind a detailed set of commands, as with many other database products. With Paradox, you simply check off the fields you want included in the results and provide examples or ranges of the data that you wish to extract. Paradox does the rest for you.

You can also use queries to add or delete records, basing the additions or deletions upon the results of the query. You can even update values in one table based upon a query directed to another table.

Displaying a Query Form

You build queries in a Query Form, which resembles the table you are using to supply the data. To display a Query Form, choose the File/New/Query option. When you do so, Paradox displays a Select File dialog box as shown here:

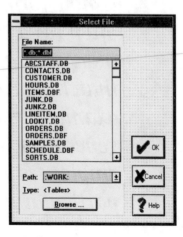

Enter the name of the desired table or choose a table from the dialog box, then click OK. Paradox displays a Query Form similar to the one shown in Figure 6-1.

The Query Form will duplicate the structure of the table that you choose. For example, the Query Form in Figure 6-1 was produced from the ABCSTAFF table. Queries of a relational nature will be covered in more detail in Chapter 11, but for now note that you can repeat this process for additional tables, and make use of examples to link common fields to build a query that provides data from more than one table.

You wouldn't select all fields and then not enter any matching expressions, as this would select the entire database.

To fill out the Query Form, you usually need to perform just two basic steps: You select the fields you want displayed in the answer by clicking in the check box to the left of the field. (Alternately, you can place the cursor in the desired field and press the Check key, F6.) If you wish to see all the fields in the answer, you can click in the check box at the leftmost field of the Query Form to place a check mark in all fields. To remove a check mark from a field, simply click the check box again. (You can also place the cursor in the field again and press F6 to remove the check mark.)

6

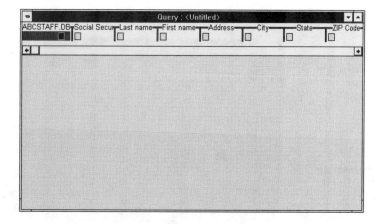

Query Form
Figure 6-1.

For the second step, simply enter a matching expression in any desired field. You only need to perform this step if you want to limit your query to include a specific subset of records; if you want to see all records, you can omit this step.

For example, if you wanted to see all employees with the last name of Robinson, you would move the cursor to the Last Name field, check the field box to select it, and type **Robinson**. To select records where the employee was hired before January 1, 1991, you would enter **< 1/1/91** in the Date Hired field. And if you wanted a list of all employees who earned between 7.50 and 9.00 per hour, you could enter **>=7.50, <=9.00** in the Salary field, as shown in Figure 6-2. You can use many variations, but these are the basic steps involved in constructing a query.

Performing the Query

Once you have filled in the Query Form, there are several methods of initiating the query. You can choose Run from the Query menu, you can click the Run Query icon in the SpeedBar, or you can press F8. The results will appear in a new table named ANSWER. Figure 6-3 shows the results of the query described in Figure 6-2. The new table, ANSWER, is a temporary table. If you perform another query, the resultant answer will overwrite the existing answer table. If you want to store the results permanently, you can first close the ANSWER table and

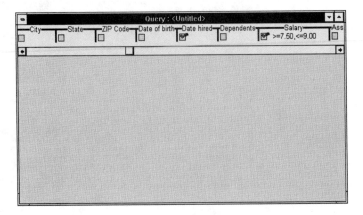

Filled-in Query
Form
Figure 6-2.

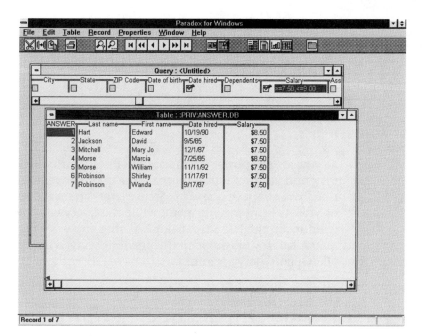

Results of example query Figure 6-3.

then choose the File/Utilities/Rename option to rename the temporary table to something more permanent.

In many cases, you can just perform these few steps to get the kind of information that you need from your database. You can quickly produce reports of critical data by designing a query with the desired fields (you may want to limit the fields so they will fit on a single page), filling in any desired conditions to isolate the needed set of matching records. Perform the query, and the results you need are displayed in the ANSWER table. At this point, you can click the Quick Report icon in the SpeedBar to produce a quick report based on your query.

While the fields in the Query Form may appear narrow, they are no more limited in size than a normal field within a Paradox table. You can enter any valid expression into any field of a Query Form. You can also widen any of the columns using the techniques covered in Chapter 4.

You can widen the columns in a query to better view the expressions you enter by dragging the right column gridline.

TIP: Use the Quick Report icon in the SpeedBar if you need a report based on the results of a query.

Saving Queries

As you use the power of Paradox queries to retrieve selected data, you may find yourself repeating the same queries over and over. To save time, you can save queries for reuse later. To save a query, choose Save or Save As from the File menu while the query window is the active window. In the File Save dialog box that appears, enter a name for the query. Later, you can open the previously saved query by choosing the File/Open/Query option.

Hands-On Practice: Performing Queries

Your first task as the personnel manager for ABC Temporaries is to find a person living in Maryland whose last name is Robinson. If necessary get into Paradox, and then follow these steps:

1. Open the ABCSTAFF table with the File/Open/Table option.
2. To begin the Query, choose the File/New/Query option.
3. When the Select File dialog box appears, choose ABCSTAFF for the table and then click OK. This brings up a Query Form.
4. In the resulting answer you want to see the Last Name and State fields, so use the mouse or the F6 key to place a check mark in the Last Name field, and enter **Robinson** in the field. Then, place a check mark in the State field, and enter the letters **MD**.
5. Finally, press F8 to have Paradox display the answer to the query, as shown in Figure 6-4.

If your results do not match those of Figure 6-4, make sure that your matching criteria in the Query Form matches the actual data in the table. For example, if you are trying to locate a record where the last name has been entered as "Robinson," you cannot find the record if you enter "robinson" or "ROBINSON" in the Query Form.

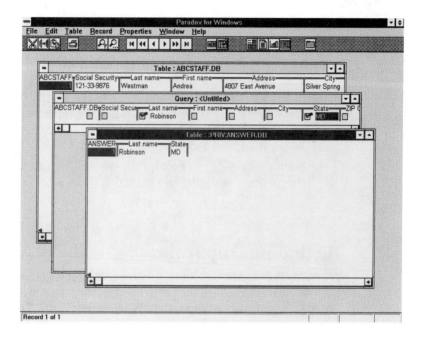

Results of first
practice query
Figure 6-4.

*The results of
queries,
stored in
answer
tables, are
temporary.
Rename the
ANSWER
table if you
want to save
it for reuse
later; choose
File/Table
Rename.*

Note that the window containing the ANSWER table is entitled
ANSWER.DB. Since ANSWER is an actual Paradox table, you can treat it
like any other Paradox table. You can add to, edit, or delete its records,
and generate reports based upon the table. However, unless you change
its name, this table will be erased if you leave Paradox or will be
replaced by the results of successive queries.

Matching on Two or More Fields

To search for records that meet criteria in two or more fields, simply
enter the criteria in the proper format within each field of the Query
Form. If, for example, you need to see all employees who live in
Virginia and earn more than $10.00 per hour, you need to place VA in
the State field and >10.00 in the Salary field of the Query Form.

To try this, first close the existing ANSWER table and the existing
query. Answer No to the prompt that asks if you want to save the Query
Form. Then follow these steps:

1. Choose the File/New/Query option to start with a fresh Query Form.

2. When the Select File dialog box appears, choose ABCSTAFF for the table and then click OK.

3. In the Query Form that appears, use the mouse or the `F6` key to place check marks in the Last Name, First Name, and State fields. While within the State field, enter the letters **VA**. Move to the Salary field, add a check mark, and enter **>10.00**.

4. Finally, press `F8` to process the query. The results will appear in the answer, as shown in Figure 6-5.

Including Duplicates

Paradox automatically filters any records that it considers to be duplicates. Depending on how you structure your query, this tendency may or may not give you precisely what you want. Try the following example to see how Paradox treats duplicates. Follow these instructions

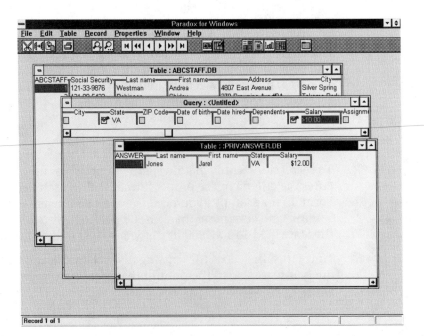

Results of
second practice
query
Figure 6-5.

to try to generate a quick count of the number of employees living in Maryland. (This is just one way to get a count in Paradox.)

Remember, one fast way to close a Query (or any window) is to press Ctrl + F4.

1. Close the existing query and the ANSWER table and then choose the File/New/Query option.
2. When the Select File dialog box appears, choose ABCSTAFF for the table and then click OK to display the Query Form.
3. Since you're only interested in the number of records, you really don't need to see any fields other than the State field. In the Query Form, use the mouse or the F6 key to place a check mark in the State field and enter **MD**.
4. Press F8 to process the query; the results should resemble those shown in Figure 6-6.

The answer, if you don't understand how Paradox operates, may appear deceptive. There is obviously more than one employee living in Maryland in the table, yet the answer indicates just one record. Because you asked for only the State field, Paradox considers all other records with MD in the State field after the first one found to be duplicates of the first one. Had you asked for additional fields, Paradox would have displayed additional records because the other records would not be considered duplicates.

There will be times, however, where you have intentional duplicates—for example, item numbers from an inventory. You can tell Paradox to display all duplicates by clicking the check box and dragging

6

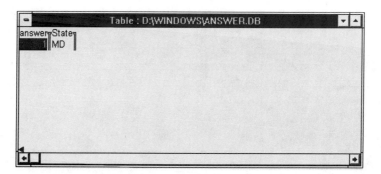

Results of third
practice query
Figure 6-6.

to the check mark-plus symbol or by using [Alt]+[F6] in place of [F6] to place a check mark followed by a plus (+) symbol in the appropriate field of the Query Form. In Paradox, this symbol is called the check-plus, as shown here:

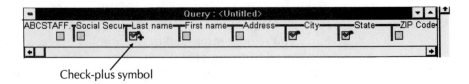

Check-plus symbol

The check-plus symbol tells Paradox to include all records matching the example conditions in the ANSWER table, regardless of what it considers to be duplicates.

To try this, follow these steps:

1. Click the Query Form to make it the active window.

2. Click and hold the mouse button in the check box of the State field of the Query Form. Drag down with the mouse until you highlight the check mark followed by the plus symbol. Then release the mouse button.

3. Press [F8] to process the query. The results, shown in Figure 6-7, indicate the number of employees who live in Maryland.

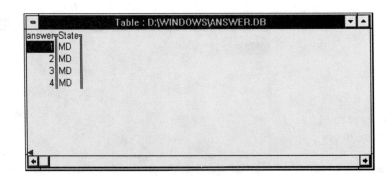

Results of
practice query
using check-plus
Figure 6-7.

If you are defining a query where several fields are selected, and you want to include duplicate records in the answer, you need only mark one of the query fields with a check-plus. The remaining fields can be marked with ordinary checks. As long as one field in the query contains a check-plus, any and all duplicates will be included in the ANSWER table.

Valid Query Symbols

You can use any of the symbols and operators listed in Table 6-1 to build your queries. These symbols let you select records based on a wide variety of numeric conditions, pattern matches, and ranges.

Using Pattern Matching

6

On occasion, you may need to find a group of records in which characters match a specific pattern. Paradox lets you use certain wildcards as a part of the query expression. The valid wildcard operators are a double period (..), which represents any number of characters; and the at-sign (@), which indicates any single character. You can use these wildcards in alphanumeric, number, or date fields. As an example, you could use the expression

J..n

to query a name field for names which might include Jackson, Johnson, and James-Albertson. To use the double period wildcard to query a number field without confusing Paradox about the location of the decimal point (which is also a period), you can enclose the decimal point in quotes. As an example, you could use the expression

.."."50

to query a currency field for all amounts ending in fifty cents (.50). In this example, the first two periods act as wildcards, telling Paradox to accept any characters to the left of the decimal point. The rest of the expression indicates that the characters "50" must appear to the right of the decimal place in the field. For dates, you could enter the expression

10/../93

Symbol	Meaning
+	Addition
−	Subtraction
*	Multiplication
/	Division
()	Operators
=	Equal to
>	Greater than
<	Less than
>=	Greater than or equal to
<=	Less than or equal to
..	Pattern matching for any characters
@	Pattern matching for any single character
like	Similar to (spelling need not be exact)
not	Not a match
blank	Contains no value
today	Date in field matches today's date
average	Average of the values
max	Maximum of the values
min	Minimum of the values
sum	Sum of the values
count	Number of the values

Valid Query
Symbols and
Operators
Table 6-1.

to specify records with any day in October of 1993 in the date field.

To experiment with pattern matching, follow these steps:

1. Choose the File/New/Query option. When the Select File dialog box appears, choose the ABCSTAFF table and then click OK.

2. In the Query Form that appears, use the mouse or the F6 key to place check marks in the Social Security, Last Name, First Name, Date Hired, and Salary fields.

3. Click the Social Security field to place the cursor there, and enter this expression:

    @@@-55-@@@@

4. Now press F8 to implement the query. You should see the records that have social security numbers with 55 as the center digits, as shown in Figure 6-8.

5. To experiment with a different query, click the Query window (or choose Query:<Untitled> from the Window menu) to get back to the Query Form, and then delete the existing entry in the Social Security field.

6. Move the cursor to the Last Name field and enter this expression in the field:

    ..n

7. Press F8 to process the query. Now you should get every last name ending in the letter "n," as shown in Figure 6-9.

8. Once again click the Query window to get back to the Query Form, delete the existing entry in the Last Name field, and place the following expression in the Salary field:

    ..".".50

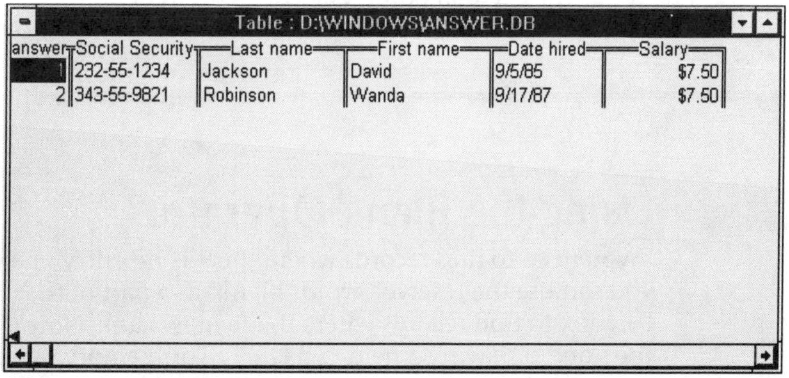

Remember, one fast way to delete an existing entry in a field of a Query is to move to that field and press Ctrl + Backspace.

6

answer	Social Security	Last name	First name	Date hired	Salary
1	232-55-1234	Jackson	David	9/5/85	$7.50
2	343-55-9821	Robinson	Wanda	9/17/87	$7.50

Table : D:\WINDOWS\ANSWER.DB

Pattern matching using any single character
Figure 6-8.

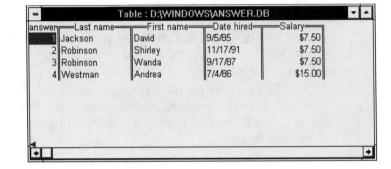

Pattern
matching using
any characters
Figure 6-9.

9. Now press ⌷F8⌷ to see every employee earning any dollar amount that ends in .50, as shown in Figure 6-10.

10. Finally, to try some date logic, click the Query window to get back to the Query Form, delete the existing entry in the Salary field, and enter this expression in the Date Hired field:

    10/../90

11. Press ⌷F8⌷ to see all employees hired during the month of October 1990, as shown in Figure 6-11.

TIP: If you need to include any punctuation marks such as the decimal point, enclose them in double quotation marks.

Using the Blank Operator

If you need to find records where there is no entry in a particular field, you can use the reserved word "blank" as a part of the expression to tell Paradox to find records where the field is blank. Note that this is not the same as leaving a field in a Query Form empty. An empty field indicates that it does not matter what is in that field of a particular record. The word "blank" in the query field indicates that the field must

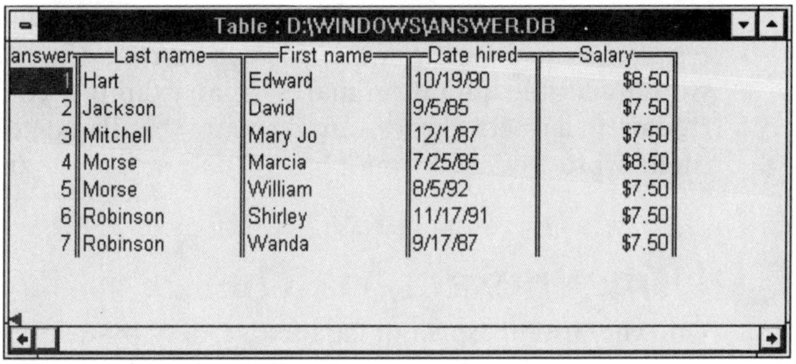

Table : D:\WINDOWS\ANSWER.DB

answer	Last name	First name	Date hired	Salary
1	Hart	Edward	10/19/90	$8.50
2	Jackson	David	9/5/85	$7.50
3	Mitchell	Mary Jo	12/1/87	$7.50
4	Morse	Marcia	7/25/85	$8.50
5	Morse	William	8/5/92	$7.50
6	Robinson	Shirley	11/17/91	$7.50
7	Robinson	Wanda	9/17/87	$7.50

Pattern matching using numeric values
Figure 6-10.

be blank (contain no entry) before the record will be selected and placed in the ANSWER table.

A Caution About Reserved Words and Wildcard Symbols

Because Paradox uses certain reserved words and symbols, you may have trouble performing a query when you want a record with the literal word and Paradox thinks that you are trying to use a reserved word. (Remember, these reserved words and symbols were shown

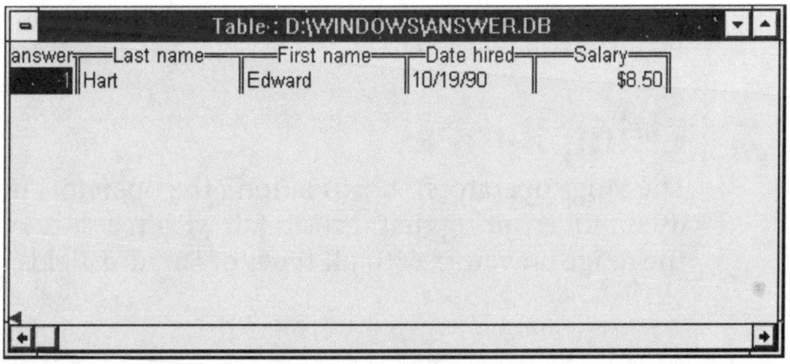

Table : D:\WINDOWS\ANSWER.DB

answer	Last name	First name	Date hired	Salary
1	Hart	Edward	10/19/90	$8.50

Pattern matching using date values
Figure 6-11.

earlier in Table 6-1.) For example, you might be searching for a text string that specifically contains the @ sign, and Paradox could take the symbol to mean any single character, possibly providing incorrect results. For such occurrences, you can surround the desired character or word in double quotation marks. As an example, you could enter "today" in a query expression to ensure that Paradox searched for the literal word "today" and not for the date stored in your PC's clock.

Using Inexact Matches

One very useful aspect of Paradox's Query-by-Example feature is its ability to use the "like" operator as a condition for finding inexact matches. For example, when you use the term "like Morrs" in the Last Name field of a query of the ABCSTAFF table, Paradox will find a record that sounds like Morrs, or Marsha Morse. To try out this feature, follow these instructions:

1. Close the existing query and choose the File/New/Query option.

2. When the Select File dialog box appears, choose ABCSTAFF for the table and then click OK to display the Query Form.

3. Now use the mouse or the F6 key to place check marks in the Last Name and First Name fields. Enter **like Morrs** in the Last Name field of the Query Form.

4. Press F8 to process the query. The answer should show the record for Ms. Marcia Morse and Mr. William Morse, because the last name Morse sounds like "Morrs."

This capability is useful for finding names when you aren't quite sure of their spelling. The like operator is also helpful for maintaining mailing lists when you are trying to weed out accidental duplicate records.

Using Ranges

The range operators, shown among the operators in Table 6-1, are very useful for ensuring that records fall within a selected range. You can use the range operators with all types of Paradox fields; they are by no means limited to numeric values. For example, try using range operators on the ABCSTAFF table to isolate the range of employees whose last names fall between the letters "M" and "Z." Follow these steps to do so:

1. Click the existing Query Form to move to it. (You can leave the existing check marks intact; if you've already cleared them, open a new Query Form and place check marks in the Last Name and First Name fields.) Add check marks to the Date Hired and Salary fields.

2. In the Last Name field of the Query Form, delete the prior expression and enter the following expression to represent "greater than 'M,' and less than or equal to 'Zz'":

   >M,<=Zz

Tɪᴘ: Note the inclusion of the second letter "z." If it were omitted, Paradox would find names up to "Z," but none after the letter "Z" alone, in effect, omitting all last names of more than one character starting with "Z."

6

3. Press F8 to process the query; the results shown in Figure 6-12 will appear.

Results of practice query with operators limiting names
Figure 6-12.

answer	Last name	First name	Date hired	Salary
1	Mitchell	Mary Jo	12/1/87	$7.50
2	Morse	Marcia	7/25/85	$8.50
3	Morse	William	8/5/92	$7.50
4	Robinson	Shirley	11/17/91	$7.50
5	Robinson	Wanda	9/17/87	$7.50
6	Westman	Andrea	7/4/86	$15.00

Table : D:\WINDOWS\ANSWER.DB

In this example, note that a comma is used to separate the two possibilities. Remember that whenever you want to enter more than one selection criteria in a field, you must separate them with commas. Another example, this time performed with dates, illustrates this point. Suppose you need a report of all employees who were hired during 1987. Follow these instructions to track down this information:

1. Click the Last Name field of the Query Form and delete the prior entry. You want to search for all employees hired in 1987, not just those with last names in the second half of the alphabet.

2. Move the cursor to the Date Hired field, press F6 to remove the check, and enter the following expression in this field:

    >=1/1/87, <=12/31/87

   You could also enter the expression ..87, which would also indicate any date value falling in 1987.

3. Press F8 to process the completed query. The result, shown in Figure 6-13, includes the employees hired by ABC Temporaries in 1987.

You may have noticed another point from this query. The limiting criteria for records was the date hired, yet the Date Hired field was not checked for inclusion in the resultant table. Paradox does not need to have the fields that are used to select the records included in the results.

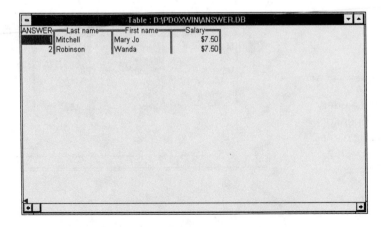

Results of query of 1987 employees
Figure 6-13.

You can also use the accepted operators listed in Table 6-1 to build queries based upon other types of ranges. Consider the common personnel problem of deciding who does and does not qualify for vacation. At ABC Temporaries, every employee with one year or more of service qualifies for vacation. If you suddenly need a list of employees eligible for vacation, a simple query will do the task. Follow these steps:

1. Move to the Date Hired field of the existing query and delete the prior expression.

2. Then enter the following expression:

   >= TODAY-365

   This means "greater than or equal to today's date minus 365 days." (Remember, Paradox uses the word "today" as a reserved word indicating today's date as measured by the computer's clock.)

3. Press F8 to process the query. Paradox will display a list of employees who have been with the firm for one year or more. Depending on the date maintained by your PC's clock and the dates you entered for the employees, this list may or may not include every employee of the company.

Matching Records Based on "OR" Criteria

You build "OR" queries by using more than one line on a query form.

The types of queries you've performed so far will work fine when you are setting one or more criteria for the same field. Such cases of criteria are also referred to as "AND" logic because you are qualifying a record where a certain condition is met "AND" another certain condition is met. But sometimes you need a different sort of qualification. Suppose you want to find records that meet more than one criteria in the same field, such as all employees who live in either Maryland or Virginia? This calls for a different type of logic known as "OR" logic. You want employees in Maryland *or* in Virginia. It's easy to fashion such queries in Paradox. You just add as many lines to the Query Form as necessary; each line contains a separate condition which can be met to qualify the records.

Follow these instructions to experiment with "OR" logic:

1. First close the existing ANSWER table and the existing Query Form. (Answer No to the prompt that asks if you wish to save the new forms or tables.)

2. Choose the File/New/Query option. When the Select File dialog box appears, choose the ABCSTAFF table and then click OK to display a Query Form.

3. Use the mouse or the F6 key to place a check mark in the first column of the Query Form. This tells Paradox to place a check mark in every field of the Query Form so that every field will be included in the answer.

4. Move the cursor down one line by pressing ⬇ once. Then click the check box at the far left or press F6 while the cursor is in the far left column. You should now have two rows in the Query Form, each with check marks in every field, as shown here:

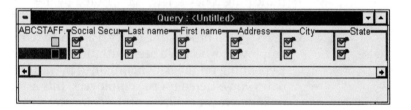

5. Next, place the cursor in the State field in the first row and enter **MD**.

6. Now move the cursor down one line by pressing ⬇ once, and then enter **VA** in the State field.

7. Finally, press F8 to process the query. The results should show all the employees who live in either Maryland or Virginia, as shown in Figure 6-14.

Complex Matching

You can use Paradox's powerful Query-by-Example facility to match criteria for various fields to set up very complex searches. And you can combine AND and OR logic to isolate the precise records you need. Suppose, for example, that you wish to see all the employees who live in Virginia or in Maryland, were hired in 1992, and are earning more than $10.00 per hour. If this sounds like overkill, rest assured that it

Social Security	Last name	First name	Address	City	State	ZIP
121-33-9876	Westman	Andrea	4807 East Avenue	Silver Spring	MD	2091(
121-90-5432	Robinson	Shirley	270 Browning Ave #2A	Takoma Park	MD	2091:
123-44-8976	Morse	Marcia	4260 Park Avenue	Chevy Chase	MD	2081!
232-55-1234	Jackson	David	4102 Valley Lane	Falls Church	VA	2204-
495-00-3456	Abernathy	Sandra	1512 Loiza Way	Herndon	VA	2207:
805-34-6789	Morse	William	4260 Park Avenue	Chevy Chase	MD	2081!
876-54-3210	Hart	Edward	6200 Germantown Road	Fairfax	VA	2220!
901-77-3456	Mitchell	Mary Jo	617 North Oakland Street	Arlington	VA	2220:
909-88-7654	Jones	Jarel	5203 North Shore Drive	Reston	VA	2209(

Table : D:\WINDOWS\ANSWER.DB

Results of an
"OR" query.
Figure 6-14.

isn't. Often real-world management reports require more complex conditions than these before upper management is satisfied with the results.

In this example, what Paradox needs to know as selection criteria are states equal to MD or VA; a date hired that is >=1/1/92 AND <=12/31/92; and a salary value that is <=$10.00.

1. To begin, close the existing ANSWER table and the existing Query Form to get a fresh screen.

2. Choose the File/New/Query option.

3. When the Select File dialog box appears, choose the ABCSTAFF table and then click OK.

4. In the Query Form that appears, enter the following matching criteria:

✦ In the Last Name and First Name fields of *both* rows 1 and 2, enter a check mark with the mouse or with F6 .

✦ In the State, Date Hired, and Salary fields of *both* rows 1 and 2, enter a check mark.

✦ In the State field on the first row, enter VA. On the second row of the same field, enter MD.

✦ In the Date Hired field on both the first and second rows, enter the expression >=1/1/92, <=12/31/92.

6

♦ In the Salary field on both the first and second rows, enter the expression **<= 10.00**

5. Finally, implement the query by pressing ⌴F8⌴. The results should be similar to those shown in Figure 6-15.

An Important Reminder

This has been mentioned before, but it is of such importance that one more reminder here may save you problems later. All of your queries are stored in a temporary table named ANSWER, and this table is erased or overwritten whenever you leave Paradox, change directories, or perform another query. If you want to save the results of any query, be sure to rename the ANSWER table with the File/Table-Utilities/Rename option.

Using Query-by-Example

Query-by-Example makes use of example elements instead of selection conditions in the fields of the Query Form. The concept of Query-by-Example is an important one to understand, because it adds flexibility to the ways in which you can use queries in Paradox. Think of *example elements* as a special type of query entry that lets you relate entries in one field of a table to entries in another field. Example

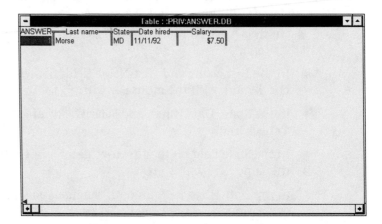

Results of
complex query
Figure 6-15.

elements are simply characters that you enter to draw examples between fields. You'll use example elements again in Chapter 11 to link multiple tables. But you can use Query-by-Example with a single table whenever you want to base a query on a relationship between two fields.

As an example, consider the Salary and Hourly Rate fields of the ABCSTAFF table. Perhaps you would like to know which employees have an hourly rate that is at least 1.5 times their salary. This is an ideal task for Query-by-Example because you are asking a question that is based on a relationship between two fields: the Salary field and the Hourly Rate field. To build a query using Query-by-Example, you use the Example key ([F5]) to start an example in a column. You then enter the example along with any expressions needed to define the desired data.

See Chapter 11 for important details on how you can link multiple tables using Query-by-Example.

An example will make this concept easier to understand, so clear the desktop now by closing any existing queries and ANSWER table. Then follow these steps:

6

1. Choose the File/New/Query option.

2. When the Select File dialog box appears, choose the ABCSTAFF table and then click OK.

3. In the Query form that appears, use the mouse or the [F6] key to add a check mark to all columns. (You don't need to check all columns to use Query-by-Example; it is done for simplicity in this example.)

4. Next, move the cursor to the Salary field and press Example ([F5]). Then type the letters **ABC**. Note that as you type, the letters appear in a different color or shading on your monitor. Because you pressed [F5], Paradox assumes that you are entering an example element, and therefore changes the color or shading of the letters used as an example.

5. Now click the Hourly Rate field to move the cursor there. Type a greater-than symbol (>). Then press Example ([F5]) and type the letters **ABC**. Then type an asterisk followed by the value **1.5**. (As soon as you type the asterisk, the letters you type will no longer be colored or shaded differently, because Paradox allows only characters for example elements.) At this point, your Query Form should resemble the example shown in Figure 6-16.

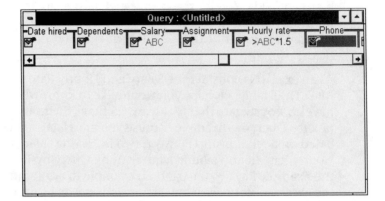

Query Form
using example
elements
Figure 6-16.

6. Press [F8] to process the query. Your results should resemble those in Figure 6-17. Only those records where the Hourly Rate entry is more than 150% above the Salary entry have been included in the ANSWER table.

Take a moment to review the query that you just constructed. Since all fields were checked, all fields of the ABCSTAFF table appeared in the ANSWER table. What's different about this query is the way it selects the desired records. In this query, an example (represented by the

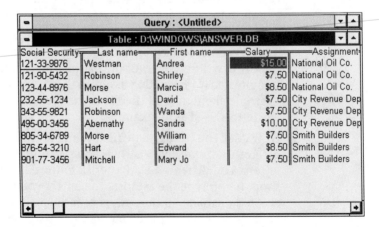

Results of
Query-by-
Example
Figure 6-17.

letters "ABC") is used to draw a relationship between two fields of the table. The query is asking for all records where the amount in the Hourly Rate field is greater than 150% of the rate in the Salary field.

For one more example that will help reinforce the concept of Query-by-Example, consider a more complex query that uses two lines of a Query Form. In this example, you want to see which employees are earning more than Marcia Morse. You can draw an example between Marcia Morse's salary and the other salaries in the table. Follow these instructions to do so:

1. First, close the existing query and the ANSWER table.

2. Choose the File/New/Query option. When the Select File dialog box appears, choose the ABCSTAFF table and then click OK.

3. In the Query Form that appears, use the `Tab` key to move to the Last Name field of the first row and enter **Morse**. Then, move the cursor to the First Name field of the first row and enter **Marcia**.

4. Now click the Salary field of the first row and press Example (`F5`). Then type the word **MONEY**.

5. Next, press `Ctrl`+`Home` to return to the far left side of the Query Form and press `↓` to move down by one row. With the cursor still on the left edge of the Query Form, press Check Mark (`F6`) to add a check mark to every field.

6. Move the cursor over to the Salary field; you should be one row below the example element you entered earlier. Type a greater than symbol (>) and then press Example (`F5`) to begin another example element. Type the word, **MONEY**.

7. Press `F8` to process the query. Your results should resemble those shown in Figure 6-18. All employees who earn a salary greater than that of Marcia Morse are displayed in the ANSWER table. (In the figure, some columns have been rotated with `Ctrl`+`R` so that the names and salaries are visible at the same time.)

A special word of explanation about this query is in order. Whenever you use a two-line query and you use example elements, Paradox considers the first line of the query as a definition of the example. The second line of the query contains a selection condition that uses the example element as part of its expression. This is different than the two-line queries shown earlier in this chapter. If example elements are

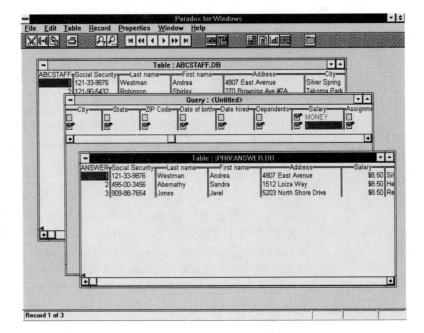

Results of
second
Query-by-
Example
Figure 6-18.

not used, Paradox considers a two-line query to be using OR logic, as
described earlier. In our first demonstration of Query-by-Example
(shown in Figure 6-17), only one row was needed in the query form
because the relationship was between two different fields of the table.
In this example, two rows were needed, because the relationship drawn
by the example uses the same field twice.

Chapter 11 includes additional examples that highlight the use of
Query-by-Example. Until then, remember that the example element (in
the first case, the letters "ABC") is not some arbitrary value that you
must use. Paradox is only concerned with what the examples represent;
in other words, when Paradox sees one example element in a query, it
looks for a matching example element in the same query. In the first
example, the letters "ABC" could have been entered as "XYZ," "1234," or
"nonsense." What is important is that Paradox must find at least two
matching example elements in the query. (Since Query-by-Example
compares one field to another, it would make no sense to have only
one example element in a query.) Once Paradox finds the matching
examples, it will perform whatever operation is indicated by the
expressions you enter in the Query Form.

Quick Summary

Building a Query

Choose File/New/Query. When the Select File dialog box appears, choose the desired table by name, then click OK to bring up the Query Form. Choose the fields you want displayed in the answer by clicking in the check box to the left of the field (or by tabbing to the field and pressing F6). To select specific records for inclusion in the answer, enter a matching expression in any desired field (omit this step if you want to see all records). Finally, press F8, or choose Query/Run, or click the Run Query icon in the SpeedBar.

Saving a Query

While the query window is the active window, choose File/Save or File/Save As. In the File Save dialog box which appears, enter a name for the query, then click OK.

Opening a Saved Query

Choose File/Open/Query from the menus. Select the query by name in the list box which appears, then click OK.

Including Duplicates in a Query

Add a check-plus symbol (click in the check box of the query field and choose it from the menu that opens, or press Alt+F6 instead of F6) when indicating the desired fields.

Using Query-by-Example

Build your query using the steps outlined above. Use the Example key (F5) to start an example in the desired column, then enter the example. Repeat this process for each example needed.

6

CHAPTER

7

USING CUSTOM FORMS

So far, when adding new records or making changes to a table, you have used the Quick Form key (F7) to switch from Table mode to a simple on-screen entry form. This form listed the various fields and displayed highlighted areas that contained the actual data. When you were learning how to add or change data within a database, this approach was sufficient. However, there can be problems with such a straightforward approach to adding data to a table.

One drawback is in the unfriendly screen that this presents to the computer user. If an ABC Temporaries employee does not know whether the hourly or weekly salary belongs in the Salary field, the help screens or the Paradox manual won't offer any assistance. Another drawback is the lack of editing control offered by Paradox's default entry form. Since all fields are present in the form, you cannot prevent a particular field from being edited in the default form.

The appearance of your forms can be enhanced by adding graphics.

To overcome such limitations, Paradox provides a flexible way to build custom forms. A *custom form* is simply a form which you design that appears on the screen for data display and data entry. Using Paradox, you can build custom forms that resemble printed forms commonly used in an office. Figure 7-1 shows an example of such a form. You can also restrict data entry by omitting certain fields while including other fields in the form. You can add *calculated fields,* which are fields that present a value based on a calculation between the contents of one or more fields in a table. And you can enhance the appearance of forms by adding lines or boxes, by changing the display properties of fields and labels in the form, and by adding graphics to a form.

If you're not already in Paradox, load the program now.

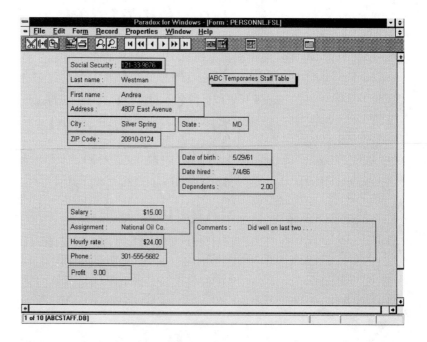

Sample custom form
Figure 7-1.

About Documents

In Paradox for Windows, both forms and reports are documents. Any view of your data through a special layout is considered a *document* in Paradox. The advantage to this is that when you are familiar with designing your own custom forms, you will understand much about designing your own customized reports since you use many of the same techniques to design forms and reports. (Designing customized reports is covered in Chapter 9.)

Creating a Custom Form

This section provides specific steps you can use to create custom forms. The following section of the chapter will demonstrate how you can use these techniques to create a custom form for the ABC Temporaries table. To create a form, from the menus, choose the File/New/Form option to display the Data Model dialog box shown in Figure 7-2. You use this dialog box to supply a data model, or the source of the fields, for the form. In Paradox, a data model is simply a model of the exact data types (fields) used in a form or report. Chapter 11 will describe in

7

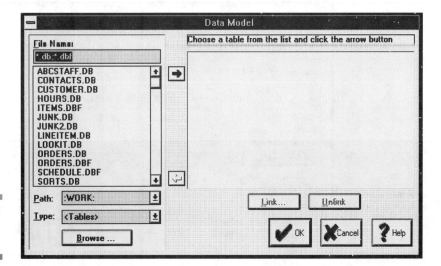

Data Model dialog box
Figure 7-2.

detail how you can use this dialog box to design forms that work with more than one table. For the remainder of this chapter, you will be working with forms that use only one table at a time as a source of data.

Click the desired table name within the File Name portion of the dialog box; that table will appear on the right side of the dialog box. Then click OK to close the Data Model dialog box.

NOTE: If you want to search a different drive or directory for a file, you can click the Browse button to bring up the File Browser. Then change to the desired drive or directory by clicking on them from the File Browser.

When the Data Model dialog box closes, the Design Layout dialog box shown in Figure 7-3 appears in its place.

By default, labels and fields for the table you selected in the prior step will appear as a sample form on the right side of the Design Layout

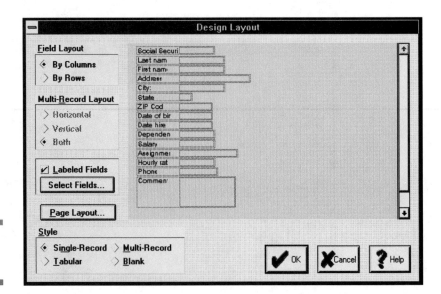

Design Layout
dialog box
Figure 7-3.

dialog box. You use the options on the left side of this dialog box to quickly design the initial layout for the form. Under Field Layout, you can click the By Columns button to provide a column-oriented layout with fields appearing in one or more columns; the first field will appear at the top of the first column, the second field below it, and so on. (This is the type of layout you see in Figure 7-3.) Or, you can click the By Rows button to provide a row-oriented layout, with fields appearing in rows; the first field will appear at the far left of the first row, the second field to the right of the first, and so on. Figure 7-4 shows a row-oriented layout.

The Multi-Record Layout section of the dialog box is used for multi-record forms, a subject that will be covered later in this chapter.

You can turn on or off the Labeled Fields button to display or remove labels, or field names, from the fields.

When you click the Select Fields button, a Select Fields dialog box appears, as shown in Figure 7-5. You can use this dialog box to change the order of fields in the layout or to remove fields. To change the

7

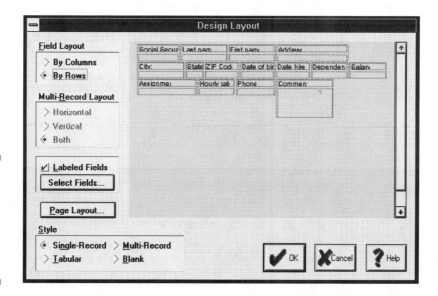

Design Layout window containing a form that will be oriented by rows

Figure 7-4.

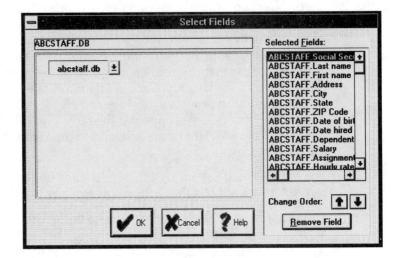

Select Fields
dialog box
Figure 7-5.

order, click the desired field name and then click the up or down
arrows next to the words "Change Order" in the lower-right corner of
the dialog box until the field moves to the desired location among the
other fields. To remove a field from the layout, click the desired field
name and then click the Remove Field button. When you have
accomplished the desired changes, click OK.

Note that if you have removed some fields and want to return them to
the layout, you can also do this from the Select Fields dialog box. To do
so, click the downward-pointing arrow next to the table name
(ABCSTAFF.DB) to open the pull-down list box, and then click the field
you want to add.

The Page Layout button in the Design Layout dialog box brings up
another dialog box, the Page Layout dialog box, as shown in Figure 7-6.
You can use this dialog box to change the page dimensions for the form.

By default, Paradox assumes that you are using the form as an
on-screen display of data, so the Screen button under Design For is
turned on automatically. You can turn on the Printer button instead. If
you do so, the Portrait and Landscape buttons under Orientation,

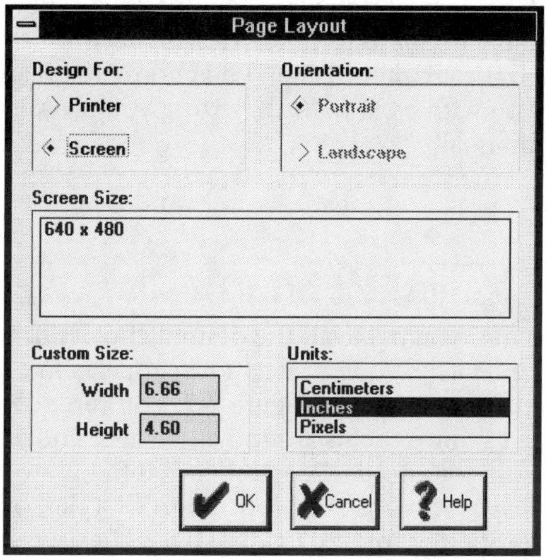

Page Layout
dialog box
Figure 7-6.

*You may find
the Printer
option handy
if you want to
design a
form that is
to be used
for printing
one record at
a time, but
this less-used
technique will
not be
described
further in this
text.*

which are dimmed by default, become enabled. At this point you can
select whether the page orientation is to be vertical (portrait) or
horizontal (landscape). The Screen Size box simply indicates current
screen resolution; for example, if you are running in VGA video mode,
a value of 640X480 (which is standard VGA resolution) appears in the
Screen Size box. The Custom Size and Units choices let you specify a
nonstandard size, if you need to do so. The units are in inches,
centimeters, or pixels, depending on the units of measurement that you
select in the dialog box. When you are done filling out the Page Layout
dialog box, click OK to close it and return to the Design Layout dialog
box.

Finally, the Style area of the Design Layout dialog box offers you the
choices Single-Record, Multi-Record, Tabular, and Blank. The Single-
Record button (which is selected by default) provides a layout like the
ones shown so far in this chapter, where only one record of a table is
displayed in each form. The Multi-Record button lets you design a
multi-record form, which displays more than one record at a time; this
topic is covered later in the chapter. The Tabular option lets you design

a form using a table-oriented format (much like that of a normal Paradox table). This can be helpful if you want to view your records in a table format, but want to omit certain fields, or design a customized table-oriented form for viewing records (this topic is also covered later in the chapter). When you choose the Blank option, Paradox presents you with a blank form, letting you place all desired fields in the form manually.

Fields are objects and have properties like fonts, border styles, and colors.

Using the Form Design Window

Once you make all the desired choices in the Design Layout dialog box and click OK, your new form appears in a Form Design Window like the one shown in Figure 7-7. You can now use the window as a drawing area, move fields around as desired, and add lines, graphics, or labels to suit your needs. Remember that fields are objects, and as such, they have properties like fonts, border styles, or colors. You can change the properties for any field by right-clicking the field and choosing the desired option from the properties menu that appears.

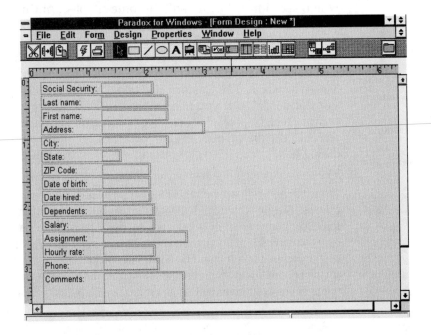

Form Design window for a new form
Figure 7-7.

Moving and Sizing Fields

To move fields in the form, first click the desired field. When you do so, the field will be surrounded by handles, as shown here:

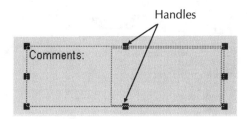

When the field is surrounded by handles, you can click anywhere on the field (avoiding the selection handles) and drag it to the desired location on the form.

To size a field, click the field to select it, then drag any of the handles. Figure 7-8 shows how you can use the handles to size a field.

Placing New Fields

To place a new field on the form, first click the SpeedBar's Field tool. Then click in the form, where you want to place the field, and drag until the new field reaches its desired size. You can then right-click the field to open a properties menu that will let you define the field, or tell Paradox which field of the database to use for the new field.

Using the SpeedBar Design Tools

When the Form Design window is open, the SpeedBar displays a set of tools that are specifically for designing forms. You can use these tools to place on a form various objects such as fields, lines, boxes, ellipses, or graphics. Figure 7-9 shows the SpeedBar that appears when a Form Design window is active.

To place an object in the form, first click the desired tool; then click and drag in the Form Design window to create the desired object. For example, to create a rectangle, just click the Box tool and then click and drag within the form to create a rectangle of the desired size. If you want to create more than one object of the same type, hold down the

7

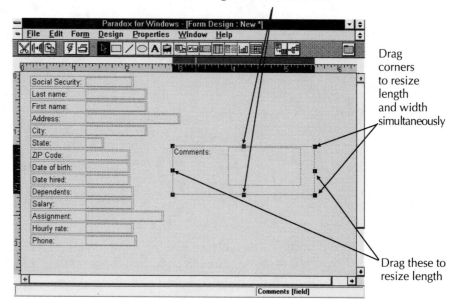

Drag these to resize width

Drag corners to resize length and width simultaneously

Drag these to resize length

Resize fields by dragging on handles
Figure 7-8.

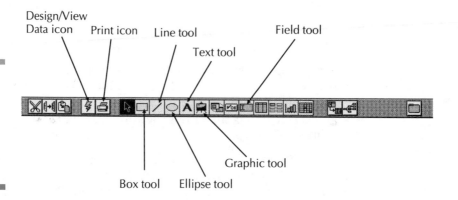

Design/View Data icon Print icon Line tool Field tool

Text tool

SpeedBar displayed whenever a Form Design window is active
Figure 7-9.

Box tool Ellipse tool Graphic tool

Shift) key as you click the tool. The tool will then remain active until you click a different tool or the selection arrow.

Adding Text

A

To add text to a form, first click the Text tool in the SpeedBar. Then click and drag in the Form Design window until the text frame that appears is as large as desired. When you release the mouse button, start typing text. As you reach the border of the frame, Paradox automatically wraps the text. If you reach the bottom of the frame, Paradox automatically scrolls the text upward. (If the box is too small, the text will scroll out of view: you can enlarge the text frame to fit the text.) You can resize the text frame at any time; just select the frame and then click and drag on a handle.

Drawing Lines, Boxes, or Ellipses

The SpeedBar provides three tools for drawing lines, boxes, and ellipses. You can heighten the visual interest of your forms by adding these shapes to them. To add a line, box, or ellipse, first click the desired tool in the SpeedBar (the Line, Box, or Ellipse tool). Then click at the desired starting location in the form and drag until the line, box, or ellipse reaches the desired size. Figure 7-10 shows a form containing lines, a box, and an ellipse as design elements.

7

Adding Graphics to a Form

You can use the SpeedBar's Graphic tool to add a graphic to a form. Figure 7-11 shows an example of a form that uses a graphic, pasted from a Windows bitmap file, as a design illustration.

To add a graphic, first click the Graphic tool in the SpeedBar. Then click at the desired starting location in the form and drag until the box that is to contain the graphic reaches the desired size.

When you release the mouse button, the box will contain the label "undefined graphic." To define the source of the graphic, right-click the undefined graphic to open its properties menu. Choose Define Graphic. From the next menu to appear, choose Paste to paste the contents of the Clipboard (if the Paste option is dimmed, the Clipboard is empty).

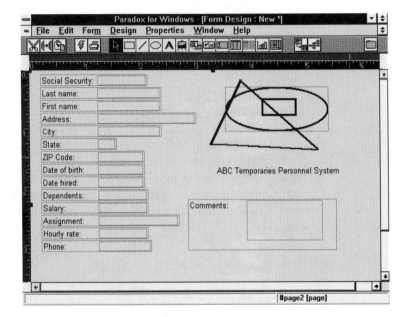

Form
containing
lines, box, and
ellipse
Figure 7-10.

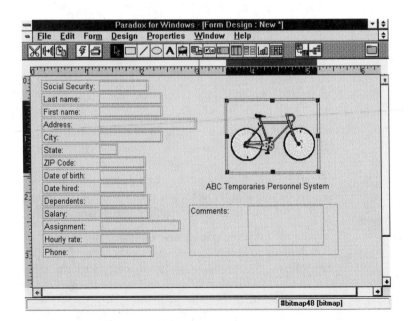

Form using
Windows
bitmap as a
graphic
Figure 7-11.

Alternately, choose Paste From to paste from a graphic image file. If you choose Paste From, a Select File box appears, and you can choose the name of the graphic file you want to paste into the undefined graphic.

NOTE: Acceptable graphic types in Paradox include .BMP, .PCX, .TIF, and .CGM (metafile).

Testing the Form During the Design Process

You can test the form with real data by choosing the View Data option from the Form menu or by clicking the View Data icon in the SpeedBar. A record will appear in the form, and you can use the `Pg Up` and `Pg Dn` keys to view additional records. You can return to the form design process at any time; simply choose Design from the Form menu, press `F8`, or click the Design icon in the SpeedBar.

Saving Your Form

When you are satisfied with the appearance of your form, you can save it by choosing Save or Save As from the File menu. If you choose Save As or if you choose File Save when saving a form for the first time, the Save File As dialog box appears, as shown in Figure 7-12.

Enter the name for the form (using DOS file naming conventions of eight characters or less and no spaces) in the New File Name text box, and then click OK. Paradox automatically adds the .FSL extension to the filename, saving the file under the assigned name in the working directory.

NOTE: You cannot save a form while the Form Design window is still active and you are viewing data. You must switch from viewing data back into Design mode before you can save the form.

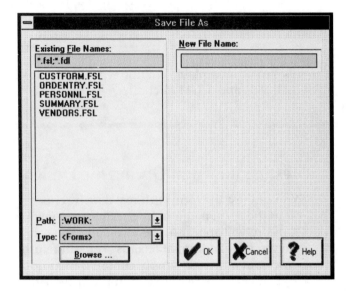

Save File As
dialog box
Figure 7-12.

Using an Existing Form

To use an existing form, use the File/Open/Form option, choose the
form by name from the Open Document dialog box that appears, and
then click OK. The form will appear, containing a record from within
the table. You can use the editing techniques discussed in Chapters 3
and 5 to edit the data as desired.

Hands-On Practice: Creating the Personnel Form

You can practice creating custom forms by designing a form for use
with the ABC Temporaries staff table. When you complete this form, it
will resemble the example shown in Figure 7-13.

   1. To begin designing the form, choose the File/New/Form option.

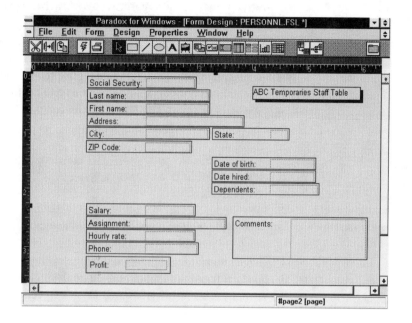

Sample
personnel form
Figure 7-13.

2. When the Data Model dialog box appears, click ABCSTAFF.DB in the File Name list box, and then click OK. In a moment, the Design Layout dialog box appears.

3. The form you will design is based on a columnar, single-record layout. However, while the Design Layout dialog box is visible, try clicking the By Rows option button under Field Layout to see the difference in layout styles. Also, after changing the Field Layout to By Rows, change the Style from Single-Record to Tabular (by clicking the Tabular button) to see the difference between the single-record and the tabular style. When you are done experimenting, click the Single-Record option button under Style and click the By Columns button under Field Layout.

4. The design layout that is now shown in the Design Layout dialog box is close to what you need for the finished form, so click OK to close the window.

5. In a moment, a Form Design window appears. If the window is not already full-screen size, expand it by clicking its Maximize button;

this will give you plenty of room to work with. At this point, your
screen should resemble the example shown in Figure 7-14.

6. To practice moving fields, you can move the fields towards the
   center of the form. You can move all of the fields to the right
   slightly by selecting them all and dragging them. With no fields
   currently selected, choose Select All from the Edit menu; handles
   will appear around all of the fields in the form.

NOTE: Make sure no fields are selected before you choose Select All.
If a field is selected and you choose Select All, Paradox simply
selects that entire field.

7. Next, click anywhere near the center of the form and drag to the
   right about an inch. As you do so, all of the fields will move to the
   right by the amount that you drag. (You can tell the approximate

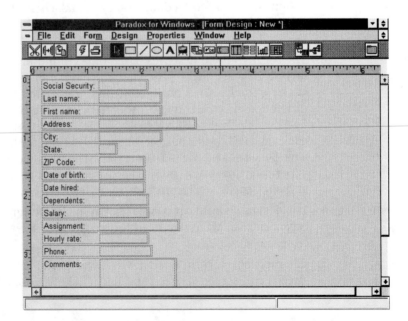

Form Design
window for
ABCSTAFF table
Figure 7-14.

distance moved by looking at the ruler at the top of the design window.)

8. Release the mouse button when you are done, and then click anywhere other than on a field to deselect the fields (the handles will vanish). You should now have some room at the left side of the form.

9. Click the Text tool in the SpeedBar (remember, it contains an uppercase "A"). Then click in the blank space about one inch to the right of the Last Name field and drag to the right until you have a text frame about two inches wide and about one-quarter inch in depth.

10. After releasing the mouse button, type **ABC Temporaries Staff Table**.

11. If the frame you created is not large enough to hold all of the text without its wrapping, click the lower-right corner of the text frame and drag until the frame is large enough to hold all the text on a single line.

12. Next, click the Comments field to select it. Then click and drag the field up and to the right until its upper-left edge is just to the right of the upper-right edge of the Assignment field.

7

13. Click the State field to select it. Then click and drag it to a new location immediately to the right of the City field.

14. Using the same select and drag technique, move the ZIP Code field immediately underneath the City field.

15. Click the Date of Birth field to select it. Then hold down the Shift key and click the Date Hired and Dependents fields. All three fields will be selected.

16. Click anywhere within the selected fields and drag them upwards and to the right until they are approximately one-half inch below the State field.

17. Finally, click once in any blank area to deselect the fields. At this point, your screen should resemble the one shown in Figure 7-15.

To try the form with real data, choose View Data from the Form menu; you can also click the View Data icon in the SpeedBar or press F8. In a moment, a record from the ABC Temporaries table appears in the form, as shown in Figure 7-16. Try the Pg Up and Pg Dn keys to view additional

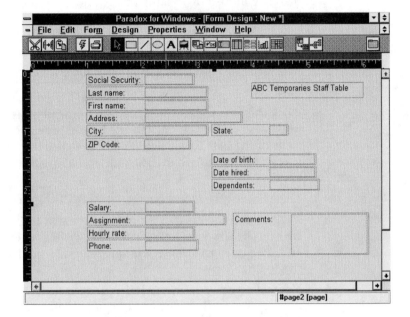

Form Design
window after
fields have
been moved to
new locations
Figure 7-15.

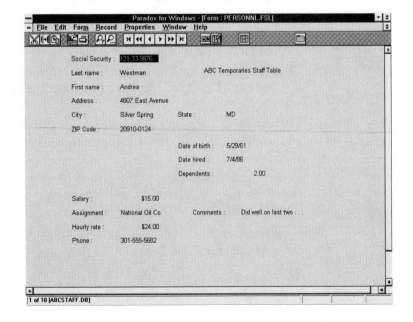

A record of the
ABCSTAFF
table as
displayed
through the
new form
Figure 7-16.

records in the form. When you are done, either choose Design from the Form menu, click the Design icon in the SpeedBar, or press F8 to return to the Form Design window.

Saving the Example Form

To save the form, choose Save from the File menu. In a moment, the File Save As dialog box appears, with the cursor flashing in the New File Name text box. Enter **PERSONNL** as a filename and then click OK to save the new form. Paradox displays the message "Form successfully saved" in the status bar to inform you that the form has been stored to disk.

Once you save the form, you can use it at any time by choosing the File/Open/Form option and selecting PERSONNL from the Open File list box that appears.

Editing an Existing Form

7

As long as you are in the Form Design window, you can make any desired changes to an existing form. To open an existing form, choose the File/Open/Form option. Once the form appears on your screen, you can choose Design from the Form menu or click the Design icon in the SpeedBar to make changes to the form's design. (You don't need to do this now, since you are still in the Paradox's Form Design mode.)

Adding a Calculated Field

As mentioned, Paradox lets you add calculated fields to a form. These fields are used to display the results of calculations that are usually based on the contents of other fields in the database. Calculated fields are not stored in any permanent location in the database. They do not consume space because they are not stored in the database file; they only exist on the form. Adding a calculated field simply tells Paradox to perform a calculation and to display the results in the calculated field of the form.

When you create a calculated field, you need to tell Paradox the expression that provides the basis of the calculation. As a part of an expression, you can use field names spelled as they appear in the table structure, surrounded with brackets; math operators, which include + (addition), − (subtraction), * (multiplication), and / (division); and constants, such as "James", 4.75, or 3/12/93. For example, here are some valid expressions:

"Mr./Ms." + [First name] +"" + [Last name]
[Salary] * [Hours worked]

As indicated by the examples, you can use the + operator to combine text strings as well as to perform mathematical operations.

In the example, the managers at ABC Temporaries want a "profitability" field, which will display the difference between the hourly rate charged to the customer and the employee's salary. It would be a waste of time to add to the table a new field for this information, since you can readily obtain the information by subtracting the salary amount from the hourly rate amount. The result can be displayed as a calculated field.

You can add a field with the Field tool on the SpeedBar. Click the Field tool now, and as you move the mouse pointer into the form design area, it will change to resemble a field containing an insertion pointer.

About one-quarter inch below the existing Phone field, click and drag until you have a field approximately one-quarter inch high and two inches long. (Remember to use the rulers at the edge of the Form Design window as a guide.) When you release the mouse button, the new field is still selected and you can right-click it to open its properties menu. From the menu, choose Define Field; when you do so, another menu appears.

ABCSTAFF.DB.Social Security
ABCSTAFF.DB.Last name
ABCSTAFF.DB.First name
ABCSTAFF.DB.Address
ABCSTAFF.DB.City
ABCSTAFF.DB.State
ABCSTAFF.DB.ZIP Code
ABCSTAFF.DB.Date of birth
ABCSTAFF.DB.Date hired
ABCSTAFF.DB.Dependents
ABCSTAFF.DB.Salary
ABCSTAFF.DB.Assignment
ABCSTAFF.DB.Hourly rate
ABCSTAFF.DB.Phone
ABCSTAFF.DB.Comments
√ Undefined Field

Note that the first option in this menu consists solely of three dots or periods. Clicking this option displays a Define Field Object dialog box, as shown in Figure 7-17.

To use a calculated field, you simply turn on the Calculated option and type the desired calculation into the Calculated text box. You can easily insert a field name in the calculation by choosing the field name from the table's drop-down list box. The field name then appears in the text box at the top of the dialog box; choose Copy Field to insert that field into the expression.

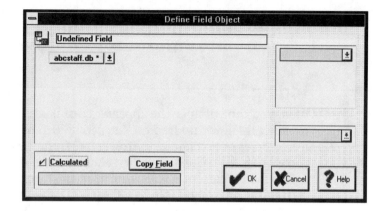

**Define Field
Object dialog
box
Figure 7-17.**

For this example, click Calculated to turn on the option. Then click the downward-pointing arrow in the ABCSTAFF.DB list box to open the drop-down list box, and double-click the Hourly Rate field. When you do so, "ABCSTAFF.Hourly Rate" appears in the text box at the top of the dialog box. Click the Copy Field button to insert the field name into the expression in the Calculated text box.

Click at the end of the entry you just inserted to place the insertion pointer at the end of the words "ABCSTAFF.Hourly Rate." Type a hyphen (the minus symbol) and click the downward-pointing arrow in the ABCSTAFF.DB list box to open the drop-down list box. Double-click the Salary field to display ABCSTAFF.Salary in the text box at the top of the dialog box. Then click the Copy Field button to insert the field name into the expression in the Calculated text box.

NOTE: The list box provides a fast way to enter field names into the Calculated text box. However, you can also type the field names manually. If you do so, be sure to enclose them within brackets.

This completes the expression needed for this example, so click OK. When the design layout is again visible, double-click in the field name for the new field to place the insertion point in the existing field name. Use the (Backspace) or (Del) key to erase the existing field name, and type the word **Profit:** in its place.

Adding Frames

Often, you can enhance the appearance of fields or text in a form by enclosing them within frames. You can do this by right-clicking the desired fields or text and choosing Frame from the properties menu that appears. To try this now, first click anywhere outside of a field so that no field is currently selected within the form. Then choose Select All from the Edit menu to select all fields in the form (handles will appear around all the fields). Next, right-click any field and a properties menu for the field will open.

Address
Define Field ▶
Color ▶
Pattern ▶
Frame ▶
Display Type ▶
Horizontal Scroll Bar
Vertical Scroll Bar
Design ▶
Run Time ▶
Methods...

(While the properties menu is named after the field you clicked, the frame that you choose will be applied to all fields because all fields are currently selected.) From the properties menu, choose Frame, choose Style, and then choose the second frame from the top in the menu of frames that appears. As a result, a frame will appear around every field, as shown in Figure 7-18.

You're going to make one more change to the form. The text box containing the title "ABC Temporaries Staff Table" currently appears in the same type of frame as the other fields. To distinguish it from the fields, you will add a shadow to its frame.

Right-click the text box now to open its properties menu. Choose Frame, choose Style, and then choose the third frame from the bottom from the menu of frames that appears. When you do so, a shaded frame appears around the text.

When you are done, save this latest version of the form by choosing Save from the File menu. You can then choose Close from the Control menu (or press (Ctrl)+(F4)) to close the design window. To use the form for viewing or editing data, choose the File/Open/Form option and select PERSONNL in the Open Document dialog box that appears.

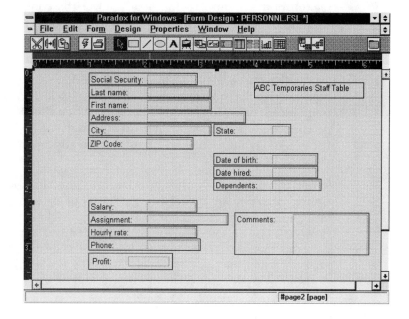

Form Design
window with
frames added to
fields
Figure 7-18.

Designing Multi-Record Forms

Paradox enables you to create *multi-record forms*. These are forms that show more than one record at a time, much like the tabular display that appears by default when you first begin viewing a table. One important difference between an ordinary view of a table and a multi-record form is that you can design the form to show the data in the format you prefer. Another important difference is that, as with any form, you can add calculated fields, something that you cannot do in Table mode.

Multi-record forms are very useful when you want to be able to view many records on the screen at once. You can also use multi-record forms to relate a number of records—such as those containing week ending dates and hours worked—to a single record in another table, such as the name of an employee. You'll learn how to design multi-record forms that are linked to more than one table in Chapter 11.

Any multi-record form has two areas: an original region, where fields from the first record to appear are placed on the form, and repeating

7

regions of the original region. Users of DOS-based versions of Paradox should note that Paradox for Windows does not require that you place all repeating regions directly below the original region, as do the DOS versions of Paradox.

To create a multi-record form, you start designing the form in the usual manner; simply choose the File/New/Form option and choose a table name from the dialog box that appears. When the Design Layout dialog box appears, click the Multi-Record button in the Style area. This causes the design layout to assume a multi-record appearance, as illustrated in Figure 7-19.

When you select the Multi-Record button, the Multi-Record Layout options are enabled. By default, the Both button is enabled, but you can also choose either Vertical or Horizontal by clicking the appropriate button. If you choose Horizontal, the records will repeat horizontally, or across the page. If you choose Vertical, the records will repeat vertically, or down the page. If you choose Both, the records will repeat both horizontally and vertically, across and down the page. Figure 7-20 illustrates this concept.

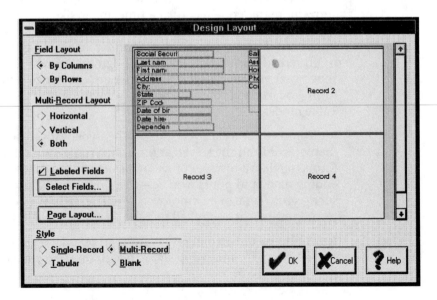

Design layout for a form using the Multi-Record layout option
Figure 7-19.

Once you are satisfied with the layout, click OK and the multi-record form will appear within a Form Design window. You can use any of the techniques outlined earlier in the chapter to modify the form's design. Remember, as you work with the form, you can choose View Data from the Form menu, press F8, or click the View Data icon in the SpeedBar to view actual data through the form. When you are done, remember to save the completed form by choosing Save or Save As from the File menu.

Hands-On Practice: Designing a Multi-Record Form

The managers at ABC Temporaries would like to be able to use a multi-record form for editing employee records. The fields most often edited are the Salary, Assignment, and Hourly Rate fields, so these fields will be included in the form. Also, the name fields are needed so the

Horizontal

Name:	Name:	Name:
City:	City:	City:
State:	State:	State:

Vertical

Name:
City:
State:
Name:
City:
State:
Name:
City:
State:

Horizontal and Vertical

Name:	Name:
City:	City:
State:	State:
Name:	Name:
City:	City:
State:	State:
Name:	Name:
City:	City:
State:	State:

Types of
multi-record
layouts
Figure 7-20.

managers can see which employee record is being edited. Follow these steps to create such a multi-record form:

1. Choose the File/New/Form option. In the dialog box that appears, click ABCSTAFF.DB and then click OK.

2. When the Design Layout dialog box appears, click the Multi-Record button in the Style area. In the Multi-Record Layout area, click the Both button if it is not already selected.

3. In this case, only certain fields are required, so click the Select Fields button to display the Select Fields dialog box (Figure 7-21). Using this dialog box, you can remove unwanted fields from the design layout.

4. In the Selected Fields list box at the right side of the dialog box, click the Social Security field. Then click the Remove Field button to remove that field from the layout.

5. Using the same process, remove all the remaining fields except for the Last Name, First Name, Salary, Assignment, and Hourly Rate fields. When you are done, these fields should be the only ones remaining in the Selected Fields list box.

6. Click OK. The Design Layout window will reappear and will contain only the selected fields, as shown in Figure 7-22.

7. Click the OK button in the Design Layout window. In a moment, a new Form Design window appears, containing the multi-record layout. Click the window's Maximize button to increase the size of the window.

8. At this point you can make any other changes to the form to enhance its appearance. In this case, add borders around the fields to better differentiate one field from another. Click the Last Name field to select it. Then hold down the Shift key and click the remaining fields in the form to select all of them.

9. With all the fields selected, right-click any field to open a properties menu.

10. Choose Frame, choose Style, and then choose the second frame from the top within the menu of sample frame styles that opens. This will place a single-line frame around all of the fields.

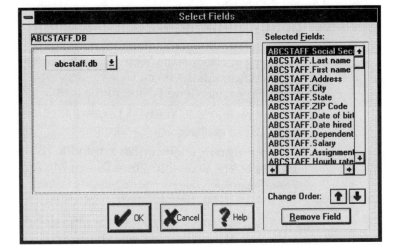

Select Fields
dialog box
Figure 7-21.

7

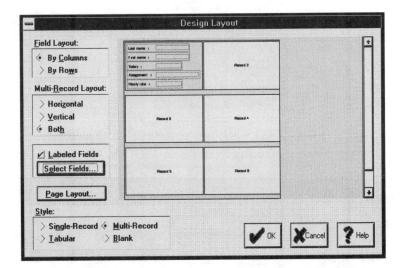

Design Layout
window
containing only
selected fields
Figure 7-22.

11. Click outside of any field anywhere in the form to deselect the fields; when you do so, your example should resemble the one shown in Figure 7-23.

12. Press F8 or click on the View Data icon on the SpeedBar to view the data through the form. Figure 7-24 shows some data from the ABCSTAFF table viewed through the form.

13. When you are done, press F8 or click the Design icon in the SpeedBar to get back into Design mode.

14. Save the form by choosing Save from the File menu. Call this form **PEOPLE**. Then close the Form Design window by pressing Ctrl + F4.

Note that you can make changes to a multi-record form at any time by using the same techniques you would use to change other forms. You change properties such as fonts or colors just as you do in other forms, as described earlier in this chapter.

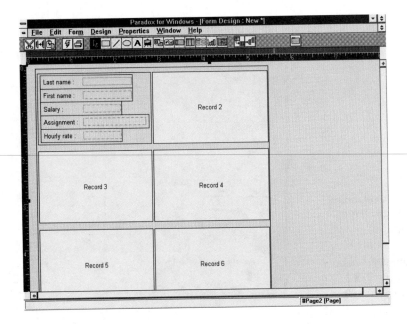

Completed
multi-record
form design
Figure 7-23.

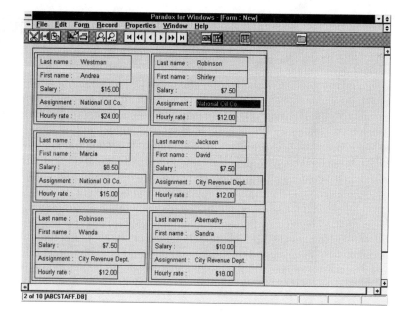

View of data
through a
multi-record
form design
Figure 7-24.

Designing a Tabular Form

Paradox also lets you design forms using a tabular layout. You start the process using the same initial steps as with other forms. First, you choose the File/New/Form option, and then you select a table on which to base the form from the Data Model dialog box. Paradox will bring up the Design Layout dialog box. Next, click the Tabular button in the Style area of the dialog box. This displays a table-based representation of the form in the Design Layout dialog box, as shown in Figure 7-25.

Note that the layout consists of rows of records and columns of fields, just as within a Paradox table. If you want to include only specific fields in the form, click the Select Fields button to display the Select Fields dialog box. Remove any unwanted fields from the layout by clicking the field name and then clicking the Remove Field button.

7

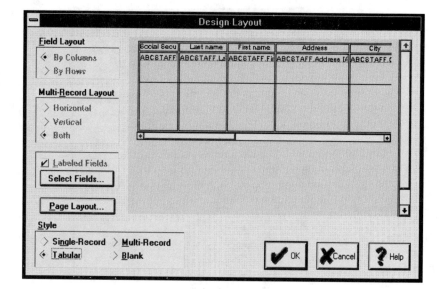

Design Layout dialog box with Tabular option selected
Figure 7-25.

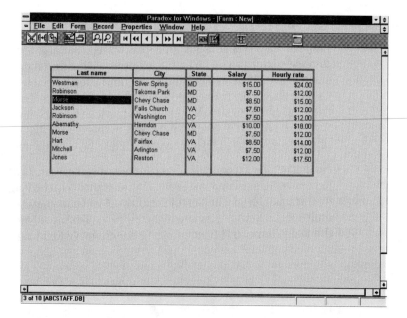

Sample tabular form with selected fields from ABCSTAFF table
Figure 7-26.

As with any form, you can make changes to the layout of a tabular form by moving fields, changing styles or fonts, adding borders, and so on. When you are done, save the form with the Save or Save As option in the File menu. Figure 7-26 shows a sample tabular form with just the Last Name, City, State, Salary, and Hourly Rate fields from the ABCSTAFF table.

Quick Summary

Creating a Custom Form

Choose the File/New/Form option to display the Data Model dialog box. Click a table name under File Name to choose the table with which the form will be used, and then click OK. This opens the Design Layout window for the form. Use the options at the left side of the Design Layout window to quickly design the initial layout for the form, and then click OK. This displays a Form Design window for the new form. Using this window as a drawing area, move fields around as desired and add any desired lines, graphics, or labels (additional text). Store the form by choosing Save or Save As from the File menu.

Designing a Form

Choose the File/New/Form option. In the Data Model dialog box that appears, choose the table on which the form will be based, and then click OK. Use the options at the left side of the Design Layout dialog box that appears to design the initial layout for the form, and then click OK. In the Form Design window that appears, move fields around as desired and add any desired lines, graphics, or labels.

7

Quick Summary *(continued)*

Modifying an Existing Form

Choose the File/Open/Form option. Once the form appears on screen, choose Design from the Form menu (or click the Design icon in the SpeedBar) to make changes to the form's design.

Placing Fields in a Form

Click the Field Tool icon on the SpeedBar and then click in the desired location and drag until the new field reaches the size you want. Right-click the field to open a properties menu for defining the field.

Adding Labels or Text in a Form

Click the Text tool in the SpeedBar. Then click and drag in the Form Design window until the text frame that appears is as large as desired. Release the mouse button and start typing the text. You can resize the text frame at any time by first selecting the frame and then clicking and dragging on a corner handle. You can move the frame by first selecting it and then clicking and dragging it to its desired location.

Drawing Boxes, Lines, or Ellipses in a Form

First click the Line, Box, or Ellipse tool in the SpeedBar. Then click in the desired starting location in the form and drag until the line, box, or ellipse reaches the desired size.

Adding Graphics to a Form

First click the Graphic tool in the SpeedBar. Then click at the desired starting location in the form and drag until the box that is to contain the graphic reaches the desired size. To define the source of the graphic, right-click the undefined graphic to open its properties menu. Choose Define Graphic. Then, from the next menu to appear, choose Paste to paste the contents of the

Quick Summary *(continued)*

Clipboard. Alternately, choose Paste From to paste from a graphic image file. If you choose Paste From, a Select File box will appear, and you can choose which graphic file to paste into the undefined graphic.

Saving a Form

Choose Save or Save As from the File menu. The File Save As dialog box appears when you choose File Save As or when you choose Save if you're saving a form for the first time. Enter the desired name for the form (using DOS file naming conventions of eight characters or less and no spaces) in the New File Name text box and then click OK.

Placing an Existing Form in Use

Choose the File/Open/Form option, choose the form by name from the Open Document dialog box that appears, and click OK. The form will appear, containing a record within the table.

7

CHAPTER

PARADOX WINDOWS PARADOX WINDOWS PARADOX WINDOWS PARADOX WINDOWS PARADOX WINDOWS PARADOX WINDOWS

8

USING GRAPHIC AND OLE FIELDS IN TABLES

In its discussion of table creation, Chapter 3 introduced the topic of graphic and OLE fields. These are special types of fields that you can use in Paradox to store different kinds of data. While graphic fields contain graphics, OLE fields can contain any type of data, including graphic images, spreadsheet cells, or word processed text. OLE is an abbreviation for object linking and embedding, *a Windows technique that is used to share data between applications.*

Graphic and OLE Fields Defined

Graphics are images or artwork that you insert into graphic fields within a Paradox table. You can also place graphics as objects in a form or report. Paradox accepts graphics in either of two ways: pasted in from the Windows Clipboard, or as a graphics file created in a different software package. If you insert a graphic as a file, you can use graphics files in any of the supported graphic formats: .BMP, .PCX, .CGM (metafile), and .TIF. If you insert a graphic from the Windows Clipboard, it does not matter what format the original application uses, but you can only use this technique with other Windows applications. Figure 8-1 shows a table containing data pasted into a graphics field from a Windows paint program.

OLE fields can store any kind of data, from graphics to text to sound.

OLE fields contain objects placed in your table from other Windows applications. OLE fields can be thought of as containers in which you can store entire files from other Windows applications. When you paste data from another Windows application into an OLE field, Paradox treats that data as an object, and embeds it into the Paradox table, establishing a two-way link between the object (in Paradox) and the source application and file. As an example, you could place an entire word processed document created in a Windows word processor in an OLE field in a Paradox table.

There are two advantages to using an OLE field. One is that the OLE field provides you with a link to the original file, in the original application. Any changes to the original file (using the original

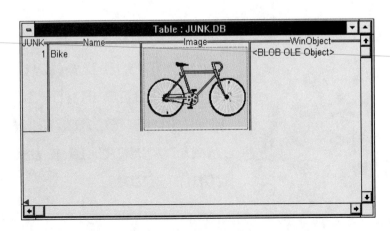

Table containing objects in a graphic field
Figure 8-1.

application) will be reflected in the OLE field in Paradox. For example, if you inserted a word processing file into an OLE field, you could later change that file using your word processor, and the change would be reflected in the document within Paradox.

The other advantage of using OLE fields is that you can change the data in the OLE field directly from Paradox; when you double-click the field containing the OLE data, the program you used to create the OLE data opens a window, and you can use that program to make the desired changes. Figure 8-2 shows a table containing OLE objects pasted into an OLE field; in this example, the objects are word processed documents from Microsoft Word.

NOTE: When you are working with OLE fields in Paradox, the other software package you're using must support OLE under Windows.

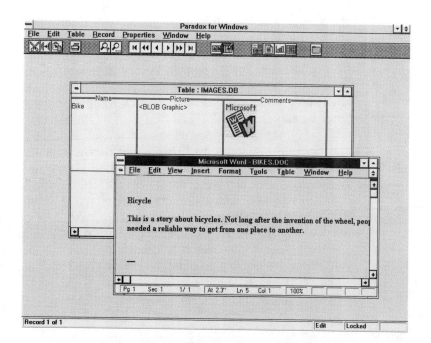

Table containing objects in an OLE field **Figure 8-2.**

8

In general, you use OLE fields in Paradox whenever you want to be able to open the source application directly from Paradox. Since graphics can be inserted into graphic fields or into OLE fields (when the application used to create the graphics supports OLE), you may wonder which type of field you should use to store graphics. If the graphic software does not support OLE, of course, there is no question; in such cases, you can only use a graphic field. If the graphic software supports OLE, the choice is up to you; there are advantages and disadvantages to the use of the OLE field over the graphic field for storing graphics. The advantage is that from Paradox, you can easily change the graphic images stored in the field by double-clicking on the field. The disadvantage is that in reports, the actual graphics will not be displayed or printed in an OLE field placed in a form or report. In a report, an icon representing the OLE object appears, but the actual contents of the object do not appear, since the object is simply a link to another program. So, if you want your graphics to appear or be printed within a form or report, you should use graphic fields.

About OLE Servers and Clients

Paradox for Windows is an OLE client but not an OLE server.

If you make extensive use of OLE capabilities under Windows, you should note that Paradox is an OLE client. Under Windows, an OLE *client* is an application that receives data, using the rules of object linking and embedding. An OLE *server* is an application that sends data using OLE rules. Some applications are OLE clients, some are OLE servers, and some are both. Paradox is an OLE client, while Borland's Quattro Pro for Windows is both an OLE client and an OLE server. Since Paradox is an OLE client (but not an OLE server), it can receive OLE data from other applications, but it cannot provide OLE data to another Windows program. This means that you could not copy part or all of a Paradox table into an OLE container in another Windows application (such as a word processor). This limitation should not present a major problem, since there are effective ways of sharing Paradox data with other applications. You could, for example, simply select and paste the desired Paradox data into the Windows Clipboard, and then paste it into the other application (but not into an OLE container). For additional details on using Paradox data in other applications, see Chapter 13.

Different types of programs that are OLE clients make use of different types of OLE containers. (An OLE *container* is any place in a program designed to store the OLE data provided by the other application.) Because Paradox is a database and databases store data in fields, Paradox uses OLE fields as containers. In Microsoft Word for Windows, special boxes within documents are OLE containers. In Borland's Quattro Pro spreadsheet, the cells of the spreadsheet can be used as OLE containers.

Defining Graphic and OLE Fields Within a Table

You can specify that a table's fields are to contain graphic or OLE data during the table creation process. To do so, choose the File/New/Table option and then click OK to begin creating the table. The Create Paradox for Windows Table dialog box appears. (See Chapter 3 for additional details about creating tables.)

After entering the name of the field in the Field Name column, press [Tab] to move over to the Type column and press the [Spacebar]. This should bring up the Type menu, as shown in Figure 8-3.

8

Choose Graphic to define a graphic field or choose OLE to define an OLE field. You needn't specify a size for either of these field types, since such fields have no specific sizes in terms of characters. When you are done defining the table's fields, click OK and enter a name for your table in the Save As dialog box.

Adding Graphic Data to a Table

As mentioned, Paradox lets you insert graphic data into a table in either of two ways: You can paste the graphic in from the Windows Clipboard (assuming you are using another Windows program to create the graphic), or you can insert the graphic as a graphic file. If you choose the graphic file method, the file must be in one of the formats supported by Paradox. (Remember, these formats are . BMP, .PCX, .CGM, and .TIF.)

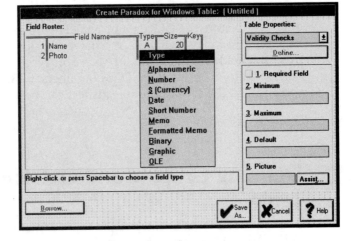

Create Table
dialog box with
Type menu
open
Figure 8-3.

Pasting a Graphic from the Windows Clipboard

To paste a graphic from the Windows Clipboard, use the following
steps:

1. Open the graphics file, using the source application under
   Windows. (The source application must be an application in which
   you can cut and paste data into the Windows Clipboard.)

TIP: In Windows, you can use [Alt]+[Esc] or [Alt]+[Tab] to switch
between applications.

2. Select the graphic, and use the Cut or Copy command from the
   Edit menu to cut or copy the graphic to the Windows Clipboard.

As an example, Figure 8-4 shows a graphic image selected in Paintbrush. If you choose Cut from the Paintbrush Edit menu, the selected image is removed from its present location and copied into the Windows Clipboard. If you choose Copy from the Paintbrush Edit menu, the selected image is copied into the Windows Clipboard and the original is left in its present location.

3. Assuming Paradox is up and running, use the mouse or the Windows Task Switcher (press $\boxed{\text{Ctrl}}$+$\boxed{\text{Esc}}$) to switch to Paradox.

4. Once you're in Paradox, open the table (or form) into which you want to insert the graphic.

5. Select the graphic field, and enter Edit mode by pressing $\boxed{\text{F9}}$.

6. Choose Paste or Paste Link from the Edit menu. (Some applications do not support the Paste Link option, in which case it will be dimmed. The difference between these two options is described under "Edit Paste Versus Edit Paste Link" later in this chapter.)

8

Selected image
in Paintbrush
Figure 8-4.

Paradox places the graphic in the field of the table. In Figure 8-5, the image previously pasted into the Clipboard has been inserted into a graphics field of a Paradox table.

TIP: A shortcut for choosing Paste from the Edit menu is to click the Edit Paste icon in the SpeedBar.

Inserting a Graphic from a File

In some cases, you may prefer to insert a graphic from a graphic file. Perhaps you know the name of the file (and just typing a filename is faster than opening another application and selecting and copying data into the Clipboard). Or, perhaps the graphic was created in a DOS application, so you cannot use the Windows Clipboard to copy the graphic. In such cases, you can insert the graphic from a graphic file that is compatible with Paradox.

Table
containing
graphic field
with graphic
pasted in from
the Clipboard
Figure 8-5.

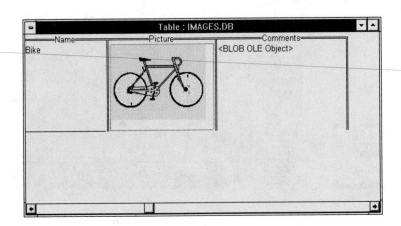

To insert a graphic from a file, start Paradox in the usual manner and open the desired table. Then, use the following steps:

1. Select the graphic field and enter Edit mode by pressing [F9].
2. Choose Paste From from the Edit menu. The Paste From Graphic File dialog box will appear, as shown in Figure 8-6.

In the dialog box, Paradox automatically displays file types that match the acceptable graphic formats. To change disk drives and/or directories, click the Browse button to bring up the File Browser, and click the desired drives and/or subdirectories. Once you locate the desired graphic file, click it, and then click OK to paste the graphic into the selected field.

NOTE: Paradox supports graphic files in .BMP, .PCX, .CGM, and .TIF file formats. Graphics files that you insert into graphic fields must be in one of these formats.

8

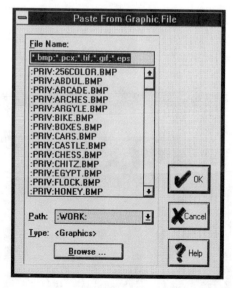

Paste from
Graphic File
dialog box
Figure 8-6.

TIP: When you place a graphic into a field, you may not be able to see as much of the graphic as you would like. Remember that you can resize the fields of a table or form as desired. If you are viewing a table, resize the column width and/or the line spacing to see more of the graphic. When using a form, switch to form design mode, and resize the graphic field as desired by clicking the field and dragging the handles. For details on resizing the magnification of the graphic, see the section "Changing Magnification" later in this chapter.

Adding OLE Data to a Table

To place text, spreadsheet data, or graphics in OLE fields, you must first open the source application that is the OLE server. Use the following steps to place OLE data in a field:

1. Open the source application containing the desired data. (The source application must have OLE capability.)

2. Select the desired value or object in the source application, and use Cut or Copy commands on the Edit menu to cut or copy the data to the Windows Clipboard. As an example, Figure 8-7 shows a selection from a paragraph of a Microsoft Word for Windows

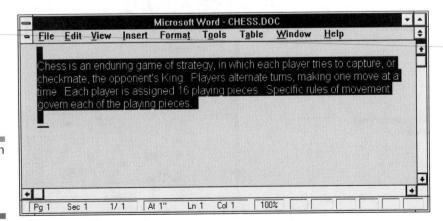

Selected text in
Word for
Windows
Figure 8-7.

document. If you choose Copy from the Word for Windows Edit menu, the selected text will be copied into the Windows Clipboard, ready for pasting into a Paradox field as an OLE object.

3. Assuming Paradox is up and running, use the mouse or the Windows Task Switcher (press Ctrl+Esc) to switch to Paradox.

4. Once you are in Paradox, open the table (or form) into which you want to insert the text, data, or graphic.

5. Select the OLE field, and enter Edit mode by pressing F9.

6. Choose Paste or Paste Link from the Edit menu. (The differences between these two options are described in a moment.) Paradox places the OLE object in the selected field. In Figure 8-8, an icon representing a Word for Windows document appears in the OLE field of the Paradox table, representing the OLE link to the source application (in this case, Word for Windows). Note that if you place a graphic into an OLE field, the graphic appears instead of an icon representing the source application.

Edit Paste Versus Edit Paste Link

The Paste and Paste Link options on the Edit menu both insert material from the Clipboard into your Paradox form or table. However, when

8

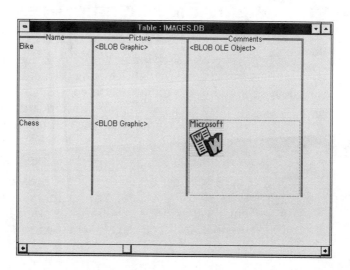

Table
containing OLE
field with Word
for Windows
object inserted
Figure 8-8.

you use the Paste option, you paste a copy of the original data. (If you later change the original data using the source application, the copy stored in Paradox will not be changed.) On the other hand, when you use the Paste Link option, you forge a link to the original application's source file. (The link is provided through the DDE, or Dynamic Data Exchange, capability of Windows.) Later, if you make changes to the data in the source application, the changes automatically appear in the data that is in the Paradox table. If the Paste Link option is dimmed when you attempt to paste the data into the Paradox table, the source application does not support Windows DDE. (Some older applications do not support Windows DDE.)

Editing OLE Data

Since OLE represents a direct link to the source application, you can edit any data in an OLE field simply by selecting the field, pressing `F9` to enter Edit mode, and then double-clicking the field. When you double-click the field, the data will appear in a window of the source application. Figure 8-9 shows the results of double-clicking an OLE field containing a Word for Windows document. You can use the usual techniques in the source application to change the data as required. As you make changes in the source application, the changes automatically appear in the OLE field within the Paradox table.

Changing the Magnification and the Default Display of Graphic and OLE Fields

As described in earlier chapters, you can change the properties associated with fields by right-clicking the field to open its properties menu. The properties menu associated with any graphic or OLE field

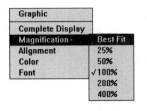

has two options not found in standard properties menus: Magnification and Complete Display. If you right-click a graphics field to open its properties menu and choose Magnification, a second menu appears.

Using this menu, you can reduce the size of the graphic or OLE object to 25% or 50% of its original size. Alternately, you can enlarge it to 200% or 400% of its original size. (The default is 100% of original size.) You can also choose the Best Fit option, in

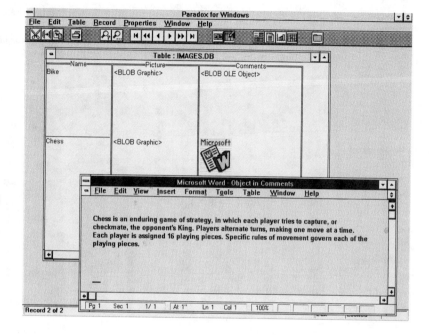

Double-clicking the OLE field opens the application containing the original file
Figure 8-9.

8

which case Paradox shrinks or expands the graphic or OLE object to best fill the dimension of the field without extending beyond it.

Using the Complete Display choice in the properties menu, you can determine whether Paradox displays the contents of every visible graphic or OLE field in a table, or just the field in the current record. If you right-click a graphics or OLE field to open the properties menu and turn on Complete Display, Paradox displays every visible graphic field. (The option is a toggle, so choosing Complete Display repeatedly turns the option on or off. In Figure 8-10, the Complete Display option has been turned off; hence, the graphic field displays its contents only when it is selected. Turn on the option if you want all visible records to display any graphics and/or OLE fields. In Figure 8-11, the Complete Display option has been turned on; hence, the field displays its contents at all times. Note that displaying graphics takes time, so if you want the fastest response possible when scrolling through a database containing graphic or OLE fields, you should turn off the Complete Display option.

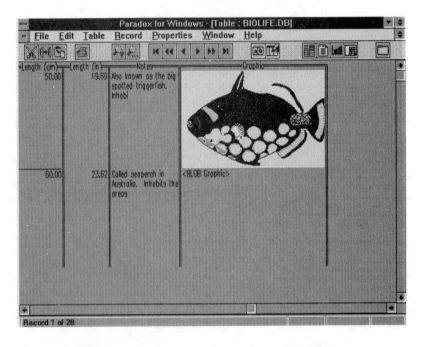

Table
containing a
graphic field,
with
Render/Current
selected from
the properties
menu
Figure 8-10.

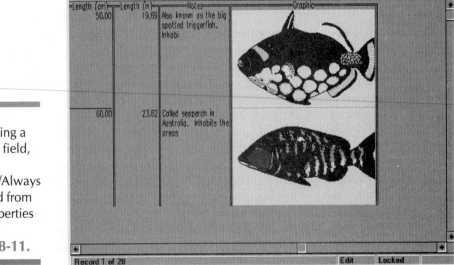

Table
containing a
graphic field,
with
Render/Always
selected from
the properties
menu
Figure 8-11.

Working with Graphic and OLE Fields in Forms and Reports

You can use the graphic tool on the SpeedBar to add a graphic to a form or a report during the design process. (For complete details on designing forms, see Chapter 7; for complete details on designing reports, see Chapter 9.)

To add a graphic while designing a form or report, click the graphic tool in the SpeedBar. Then click the desired starting location in the form and drag until the container that will contain the graphic is the desired size. When you release the mouse, the container will contain the label "undefined graphic."

To speed up the response when scrolling through databases with graphic fields, right-click the graphic field to open the properties menu, and turn off Complete Display.

To define the source of the graphic, first, if you are using the Clipboard as a source, paste the desired graphic into the Clipboard from the original application. Then, switch back to Paradox, and right-click the graphic container to open its properties menu. Choose Define Graphic and then perform either of the following:

✦ Choose Paste to paste the contents of the Clipboard. (If the Clipboard is empty, the Paste option will be dimmed.)

✦ Choose Paste From to paste from a graphic image file. If you choose Paste From, Paradox displays a Select File box. Now you can choose the graphic file that you want to paste into the graphic container.

8

You can move the graphic within its container by clicking and dragging it to the desired location (the cursor changes to the shape of a hand when dragging the graphic is possible). If you want to move the container as a whole, select the entire container by clicking it, and drag it to the desired location in the document.

Quick Summary

Defining a Graphic or OLE Field

When you're creating a table, move the cursor to the Type column of the Table Structure dialog box and press the [Spacebar] to open the Type menu. Choose either Graphic or OLE from the Type menu to identify the field type.

Inserting the Contents of the Windows Clipboard into a Graphic Field

In the source application, use Cut or Copy on the Edit menu to place the image in the Windows Clipboard. Then switch to Paradox, select the desired field of the desired record, press [F9], and choose Paste or Paste Link from the Edit menu.

Inserting a Graphics File into a Graphic Field

Select the desired field of the desired record, and press [F9] to begin editing. Choose Paste From from the Edit menu. In the Select File dialog box that appears, choose the desired graphics file (use the Browse button to view other drives and/or directories). Once you locate the desired graphics file, click it, and then click OK to paste the graphic into the field.

CHAPTER

PARADOX WINDOWS PARADOX WINDOWS PARADOX WINDOWS PARADOX WINDOWS PARADOX WINDOWS PARADOX WINDOWS

DESIGNING AND USING REPORTS

Creating reports is, for many users, what database management is all about. Although a Paradox query is a powerful tool for gaining immediate answers to specific questions, much of your work will probably involve generating reports.

Detailed reports are easy to produce with Paradox, due in no small part to the program's philosophy of designing visually, by manipulating objects with the mouse to get the job done.

To select records for inclusion in a report, you can design a query using the tools you have already learned from Chapter 6. Once those records are contained in a table, you can print a standard tabular report by clicking the Quick Report icon in the SpeedBar. For greater flexibility, you can use Paradox's report creation features to design custom reports that meet your specific needs.

Paradox offers two overall types of reports: quick reports and custom reports. *Quick reports* are reports that Paradox creates automatically whenever a table is active and you click on the Quick Report icon in the SpeedBar, press [Shift]+[F7], or choose Print from the File menu while a table is open in the active window. Such reports contain all of the field names in a table, and the field names that you supplied during the table design are used as headings for the fields.

You can design custom reports that meet your specific needs, using Paradox's report creation features.

Custom reports, by comparison, are reports that you modify in some way to better fit your specific needs. Unlike many competing database managers, Paradox for Windows does not force you to design a report from scratch, and it does not limit you to one or two predefined report layouts (many other programs offer only a row-oriented layout and a column-oriented layout). When you create a custom report in Paradox, you can use a Design Layout screen to create an initial report design using one of a large number of styles. You can add or remove fields from the report, change headings, lengthen or shorten columns, change formatting attributes, and save the design as a custom report. Figures 9-1 through 9-3 are examples of some of the types of reports that you can produce in Paradox.

Generating a Quick Report

By far the fastest way to produce printed reports in Paradox is to use the Quick Report icon on the SpeedBar (or press [Shift]+[F7]) because you don't need to design such reports in advance. To produce a quick report, simply activate the window containing the table, turn on your printer, and click the Quick Report icon on the SpeedBar. After the report appears on the screen, click the Print icon on the SpeedBar. When the dialog box appears, click OK. You can also generate a quick

Wednesday, September 9, 1992   ABCSTAFF   Page 1

Social Security	Last Name	First Name	Address	City	State	ZIP Code
121-33-9876	Westman	Andrea	4807 East Avenue	Silver Spring	MD	20910-0124
121-90-5432	Robinson	Shirley	270 Browning Ave #2A	Takoma Park	MD	20912
123-44-8976	Morse	Marcia	4260 Park Avenue	Chevy Chase	MD	20815-0988
232-55-1234	Jackson	David	4102 Valley Lane	Falls Church	VA	22044
343-55-9821	Robinson	Wanda	1607 21st Street, NW	Washington	DC	20009
495-00-3456	Abernathy	Sandra	1512 Loiza Way	Herndon	VA	22071
805-34-6789	Morse	William	4260 Park Avenue	Chevy Chase	MD	20815-0988
876-54-3210	Hart	Edward	6200 Germantown Road	Fairfax	VA	22025
901-77-3456	Mitchell	Mary Jo	617 North Oakland Street	Arlington	VA	22203
909-88-7654	Jones	Jarel	5203 North Shore Drive	Reston	VA	22090

Sample of tabular report based on ABCSTAFF table
Figure 9-1.

report by activating the window containing the table and then choosing Print from the File menu.

Tıp: To get a Quick report, you can 1) click the Quick Report icon, or 2) press Shift+F7, or 3) choose File/Print while a table is open in the active window. Then click OK in the dialog box that appears.

The report shown in Figure 9-1 was produced from the ABCSTAFF table by means of the Quick Report option. Note that this example illustrates the design of a Quick report. Paradox uses the table's name as a page header, prints page numbers in the upper-right corner, and prints the current date in the upper-left corner. The field names appear as column headings, and the data appears in rows beneath the headings in a

Wednesday, September 9, 1992   ABCSTAFF   Page 1

Social Security: 121-33-9876
Last Name: Westman
First Name: Andrea
Address: 4807 East Avenue
City: Silver Spring
State: MD
ZIP Code: 20910-0124   Comments: Did well
Date of Birth: 5/29/61   on last two assignments.
Date Hired: 7/4/86
Dependents: 2.0
Salary: $15.00
Assignment: National Oil Co.
Hourly Rate: $24.00
Phone: 301-555-5682

Social Security: 121-90-5432
Last Name: Robinson
First Name: Shirley
Address: 270 Browning Ave #2A
City: Takoma Park
State: MD
ZIP Code: 20912   Comments: Too new to
Date of Birth: 11/2/64   evaluate.
Date Hired: 11/17/91
Dependents: 1.0
Salary: $7.50
Assignment: National Oil Co.
Hourly Rate: $12.00
Phone: 301-555-4582

Sample of
form-oriented
report based on
ABCSTAFF
table
Figure 9-2.

Wednesday, September 9, 1992   HOURS   Page 1

Social Security: 121-33-9876 Weekend Date: 1/16/92 Assignment: National Oil Co. Hours Worked: 30.0	Social Security: 495-00-3456 Weekend Date: 1/16/92 Assignment: City Revenue Dept. Hours Worked: 28.0
Social Security: 121-33-9876 Weekend Date: 1/23/92 Assignment: National Oil Co. Hours Worked: 35.0	Social Security: 495-00-3456 Weekend Date: 1/23/92 Assignment: City Revenue Dept. Hours Worked: 32.0
Social Security: 121-90-5432 Weekend Date: 1/16/92 Assignment: National Oil Co. Hours Worked: 27.0	Social Security: 805-34-6789 Weekend Date: 1/23/92 Assignment: Smith Builders Hours worked: 35.0
Social Security: 123-44-8976 Weekend Date: 1/16/92 Assignment: National Oil Co. Hours Worked: 32.0	Social Security: 876-54-3210 Weekend Date: 1/23/92 Assignment: Smith Builders Hours Worked: 30.0
Social Security: 232-55-1234 Weekend Date: 1/16/92 Assignment: City Revenue Dept. Hours Worked: 30.0	Social Security: 901-77-3456 Weekend Date: 1/23/92 Assignment: Smith Builders Hours Worked: 28.0
Social Security: 232-55-1234 Weekend Date: 1/23/92 Assignment: City Revenue Dept. Hours Worked: 30.0	Social Security: 909-88-7654 Weekend Date: 1/16/92 Assignment: National Oil Co. Hours Worked: 35.0
Social Security: 343-55-9821 Weekend Date: 1/16/92 Assignment: City Revenue Dept. Hours Worked: 35.0	Social Security: 909-88-7654 Weekend Date: 1/23/92 Assignment: National Oil Co. Hours Worked: 33.0
Social Security: 343-55-9821 Weekend Date: 1/23/92 Assignment: City Revenue Dept. Hours Worked: 32.0	

9

Sample of
multi-record
report based on
HOURS table
Figure 9-3.

tabular format. If the field name is wider than the default column width, Paradox widens the column so the entire heading will fit.

The example in Figure 9-1 shows one trait of a default quick report which you may not find very appealing. Depending on the design of the table's structure, one or more columns may be cut off by the right margin of the report. In many cases, you can quickly solve this problem by performing a query that provides an ANSWER table containing just the fields you want; then, use that table to generate the quick report, as described in the following section. You can also solve this problem by changing the options in the Print the File dialog box that appears when you print a report; these techniques will also be detailed shortly.

TIP: If a report needs to be in a specific order, sort the table before producing the report.

Hands-On Practice: Producing Selective Quick Reports with Ease

Remember, for a fast, selective report, perform a query and then press Shift + F7.

If you want maximum results in a minimum of time, keep in mind the flexibility that Paradox provides by storing the results of queries in the form of temporary tables. You can use these tables to generate your reports. And, in many cases, you can solve your formatting problems by including selected fields in the ANSWER table while omitting unwanted fields.

If you produce a quick report by viewing the ABCSTAFF table and pressing Shift + F7 to print a report, not all the fields will fit on a single page. However, perhaps you are only interested in the Last Name, Salary, Hourly Rate, and Assignment fields, and you know that these will comfortably fit on a single sheet of standard paper. Follow these steps to create a quick report containing only those fields:

1. Choose the File/New/Query option.

2. When the Select File dialog box appears, click ABCSTAFF.DB and then click OK.

3. In the Query Form that appears, use the mouse or the F6 key to place check marks in the Last Name, Salary, Hourly Rate, and Assignment fields, and then press F8 to process the query. The resulting ANSWER table contains all of the records from the staff table, but with only the designated fields.

4. Press Shift+F7 to display the report, then choose Report/Print (or click the Print icon on the SpeedBar). When the Print File dialog box appears, click OK. (This dialog box is discussed in detail in the next section.) The quick report that is printed will resemble the one shown in Figure 9-4, in which all of the desired data fits on a single page.

Refer back to Chapter 6 for information regarding Query-by-Example techniques.

If you want specific records in the report, you can use the Query-by-Example techniques explained in Chapter 6 to produce a subset of records in the ANSWER table. Also, if you want to see the report in some specific order, you can sort the ANSWER table and then produce the report. Paradox's built-in flexibility lets you generate complex reports with little or no customizing.

Before proceeding, close the new reports, ANSWER table, and the existing query form (answer No to the prompt that asks if you want to save the new report or the new query form).

9

Wednesday, September 9, 1992		ANSWER	
Last Name	Salary	Assignment	Hourly Rate
Abernathy	$10.00	City Revenue Dept.	$18.00
Hart	$8.50	Smith Builders	$14.00
Jackson	$7.50	City Revenue Dept.	$12.00
Jones	$12.00	National Oil Co.	$17.50
Mitchell	$7.50	Smith Builders	$12.00
Morse	$7.50	Smith Builders	$12.00
Morse	$8.50	National Oil Co.	$15.00
Robinson	$7.50	City Revenue Dept.	$12.00
Robinson	$7.50	National Oil Co.	$12.00
Westman	$15.00	National Oil Co.	$24.00

Quick report based on query with selected fields
Figure 9-4.

About the Print File Dialog Box

Whenever you print any report, whether it is a Quick report or a Custom report, Paradox first displays the Print File dialog box shown in Figure 9-5.

You can use the options in the Print portion of the dialog box to specify a range of pages to print or to print all pages of the report. To print all the pages in a report, click the All button if it is not already selected (this is the default). To specify a range of pages, click the Page Range button. Then enter a starting page number in the From text box and an ending page number in the To text box. To print from the first page to a specific page, you can leave the From box empty and just enter a number in the To box. To print a single page, just enter the same page number in both text boxes.

TIP: The Page Range options can be useful for reprinting part of a large table after a printer jam. You can specify just those pages of the report you need, and avoid reprinting the entire report.

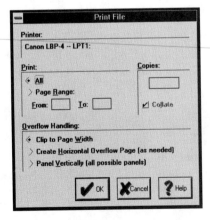

Print File
dialog box
Figure 9-5.

Use the Copies option to change the number of copies that you want printed; the default is 1. If you are printing more than one copy of a report, leave the Collate box checked if you want multiple copies to be collated into sets.

The options in the Overflow Handling portion of the dialog box let you tell Paradox how you want to treat data that is too wide to fit on a printed page. Your options here are as follows:

✦ The Clip to Page Width option clips (or, trims) all data that doesn't fit across the page.

✦ The Create Horizontal Overflow Pages (as needed) option prints additional pages to the right, only when necessary, to accommodate all the data.

✦ The Panel Vertically (all possible panels) option prints a second page for each page of the report, regardless of how many pages actually have overflow data. In other words, if you have a 3-page report and only page 1 has overflow, pages 2 and 3 will still get a second page.

After you set all options as you want them, click OK. A status message in a Preparing Report dialog box appears on the screen while Paradox sends the report to the printer. You can choose Cancel from this dialog box at any time to stop sending the report.

9

TIP: Once the Preparing Report dialog box vanishes, it is too late to cancel a report from within Paradox. However, you may still be able to cancel part or all of the report by switching to the Windows Print Manager by pressing Ctrl+Esc, choosing Print Manager from the Task Switcher, selecting the print job by name, and choosing Delete.

Creating a Custom Report

If you have worked through the examples in Chapter 7, you already know much about designing reports. Like forms, Paradox reports are a type of document that you design by placing desired objects within a design layout. Follow the specific steps below to learn how to create a Custom report for the ABC Temporaries table.

To begin the process of creating the Custom report, choose the File/New/Report option. This brings up the Data Model dialog box shown in Figure 9-6. As with forms, you use this dialog box to identify the data model, or source of the fields, for the report. This chapter describes how to create reports that make use of a single table. For details on creating reports based on more than one table, refer to Chapter 11.

In the File Name list box in the dialog box, click the desired table name to select it. Then click OK to display the Design Layout dialog box, as shown in Figure 9-7.

By default, labels and fields for the table you selected in the previous step appear in a sample report that occupies most of the Design Layout dialog box. You use the options on the left side of the dialog box to specify an initial layout for the report's design.

The options in the Style area in the lower-left corner of the dialog box control the overall style of the report. (The other options may or may not be available, depending on which of the Style options you have selected.) You have four choices: Single-Record, Multi-Record, Tabular, and Blank. By default, Tabular is selected; this provides a report oriented in tabular fashion, much like that of a Table mode in Paradox. The Single-Record option places one record at a time in the report,

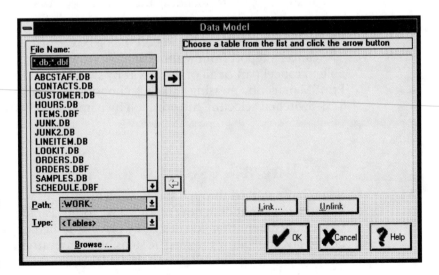

Data Model
dialog box
Figure 9-6.

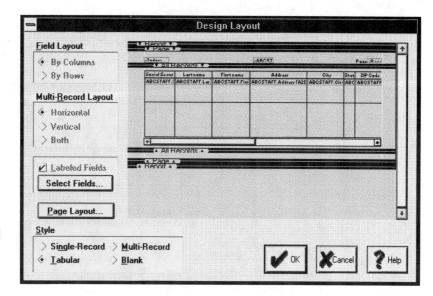

Design Layout
dialog box used
with reports
Figure 9-7.

using a free-form layout (fields do not appear in columns, but instead are placed where they are needed on separate lines). The Multi-Record option displays several records at a time. You'll use this option for Multi-Record reports, a topic covered later in this chapter. Finally, the Blank option brings up a Blank report, letting you insert and position all the fields manually. Figure 9-8 illustrates the Tabular, Single-Record, and Multi-Record report styles.

If you choose Single-Record or Multi-Record as the report's style, the Field Layout options are made available. Click the By Columns button to provide a column-oriented layout, where fields appear in one or more columns, with the first field on top, the next field below it, and so on. An example of this report layout is shown in Figure 9-9. Or, click the By Rows button to specify a row-oriented layout with fields appearing in rows, with the first field at the far left of the first row, the second field to the right of the first, and so on. Figure 9-10 illustrates this report layout.

The Multi-Record Layout section of the dialog box is used for Multi-Record forms, a subject that is covered later in the chapter. You can turn on (or off) the Labeled Fields check box to display (or remove) labels, or field names, from the report's fields.

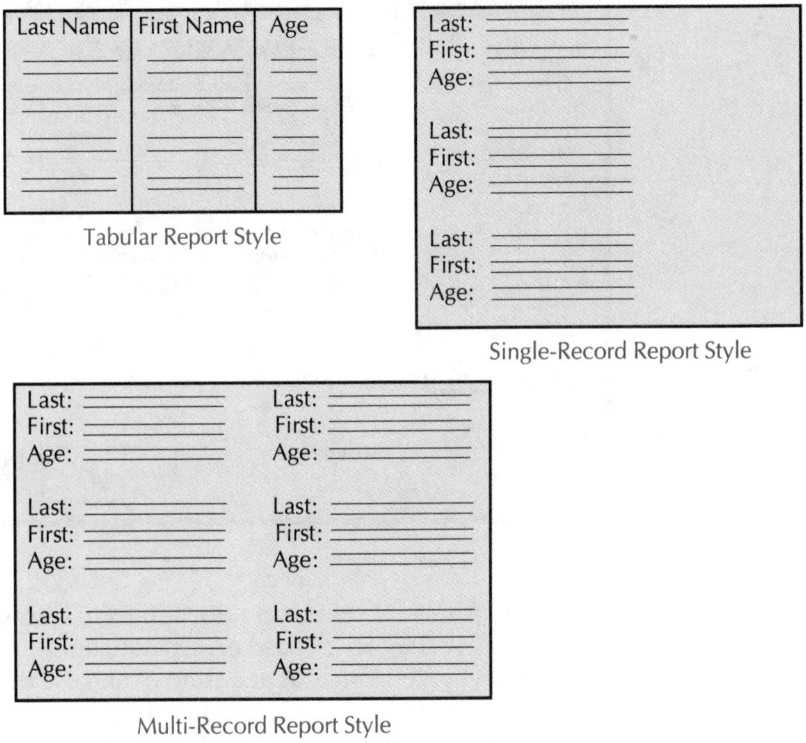

Last Name	First Name	Age
─────	─────	──
─────	─────	──
─────	─────	──
─────	─────	──
─────	─────	──

Tabular Report Style

```
Last:  ═════════
First: ═════════
Age:   ═════════

Last:  ═════════
First: ═════════
Age:   ═════════

Last:  ═════════
First: ═════════
Age:   ═════════
```

Single-Record Report Style

```
Last:  ═════════      Last:  ═════════
First: ═════════      First: ═════════
Age:   ═════════      Age:   ═════════

Last:  ═════════      Last:  ═════════
First: ═════════      First: ═════════
Age:   ═════════      Age:   ═════════

Last:  ═════════      Last:  ═════════
First: ═════════      First: ═════════
Age:   ═════════      Age:   ═════════
```

Multi-Record Report Style

Different styles of reports
Figure 9-8.

Clicking the Select Fields command button brings up a Select Fields dialog box, as shown in Figure 9-11. You can use this dialog box to remove fields, add fields, or change the order of fields in the report. To remove a field from the report's layout, click the desired field name and then click the Remove Field command button in the lower-right corner of the dialog box. To change the order of the fields in your report, click the desired field name and then click the up or down arrows to the right of the words "Change Order" until the selected field moves to the desired location. To add fields, click the drop-down list box beside the table name, and select the desired fields in the drop-down list box by clicking them.

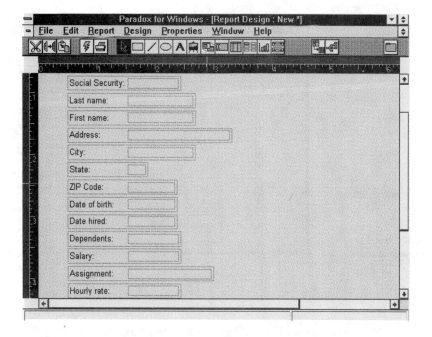

Single-record
report design
that is oriented
by columns
Figure 9-9.

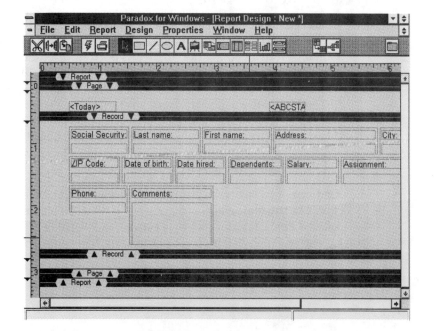

Single-record
report design
that is oriented
by rows
Figure 9-10.

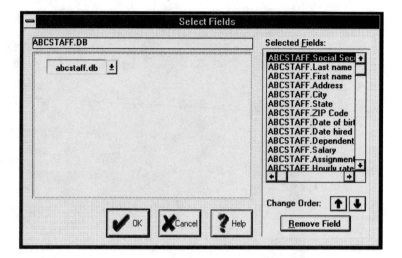

Select Fields
dialog box
Figure 9-11.

The Page Layout command button in the Design Layout dialog box brings up the Page Layout dialog box shown in Figure 9-12. Use this dialog box to change the page dimensions for the report.

Paradox assumes that you use report layouts for printing, so the Printer button is selected by default, and the portrait and landscape buttons are available, letting you choose between portrait orientation and landscape orientation. (Portrait provides a normal printing orientation, with table columns printing down the page, and rows printing with the first row near the top of the page, and successive rows underneath. Landscape rotates the printed image 90 degrees from normal printing.) If you select the Screen button, the report will be displayed on the screen rather than printed, and the Portrait and Landscape options will not be available (they'll be dimmed).

Assuming the Printer button has been selected, the list box in the center of the dialog box provides you with a choice of paper sizes. The options are U.S. letter (8.5 by 11 inch), U.S. legal (8.5 by 14 inch), U.S. Executive (7.5 by 10 inch), A4 European, B5 European, and #I0

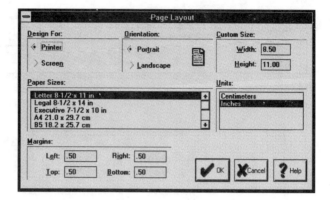

Page Layout
dialog box
Figure 9-12.

Envelope. If you need a paper size different than one of these standards, you can enter your own dimensions under Width and Height in the Custom Size box. You can enter the values in inches or centimeters by choosing between Inches and Centimeters in the Units list box. Under Margins, you can enter values for the Left, Right, Top, and Bottom margins (the default value is .5 inch for each of these measurements).

Using the Report Design Window

Once your report appears in the Report Design window you can make changes to its design.

After you make the desired choices from the Design Layout dialog box and click OK, your report appears in a Report Design window, as shown in Figure 9-13. You can now make the desired changes to the report's design, changing the width of fields or the depth of rows, rearranging the placement of fields, and adding other objects such as lines, boxes, or graphics.

As you can see from the figure, by default Paradox inserts objects representing the current date, the table name, and the page number at the top of the report. Like any other objects in a document, you can inspect these and change their properties (by right-clicking the desired object), and you can move them or delete them.

9

Report header
band

Page header
band

Record band

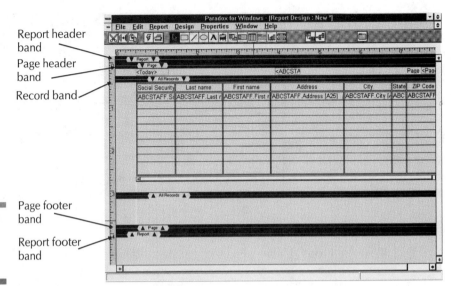

Page footer
band

Report footer
band

**Report Design
window for
new report
Figure 9-13.**

Parts of the Report Design

One major difference between forms and reports in Paradox is that a
report's design is made up of several different parts, as shown in Figure
9-13. Paradox divides a report into five individual sections. These
sections determine where the objects you place within a report appear
when the actual report is displayed or printed. As you can see, there is a
report header band, a page header band, a record band, a page footer
band, and a report footer band. The report design may also include
optional group bands. These various bands control what the report
contains and how it will appear when printed.

The *report header band* contains any information that should appear at
the start of a report. Such information can be simple (as in a series of
headings) or complex (as with a paragraph or more of explanatory
text). *Report footer bands* contain any summary information that is to be
printed at the end of a report. Often totals for number fields are
included in this area.

*Paradox
divides a
report into
five individual
sections.*

The *page header band* appears once at the start of each page of a report.
In many cases, you'll place such information as the date of the report
and a report title in this area. (By default, Paradox places the date, page

number, and table name in this area, but you can of course change this to anything you like.) The *page footer band* at the bottom of the report design contains any information that should appear at the bottom of each page.

The *record band* contains the actual information (which usually includes field objects) that will appear in the body of the report. *Group bands,* which are optional, let you arrange a report by groups. As an example, you might prefer to see a national mailing list arranged by groups of residents of each state; you would use a group band for this task. (The addition of group bands to a report is covered in the section "Adding Grouping to a Custom Report" later in this chapter.)

When you turn on the Band Labels option in the properties menu, each band in the report is clearly identified by a *boundary line* containing the name of the band and arrows pointing towards the record band, as shown in Figure 9-13. (If the option is turned off, the bands are identified by thin lines.)

TIP: You can display or hide the boundary lines by choosing Band Labels from the properties menu during the report design process.

9

Changing Column Widths and Row Heights in Tabular Reports

You change the width of a column in a tabular report using the same technique that you used in Chapter 5 to change column widths in tables. That is, you click and drag the column's right grid line while the pointer is in the heading area. The pointer is in the correct area when it changes into a double-headed arrow.

Drag the grid line to the left to decrease the column width, or to the right to increase the column width.

To change the row height, click and drag any horizontal grid line that is directly underneath a field. Drag the grid line up to decrease the row height, or down to increase the row height.

Moving Columns in Tabular Reports

To move a column, click directly on the topmost grid line of the desired column. When you first place the mouse pointer in the correct area, the pointer changes to a rectangular shape, as shown here.

Click and drag the column to the desired location. (As you drag, the pointer changes into a double-headed arrow.) When you release the mouse button, the column moves to the location of the pointer.

Moving and Sizing Fields in Nontabular Reports

To move fields in a nontabular report, first click the desired field. When you do so, the field will be surrounded by handles, as shown here.

At this point, you can click and drag the field to the desired location on the report. To size a field, click the field to select it, then drag any of the handles.

NOTE: You can delete a field at any time by clicking to select it and then pressing Del.

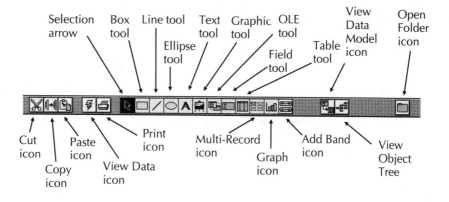

SpeedBar
displayed
whenever a
Report Design
window is
active
Figure 9-14.

Using the SpeedBar Design Tools

When the Report Design window is open, the SpeedBar displays a set of tools that are specific to the task of designing forms. You can use these tools to place various objects, such as fields, lines, boxes, ellipses, or graphics, on a report. Figure 9-14 shows the SpeedBar that appears when a Report Design window is active.

To place an object in the report, first click the desired tool; then click and drag in the Report Design window to create the desired object. If you want to create more than one object of the same type, hold down the (Shift) key as you click on the tool. The tool will then remain active until you click on a different tool or on the selection arrow. (If you don't hold the (Shift) key, the selection arrow is re-selected by default when you finish using a tool.)

Placing New Fields   To place a new field in the report, first click the Field tool on the SpeedBar. Then click in the desired location and drag until the new field reaches the size you want. At this point, release the mouse button. You can then right-click the field to open a properties menu that lets you define the field (tell Paradox which field of the database to use for the new report field).

Adding Text   To add text to a report, first click the Text tool on the SpeedBar. Then click and drag in the Report Design window until the text frame that appears is of the desired size. When you release the mouse button, you can start typing text. As you reach the border of the text frame, Paradox automatically wraps the text. If you reach the bottom of the frame, Paradox automatically scrolls the text upward. You can resize the text frame at any time. To do so, first select the frame and then click and drag on a handle.

Drawing Lines, Boxes, or Ellipses   The SpeedBar provides three tools for drawing lines, boxes, and ellipses. You can add a visual emphasis to your forms by adding these elements in appropriate locations. To add a line, box, or ellipse, first click the appropriate tool in the SpeedBar. Then click at the desired starting location in the report and drag until the line, box, or ellipse reaches the desired size.

Adding Graphics to a Report   You can add a graphic to a report, using the SpeedBar's Graphic tool. Figure 9-15 contains a report that uses a graphic, which is pasted from a Windows bitmap file.

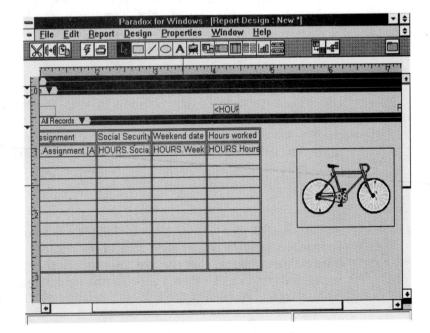

Report using
Windows
bitmap as a
graphic
Figure 9-15.

To add a graphic, first click the Graphic tool in the SpeedBar. Then click in the desired starting location in the report and drag until the box that is to contain the graphic reaches the desired size.

When you release the mouse, the box will contain the label, "Undefined Graphic." To define the source of the graphic, right-click the graphic to open its properties menu. Choose Define Graphic. From the next menu to appear, choose Paste to paste the contents of the Clipboard (if the Paste option is dimmed, the Clipboard is empty); alternately, choose Paste From to paste from a graphic image file. If you choose Paste From, a Select File box appears, and you can choose the graphic file that you want to paste into the undefined graphic.

Testing the Report

To test the report with actual data, choose Preview from the Report menu, click the View Data icon on the SpeedBar, or press F8. A preview of the report appears, as shown in Figure 9-16.

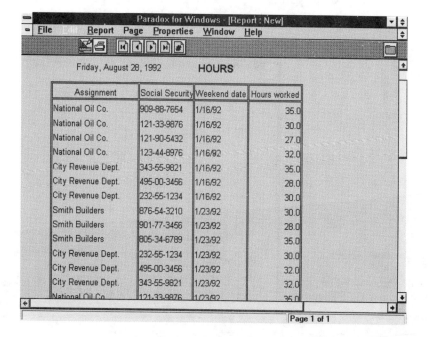

Report preview
Figure 9-16.

9

Use the scroll bars or the (Pg Up) and (Pg Dn) keys to view additional pages of the report. You can return to the report design process at any time by choosing Report/Design from the menu bar, by pressing (F8), or by clicking the Design icon in the SpeedBar.

Saving the Report

When you are satisfied with the appearance of your report, save it by choosing Save or Save As from the File menu. This brings up the Save File As dialog box, as shown in Figure 9-17.

Enter a name for the report (using the DOS file naming conventions of eight characters or less and no spaces) in the New File Name text box and then click OK. Paradox will automatically add the .FSL extension to the report name, and saves that file under the assigned name in the working directory.

Printing Stored Reports

Once you have saved a report, you can print it at any time. To print a report, choose the File/Open/Report option. In the Open Document

Save File As
dialog box
Figure 9-17.

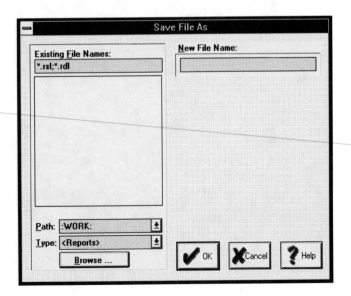

dialog box that appears, select the Print option and then click OK. When the Print the File dialog box appears, choose any desired options, and click OK to print the report.

Hands-On Practice: Creating a Custom Report

ABC Temporaries needs a personnel report that includes more than the standard quick report. The report must include the Last Name, First Name, Phone, Date Hired, Salary, and Hourly Rate fields. The date of the report should appear near the upper-right corner of the first page, and a report title should appear near the upper-left corner of the first page. Perform the following steps to design the report:

1. Choose the File/New/Report option to display the Data Model dialog box, which was shown earlier in Figure 9-6.

2. Click the ABCSTAFF filename and then click OK. In a moment, you'll see the Design Layout window, which was shown earlier in Figure 9-7.

3. Click the Select Fields button, to bring up the Select Fields dialog box, which you saw in Figure 9-11.

4. Click the Social Security field in the Selected Fields list box. Then click the Remove Field command button to remove that field. Using this same procedure, remove the Address, City, State, ZIP Code, Date of Birth, Dependent, Assignment, and Comments fields from the list box.

5. Click the Phone field in the Selected Fields list box to highlight it, and click the up arrow button to the right of the words "Change Order" until the Phone field follows the First Name field in the Selected Fields list box.

6. Click OK to close the Select Fields dialog box.

7. Click OK in the Design Layout window. In a moment, a new Report Design window appears. Click the Maximize icon to expand the window to full-screen size so you have plenty of room to work. Figure 9-18 shows an example of what your screen should look like at this point.

9

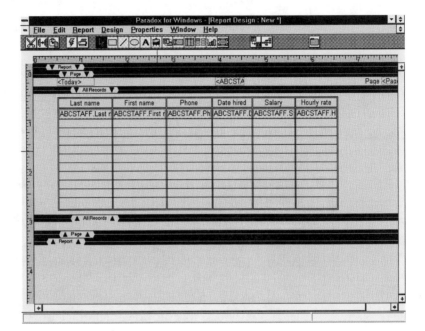

Example of
custom report
Figure 9-18.

8. Click the Date field (the box containing the label "Today") in the Page band to select it. Then click and drag it to the right side of the header area, directly above the Hourly Rate field. (You may need to use the scroll bars to view enough of the report to drag the field all the way to the right.)

9. Click the report title (the text box containing the word "ABCSTAFF" near the center of the header) to select it. Then click and drag it to the left side of the header area, directly above the Last Name field.

10. Click the Page Number field (the box containing the label "Page") in the Page band to select it. Then press the Del key to delete it.

11. To see a preview of the report, click the View Data icon in the SpeedBar or press F8. In a moment, the report preview appears, as shown in Figure 9-19. While you are previewing a report, you can click the Print icon in the SpeedBar to print the report.

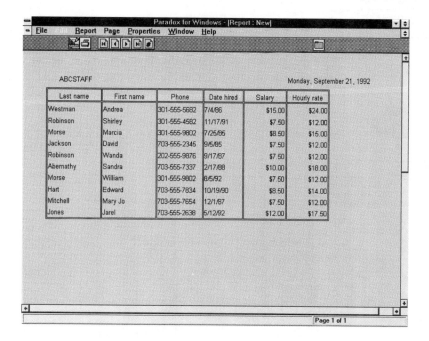

Example of
report preview
Figure 9-19.

12. When you are done previewing the report, press F8 again or click the Design icon in the SpeedBar.

9

13. Choose Save from the File menu. When the File Save As dialog box appears, enter **REPORT1** in the New File Name text box to name your report.

Adding Grouping to a Custom Report

You can use the Add Band option on the Report menu to add group bands to a report. As mentioned earlier, group bands let you further divide a report into groupings of records. Most likely, you will need to arrange reports in this fashion. As an example, you might want to see all employees divided into groups by state of residence or by the name of the assignment. Often, many levels of grouping are needed in business reports. In something as simple as a national mailing list, for example, you might need to see records by groups of states, and within

each state group by city, and within each city group by ZIP or postal
code. That represents three levels of grouping alone. Divide the data in
the table more specifically, by other categories like income levels, and
you will appreciate Paradox's ability to perform groupings effectively.

NOTE: You cannot place group bands inside the record band. You
can only insert group bands between the page band and the record
band of a report.

If you add a group band to a report, when you display or print the
report Paradox automatically sorts the table on the field used by the
group. If, as an example, you group a report using the Assignment field
of the ABCSTAFF table, the records in the report appear sorted by the
values in the Assignment field.

To create a group band while designing the report, choose Add Band
from the Report menu. This brings up the Define Group dialog box
shown in Figure 9-20.

You can group by a field value (the usual choice), or by a specific
number of records. When the Group By Field Value button is selected
(the default), you pick the field by which to group in the Field list box,
and then you click OK to add the group to the report. When the Group
By Record button is selected, you enter the desired number of records
that are to appear in each group, and then you click OK to add the
group to the report. As an example, selecting the Group By Field Value
button, clicking the State field, and then clicking the OK button would
cause a report to be grouped by the values in the State field. On the
other hand, selecting the Group By Record button, entering **5** in the #
of Records text box, and then clicking the OK button would cause every
five records in the report to appear within a group.

The Table list box in the Define Group dialog box is used to select the
table that will control the grouping. When you are working with only
one table (as is the case throughout this chapter), this is irrelevant. But
if you work with reports based on multiple tables (a topic that is
covered in Chapter 11), you can click a table in the Table list box to
display that table's fields within the Field list box.

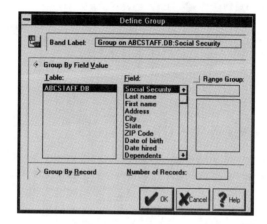

Define Group
dialog box
Figure 9-20.

TIP: Borders of group bands (and all other bands) normally appear as very thin lines. To make them clearly visible, choose Band Labels from the properties menu.

Paradox lets you add as many group bands as you like. If you are adding more than one group band, you should add the largest group bands first so the largest groups are above the smaller groups. For example, if you group a mailing list by state, then by cities within each state, you should add the group band for the states first, and then add the group band for the cities.

TIP: If you add a group band and later decide that you don't want that band in the report, you can delete it by selecting it and pressing Del.

9

Moving Group Bands

To move a group band, select the band and then drag it to its new location. You can drag from anywhere inside the band, or drag the band marker, which is the small triangle at the far left edge of the report design, outside the ruler.

 ## Previewing the Results

Once you have added the desired group band, you can check whether the results are appropriate by clicking the View Data icon in the SpeedBar or by pressing F8. The resulting report preview that appears on your screen will be divided by groups. When you are satisfied with the results, remember to save the report with the Save or Save As option in the File menu.

 ## Hands-On Practice: Grouping by the Assignment Field

Try grouping records by the Assignment field in the personnel report you created earlier in this chapter. To do so, perform the following steps:

1. If the report you created earlier in the chapter is not open in the Design mode, open it now. (If you closed the report, choose the File/Open/Report option and pick the report by name from the Select File dialog box that appears. If the report is still open but you are viewing data, press F8 or click the Design icon in the SpeedBar to get back into Design mode.)

2. Choose Add Band from the Report menu. This brings up the Define Group dialog box, as shown earlier in Figure 9-20.

3. In the Field list box, click the Assignment field (you may need to scroll down to find this field).

4. Click OK. The Assignment group band now appears in the report, as shown in Figure 9-21. (If there is not a clear definition between your bands, choose Band Labels from the properties menu.)

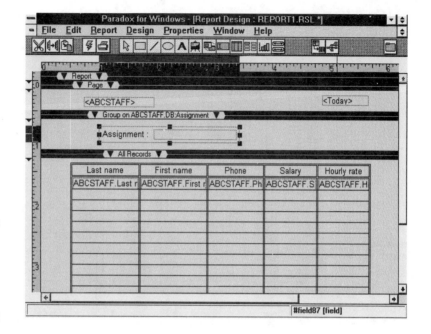

Report design
with
Assignment
group added
Figure 9-21.

5. To see the results, click the View Data icon in the SpeedBar or press F8. In a moment, the report preview appears, as shown in Figure 9-22.

6. When you are done previewing the report, press F8 again or click the Design icon in the SpeedBar.

7. Choose Save from the File menu to save this updated version of the report. Do not close the Report Design window just yet, as you will work with it again shortly.

9

Adding Summary Fields to a Report

Often you will want to add summary fields that count or total in some way the contents of number fields. Summary fields perform calculations on a set of records. With summary fields, you can sum, count, or average the values in a given field. For example, if you are printing a report of items sold to a customer and each item has an individual cost,

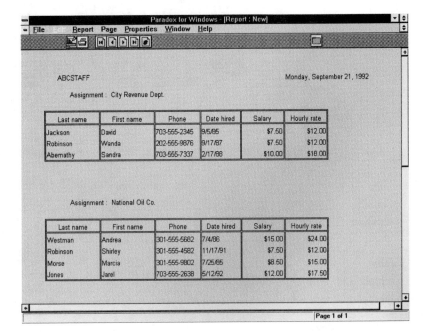

ABCSTAFF   Monday, September 21, 1992

Assignment : City Revenue Dept.

Last name	First name	Phone	Date hired	Salary	Hourly rate
Jackson	David	703-555-2345	9/5/85	$7.50	$12.00
Robinson	Wanda	202-555-9876	9/17/87	$7.50	$12.00
Abernathy	Sandra	703-555-7337	2/17/88	$10.00	$18.00

Assignment : National Oil Co.

Last name	First name	Phone	Date hired	Salary	Hourly rate
Westman	Andrea	301-555-5682	7/4/86	$15.00	$24.00
Robinson	Shirley	301-555-4582	11/17/91	$7.50	$12.00
Morse	Marcia	301-555-9802	7/25/85	$8.50	$15.00
Jones	Jarel	703-555-2638	5/12/92	$12.00	$17.50

Page 1 of 1

Preview of
report with
grouping
Figure 9-22.

you might want a summary field that shows the total cost of the items. In the case of the ABC Temporaries report, which is now grouped by assignment, it might be helpful for managers to see a total of the Hourly Rate field for each assignment, to get an idea of the total amount that will be billed each client per hour of work (assuming all employees are working). These are the kinds of tasks that can be accomplished through the addition of summary fields.

Two overall steps are involved in adding a summary field. First, use the Field tool of the SpeedBar to place a new field where desired in the report (usually this is in a group footer band or in a report footer band). Next, inspect the field by right-clicking it to open the properties menu, and use the Define Field choice of the menu to define the new field as a summary field. With the report you created still open in the report design window, perform the following steps to add a summary field that provides a sum of the Hourly Rate field:

1. Scroll the window upwards until the entire bottom of the report is visible.

2. Click the Field tool button in the SpeedBar. When you do this, the mouse pointer changes shape to resemble the Field tool.

3. Point to an area near the center of the footer for the Assignment group band (between the border labeled "All Records" and the border labeled "Group on ABCSTAFF.DB Assignment"), and click and hold the mouse button. Drag down and to the right until the box that appears is roughly 1.5 inches in length and .25 inch high (you can tell the dimensions by looking at the values in the status bar as you drag). When you release the mouse button, Paradox displays an undefined field object, as shown here:

4. Right-click the undefined field object, to open its properties menu, and choose Define Field. In the menu of fields that next appears, click the first line of the menu (the one containing the three periods). This causes the Define Field Object dialog box to appear, as shown here:

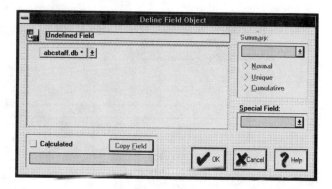

9

5. Click the arrow in the drop-down list box next to the table name (ABCSTAFF.DB) to open the list box, and choose Hourly Rate from the list box.

6. Click the arrow in the drop-down list box in the Summary area at the upper-right corner of the dialog box, and choose Sum from the list box that opens. (The remaining choices in the list box, Min, Max, Avg, and Count, let you choose to display a minimum of the

values in the field you are summarizing, a maximum of the values, an average of the values, or a count, or total number of records.)

7. Leave all other options in the dialog box set to their default values.

8. Click OK.

9. To see the results, click the View Data icon in the SpeedBar, or press F8. In a moment, the report preview appears, as shown in Figure 9-23.

10. When you are done previewing the report, press F8 again or click the Design icon in the SpeedBar.

11. Choose Save from the File menu to save this updated version of the report. Then put the report away by closing its window (press Ctrl + F4).

Experimenting with Other Report Types

As mentioned earlier in the chapter, Paradox lets you create many different types of reports. The tabular style of report created thus far in

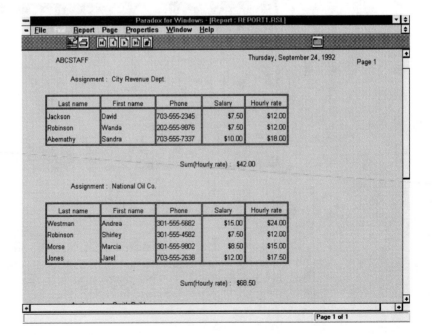

Report with summary field added
Figure 9-23.

this chapter is but one of three common report styles in Paradox; the others include single-record style reports and multi-record style reports. As noted, you can use the options in the Style area of the Design Layout dialog box to pick the desired report style. The hands-on practice sessions that follow illustrate how to create both single-record and multi-record reports. (You need both the ABCSTAFF and the HOURS tables from Chapter 3 to follow along with these examples.)

Hands-On Practice: Creating a Single-Record Style of Report

To create a single-record style report, perform the following steps:

1. Choose the File/New/Report option.
2. In the Data Model dialog box that appears, click ABCSTAFF and then click OK to display the Design Layout dialog box.
3. In the Style area of the dialog box, click Single-Record. This causes the Design Layout to display a report in which a single record appears within the record band of the report, as shown in Figure 9-24. In this example, you will use all fields of the table in the report. However, if you wanted to omit some fields, you could do so by clicking the Select Fields button and using the Select Fields dialog box to remove any unwanted fields from the layout, as described earlier in the chapter.
4. Click OK. The report will appear in a design window (Click the Maximize button so you can view more of the report.)
5. Scroll to the bottom of the report and click the Comments field to select it. Then click and drag the field until it is to the right of the Assignment, Hourly Rate, and Phone fields.
6. Choose Add Band from the Report menu to display the Define Group dialog box.
7. Select the Group By Record option at the bottom of the dialog box, and enter **2** as a value in the # of Records text box. Then click OK. (This is a fast way to have Paradox print two records on each page of the report.)

9

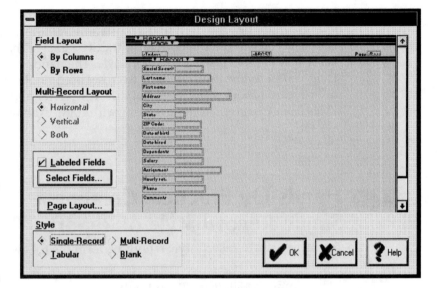

Design layout
based on
single-record
report style
Figure 9-24.

8. To see the results, click the View Data icon on the SpeedBar or press F8. In a moment, the report preview appears, as shown in Figure 9-25. If you want, you can print a copy of the report by clicking the Print icon on the SpeedBar.

9. When you are done previewing the report, press F8 again or click the Design icon on the SpeedBar.

10. Choose Save from the File menu to save the report, naming it **REPORT2**. Then put the report away by closing its window (press Ctrl+F4).

Hands-On Practice: Creating a Multi-Record Style of Report

To create a multi-record style report, perform the following steps:

1. Choose the File/New/Report option.

2. In the Data Model dialog box that appears, click HOURS and then click OK. This brings up the Design Layout dialog box.

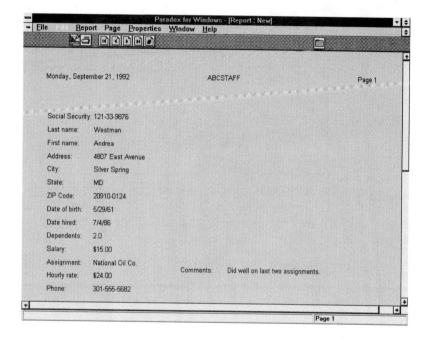

Preview of
single-record
style report
Figure 9-25.

3. In the Style area of the dialog box, click Multi-Record. In the Multi-Record Layout area of the dialog box, click Both. You should see a report design in which multiple records appear both horizontally and vertically within the record band of the report, as shown in Figure 9-26.

4. Click OK. The report will appear in a design window. At this point, you can make any other desired changes to the design of the report. For this example, no additional changes are necessary. However, feel free to make changes of your own using the design techniques you have learned throughout this chapter.

5. To see your results, click the View Data icon in the SpeedBar or press F8. In a moment, the report preview appears, as shown in Figure 9-27.

6. When you are done previewing the report, press F8 again or click the Design icon on the SpeedBar.

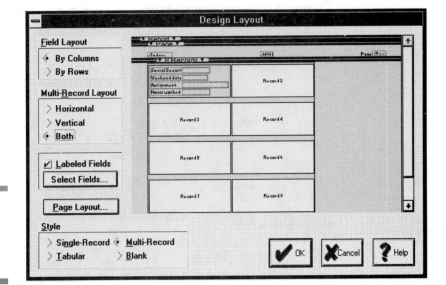

Design layout
based on
multi-record
report style
Figure 9-26.

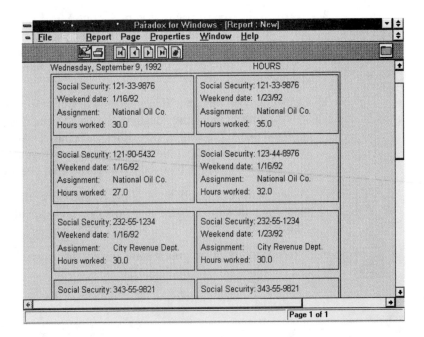

Preview of
multi-record
style report
Figure 9-27.

7. Choose Save from the File menu to save the report, naming it **REPORT3**. Then put the report away by closing its window (press [Ctrl]+[F4]).

NOTE: A multi-record style of report is very useful as part of a report that draws information from more than one table. For example, you may want to show the name of one employee, along with all the records of hours worked for that employee. Techniques for designing this type of report are outlined in Chapter 11.

Creating Mailing Labels

One very common use of database software is the creation and management of a mailing list. With mailing lists usually come the need for the printing of mailing labels. In Paradox, you can create reports that can be used to generate mailing labels, by using the multi-record report type. The basic steps in this process involve opening and defining a multi-record report (in order to generate more than one label per row of the page), setting the margins and the page band to accommodate labels, and using text objects to remove (or "squeeze") blank fields and/or lines when the labels are printed. The steps below outline how you can design a report to accommodate mailing labels, and the hands-on practice in the section that follows demonstrates the design of mailing labels for the ABCSTAFF employees table.

9

To design a report that can be used to produce mailing labels, follow these steps:

1. Open and define a multi-record report. In the Data Model dialog box, select the table(s) that you will need to insert in the mailing labels. In the Design Layout dialog box, turn off the Labeled Fields option, and use the Select Fields button to bring up the Select Fields dialog box, to remove unwanted fields.

2. In the report's design, remove the page header and the page footer by reducing the header and footer bands to minimum size.

3. Move the fields to the desired locations within the report, and if desired, inspect the fields to change their appearance as needed.

4. Resize the record region to fit a single label.

5. Resize the multi-record region to fit a row of labels.

6. Place text objects around fields that may contain blanks, so adjoining field contents will be automatically squeezed (or blank spaces removed) in the labels.

7. Preview the report to check its design, and when satisfied, save the report by choosing File/Save or File/Save As.

Hands-On Practice: Designing Mailing Labels

Consider the example of creating mailing labels for ABC Temporaries in the common "three-across" format. Laser printer mailing labels, commonly available at office supply stores, use this common format. With this format, each 8.5 by 11-inch label sheet contains 30 labels, in three columns and ten rows. Perform the following steps to create mailing labels in this format for the ABCSTAFF table.

1. Choose File/New/Report from the menu bar. This causes the Data Model dialog box to appear.

2. Click ABCSTAFF as the desired table, then click OK. In a moment, the Design Layout dialog box appears.

3. In the Style area of the dialog box, turn on the Multi-Record option by clicking its button.

4. In the Multi-Record Layout area of the dialog box, click the Both button.

5. Click the Select Fields button to display the Select Fields dialog box.

6. Click the Social Security field (if it is not already highlighted), and click the Remove Field button to remove the field. Using the same procedure, remove the Date of Birth, Date Hired, Dependent, Salary, Assignment, Hourly Rate, Phone, and Comments fields.

7. Click the First Name field to select it, then click the Up Arrow in the Change Order area of the dialog box, so that the First Name field comes before the Last Name field within the list box.

8. Click OK to put away the Select Fields dialog box.

9. Click the Labeled Fields check box in the dialog box, to turn this option off. (Doing so will remove the field labels that normally appear beside the fields in a default report's design.)

10. Click the Page Layout button to display the Page Layout dialog box.

11. Make sure that Letter (8-1/2 by 11 inch) is selected in the Paper Size list box, Orientation is set to Portrait, Units is set to Inches, and each text box in the Margins area is set to 0.50, then click OK.

12. Click OK in the Design Layout dialog box. In a moment, a new report design window opens. Click the Maximize button, so you have plenty of room to work with the new report's design. Your screen should resemble the example shown in Figure 9-28.

13. Click the date field (labeled <Today>) in the page header band to select it, and press Del to delete the field. Then, repeat this procedure to delete the title field (labeled <ABCSTAFF>) and the Page Number field (labeled <Page>), also in the page header band.

14. Select the page header band by clicking its border. (If you cannot see the border, choose Properties/Band Labels from the menu bar.)

15. Place the mouse pointer atop the page header band's border until the pointer changes shape to a double-headed arrow, then click

9

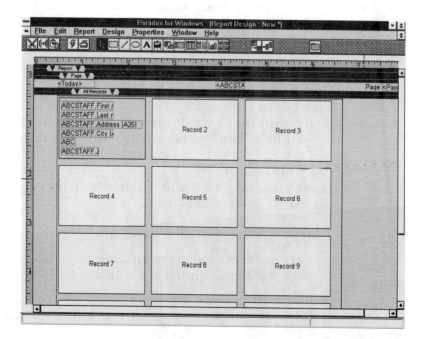

Initial mailing
label design
Figure 9-28.

and drag the header band downwards until it reaches its minimum size, then release the mouse.

16. Scroll the window contents until the footer bands are fully visible, then select the page footer band by clicking its border.

17. Place the mouse pointer atop the page footer band's border until the pointer changes shape to a double-headed arrow, then click and drag the footer band upwards until it reaches its minimum size, then release the mouse.

18. Scroll the window contents downwards until the first record is again fully visible.

19. Click the State field until just the field is selected (it is directly beneath the City field), and drag it to the right of the City field.

20. Click the ZIP Code field, and drag it upwards until it is just underneath the City field.

21. Preview your report, by clicking the View Data icon in the SpeedBar, or by pressing F8 . It should resemble the example shown in Figure 9-29.

22. When done previewing the report, click the Design icon in the SpeedBar, or press F8 , to return to designing the labels.

Enclosing Fields in a Text Object

As you can see from Figure 9-29, there is a minor problem with the initial design. The City and State names are separated by the width of the entire field, regardless of the length of the actual text stored in the City field. The labels would look considerably more attractive if extra blank spaces were removed from the City field. You can remove extra spaces by enclosing fields within a text object; the steps that follow will demonstrate how you can do this.

1. Click the Text tool in the SpeedBar.

2. Click just above and to the left of the upper-left corner of the City field, and drag down and to the right of the lower-right corner of

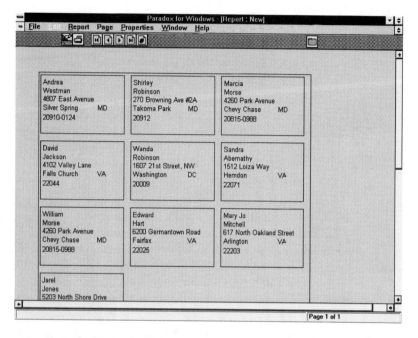

Initial preview
of mailing labels
Figure 9-29.

the State field, so that the text box fully encloses both the City and
State fields.

3. Preview your report by clicking the View Data icon in the
   SpeedBar, or by pressing F8 ; don't be surprised by the fact that
   the City and State fields now run too close together. When done
   previewing the report, click the Design icon in the SpeedBar, or
   press F8 , to return to designing the report.

9

You should have noticed (when you previewed the report) that the
extra blank spaces have been removed between the City and State
fields; however, the text in the fields now runs together; for example,
records with "Reston" and "VA" in the City and State fields appear as
"RestonVA." To correct the appearance, you will need to add
punctuation between the fields, by performing the steps that follow.

1. Click the text box to select it, then click it near the bottom-right
   corner. This places the insertion pointer after the State field.

2. Press the ← key once. This moves the insertion pointer between the City and State fields.

3. Type a comma, then a space. You will see the City and State fields are separated by the comma and space when you do this.

4. Preview your report by clicking the View Data icon in the SpeedBar, or by pressing F8. When done previewing the report, click the Design icon in the SpeedBar, or press F8, to return to designing the report. This time, you will notice that the contents of the City and State fields are properly separated by a comma and a space.

NOTE: If the City field disappears entirely after you do this, it means the text box is now too small to accommodate both the fields and the added punctuation. Click at the right edge of the text box, and drag to the right slightly to enlarge the text box to fit both the fields and the punctuation.

Making the Report Fit the Mailing Labels

The last overall step in the process of designing the report is to make the report precisely fit your mailing labels. Three specific steps are involved in this; you must first, inspect the contents of the record band, and use the Record Layout choice of the properties menu to adjust the spacing between each label; second, change the height of the multi-record region to match the height of each label; and third, change the width of the multi-record region to match the width of your labels. Perform the following steps to accomplish this for your example labels.

1. Select the contents of the entire record band by clicking anywhere in the shaded box labeled Record 2 or Record 3.

2. Right-click the same area to open the properties menu, and choose Record Layout. This causes the Record Layout dialog box to appear, as shown here:

3. Change the value in the Number Down text box to 10, to accommodate 10 rows of labels. Then, change the values in both the Separation Across text box and the Separation Down text box to zero, and click OK. Paradox will adjust the multi-record regions so there is no space separating them.

4. Choose Properties/Band Labels to turn off the Band Labels. When you do so, the top of the first record region should align closely with the zero mark on the ruler at the left edge of the design window.

5. To make your labels one inch in height, click the record object containing your fields to select it. When selected, handles will appear around the record object.

6. Place the mouse pointer over the bottom line of the record object until it changes to the shape of a double arrow, then click and drag upwards until the line aligns with the one-inch marker on the ruler at the left edge of the window.

7. To make your labels 2.5 inches wide, with the object containing your fields still selected, place the mouse pointer over the right edge of the object until the pointer changes shape to a double-headed arrow. Then, click and drag until the object is 2.5 inches wide (you can see the exact width in the status bar as you resize the object).

8. Choose File/Save from the menu bar to save the completed report. Call the report LABELS1. After saving the report, if you preview the report by clicking the View Data icon in the SpeedBar, or by pressing F8, it should resemble the example shown in Figure 9-30.

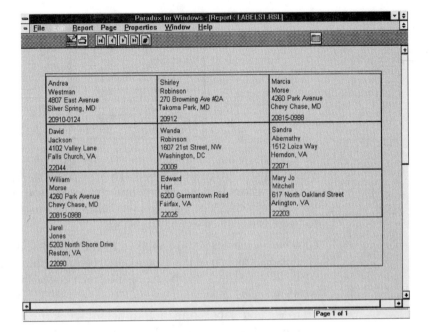

Preview of
completed
mailing labels
Figure 9-30.

Before you begin to design your own mailing labels, you should know the exact size of the labels, since mailing labels come in a wide variety of sizes. You should also take care to use the correct type of mailing labels designed for your particular printer. Laser-printer labels may not feed well into dot-matrix printers, and labels designed for dot-matrix printers will often damage laser printers if you attempt to use them.

Hints for Report Design

Before you start crafting custom reports, you should plan the design of the report. This may mean asking the other users of the database what information will actually be needed in the report. In many cases, it should help to outline the report contents and format on paper. Once you have sketched the report on paper, your outline should resemble the actual report that you will produce with Paradox's help. You can then refer to this outline while designing the report.

Quick Summary

Generating a Quick Report

Open the desired table and then click the Quick Report icon on the SpeedBar or press Shift+F7.

Designing a Custom Report

Choose the File/New/Report option. From the Data Model dialog box, choose the table with which the report will be used, and then click OK. Use the options in the Design Layout dialog box that appears to quickly design the initial layout for the report. Then click OK to display the Report Design window for the new report. Make any desired modifications to the report's design, and then store the report by choosing Save or Save As from the File menu.

Adding Groups to a Report

While designing the report, choose Add Band from the Report menu. In the Define Group dialog box that appears, choose the options that will control the basis for the grouping, and click OK.

CHAPTER

PARADOX WINDOWS PARADOX WINDOWS PARADOX WINDOWS PARADOX WINDOWS PARADOX WINDOWS PARADOX WINDOWS

10

PRESENTATION GRAPHICS

Paradox offers powerful capabilities for displaying and printing graphs. You can prepare graphs for data analysis or for presentation-quality reports. Paradox offers a wide variety of styling features and options to enhance the appearance of your graphs.

Typical Graphs

Some typical graphs that you can create with Paradox are shown in Figure 10-1. Paradox can create any of the following types of graphs:

+ Bar

+ Stacked bar

+ Rotated bar

+ 3D bar

+ 3D stacked bar

+ 3D rotated bar

+ XY graph

+ Area graph

+ Line graph

+ Pie chart

+ 3D area graph

+ 3D line graph

+ 3D pie chart

The graphs consist primarily of elements representing the data contained within the table. The appearance of the elements varies, depending on the type of graph you select. In a bar, stacked bar, or rotated bar graph, the data is illustrated with bars; in a line graph, the data appears as thin lines. An area graph combines a line graph with shadings underneath the lines to represent trends, plotting data in a cumulative fashion. In a pie graph, data is represented as wedges of the pie. Pie charts show the relationship between parts and a whole, so only a single set of values is represented by each pie chart.

All graphs except for pie graphs have two axes: a horizontal axis, called the X axis, and a vertical axis, called the Y axis. With most (but not necessarily all) graphs, the X axis is also known as the category axis, and the Y axis is also known as the value axis.

Some graphs in Paradox are combinations or variations of the types just described. Stacked bar, rotated bar, and 3D-stacked and 3D-rotated bar

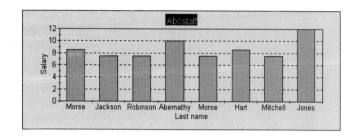

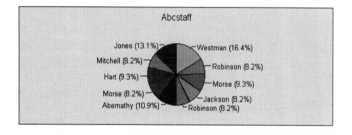

Types of graphs
created with
Paradox for
Windows
Figure 10-1.

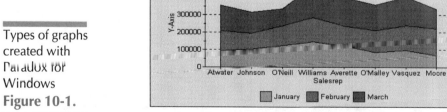

10

graphs are all variations of a bar graph. An XY graph is a line graph that
displays values along both the X and the Y axis. XY graphs are used to
show a corresponding relationship between two sets of numbers.

In Paradox, you create graphs in form documents. As such, they share common traits with forms: They appear in a Form Design window, and you modify graph characteristics by switching into Form Design mode. Once you are in Form Design mode, you can modify objects that make up the graph by right-clicking the object, just as you can with objects in a form. You save the graph by choosing File/Save or File/Save As, just as you do with other forms, and you print the graph using the same techniques you use to print a form. (See Chapter 7 for more details about custom forms.)

Making a Simple Graph

Paradox has a Quick Graph SpeedBar icon and a keyboard equivalent, Ctrl+F7, that make it easy to produce a graph. The basic steps are as follows:

1. With the desired table open in the active window, press Ctrl+F7, or click the Quick Graph icon on the SpeedBar. This causes the Define Graph dialog box to appear.

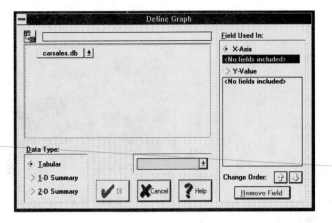

2. Click the arrow in the drop-down list box for the chosen table (at the upper-left side of the dialog box), and choose the desired field that will be used as the X axis, or horizontal axis of the graph. As mentioned, the X axis is often referred to as the category axis, because categories normally appear along this horizontal axis.

(Typically it runs along the bottom of the graph.) When you click to select the desired field, it appears at the upper-right side of the dialog box, under Field Used In X-Axis.

3. At the right side of the dialog box, click the Y-Value button to select it. Then click the arrow in the drop-down list box again, and choose the table field that will be used for the Y-axis value. As mentioned, the Y axis is often called the value axis, because values normally appear along this vertical line.

4. Click OK in the dialog box. In a moment, a new form appears, containing a bar graph similar to the one shown in Figure 10-2. (In Paradox, the bar graph is the default graph setting.)

At first glance, you might think that producing a graph must be more complicated, and it can be. The graphs themselves may be as simple or as complex as you care to make them. Thanks to the flexible options provided in Paradox, you can experiment with different types of graphs, customized text and legends, and fancy formatting. If all you need is a basic graph, however, you can use the simple steps just outlined to produce a complete graph.

One point can help get the results you want when you use this quick technique. No doubt you'll often want to graph just a subset of data from a particular database. You can use the Query-by-Example

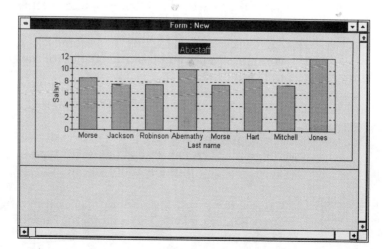

Quick Graph
created using
ABCSTAFF table
Figure 10-2.

10

techniques described in Chapter 6 to build an ANSWER table containing the desired subset of your data. Then create the graph, based on the ANSWER table, by using the steps outlined previously.

Hands-On Practice: Creating a Quick Graph

You can try the techniques just described with the ABCSTAFF table created earlier in this book. As you will see, you can quickly create a graph showing the salaries of the employees. To do so, perform the following steps:

1. Get into Paradox and open the ABCSTAFF table, if it is not already open. If it is already open, click on its window to be sure it is the active window.

2. Press Ctrl+F7, or click the Quick Graph icon on the SpeedBar. This brings up the Define Graph dialog box.

3. Click the arrow in the drop-down list box and choose Last Name from the list of fields. When you do this, Last Name appears in the upper-right side of the dialog box, under Field Used In X-Axis.

4. At the right side of the dialog box, click the Y-Value button to select it. Then click the arrow in the drop-down list box again, and choose Salary from the list of fields. You may notice that the list of available fields for the Y axis contains only the Salary and Dependents fields. Since these are the only numeric fields in the table, they are the only fields that have values which can be graphed.

5. Click OK in the dialog box. In a moment, a new form appears, containing a bar graph of the salaries for the employees, as shown in Figure 10-2.

Changing the Graph Type

With the graph still displayed, you may wish to experiment with other types of graphs. You can easily change the type of graph that is displayed by performing the following steps:

1. Choose the Form/Design option, click the Design icon in the SpeedBar, or press F8. In a moment, Paradox places you in Form Design mode.

2. Select the graph by clicking the border that surrounds the entire graph. (You can tell that the graph has been selected when handles appear around its edges.) Next, right-click within the selected area to open the properties menu for the graph.

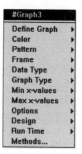

3. Choose Graph Type from the menu to open another menu displaying the available graph types.

4. Choose 2D Pie. The Form Design window is redrawn, and now contains an example of a pie chart.

5. Press F8 or click the View Data icon on the SpeedBar to exit Form Design mode. In a moment, the graph reappears as a two-dimensional pie graph, as shown in Figure 10-3.

For now, you may want to try choosing a few other graph types using the steps just outlined.

10

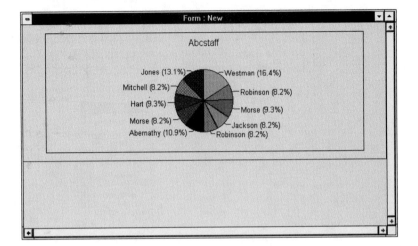

**Pie Graph of
ABCSTAFF
salaries
Figure 10-3.**

Printing a Graph

Since a graph is a Paradox document, you print it just as you would print any other document. With the window containing the graph open and active, you can choose the File/Print option. Or, click the Print icon in the SpeedBar. With either method, when the Print File dialog box appears, click OK to begin printing.

Because graphs contain large amounts of data, it may take some time for the graph to print. If you have a dot-matrix printer, the graph will probably print at slow to moderate speeds, line by line. With most laser printers, there will be no activity for a minute or two, and then the graph will be printed. Laser printers must receive and compose the entire page in memory before printing begins.

NOTE: Your printer must support graphics printing under Windows to be able to print graphs.

Parts of a Graph

Before considering the options that Paradox offers for creating graphs, you should be familiar with the parts of a graph. These are discussed here and shown in Figure 10-4.

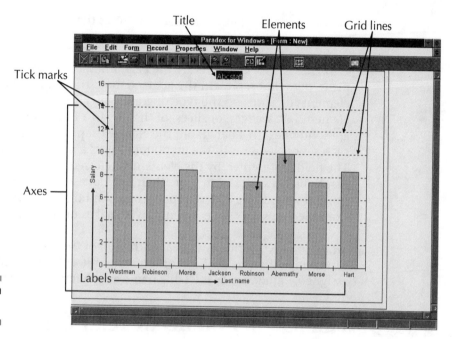

Parts of a graph
Figure 10-4.

Axes The axes are the horizontal and vertical frames of reference that appear in all types of graphs except pie charts. The horizontal (or X) axis is called the category axis because categories of data are normally plotted along this line. The vertical (or Y) axis is called the value axis because values are normally shown along this line. A variation on this rule is the rotated bar graph, where the axes are reversed, with the category axis being vertical and the value axis being horizontal. And an exception to the rule is the XY graph, which shows values along both axes.

Tick Marks Tick marks are reference marks that separate the scales of the value axis and the categories of the category axis. Tick marks make it easier to read values used in your chart. The measurements used for tick marks vary, depending on the values used in your chart.

Labels The labels describe the categories or values. By default, Paradox adds labels to the X axis of a graph based on the contents of the field you specified in the Define Graph dialog box. You can change these labels or omit them, using options described later in the chapter.

10

Grid Lines   Grid lines are reference lines that extend across the entire area of the graph.

Elements   The elements are the bars, lines, columns, shaded areas, or pie wedges that represent the actual data in the graph. The form of the elements depends on the type of graph you choose. In a pie chart, the elements are wedges, or slices, of the pie. In a line graph, the elements are solid lines. In a bar graph, the elements appear as bars. Note that each set of elements in the graph represents a field within the table. The field represented by the element is referred to as a data series. If a graph displays data from more than one data series, each data series will be represented by a different pattern or symbol. In Figure 10-4, for example, the salary for each employee makes up a different data series.

Titles   Titles normally appear at the top of the graph, although you can change the title position or omit the title entirely. If no title is assigned, Paradox uses the table name as a default for the title.

Hands-On Practice: Creating Different Graphs

To try creating different graph types, you can quickly build a table of sales figures from eight sales representatives. This table will be used in numerous examples throughout this chapter. The table will contain data for the months of January through March. To build the table, perform the following steps:

1. Choose the File/New/Table option. When the Table Type dialog box appears, click OK to accept the default table type of Paradox for Windows.

2. When the Create Table dialog box appears, enter the following specifications for the fields:

Field Name	Type	Size
SALESREP	Alphanumeric	20
JANUARY	Currency	
FEBRUARY	Currency	
MARCH	Currency	

3. Click Save As to save the new table. In a moment, the Save Table As dialog box appears.

4. In the New Table Name text box, enter **CARSALES** as a table name. Turn on the Display Table option button, so the new table is opened in a window automatically when you close the dialog box.

5. Click OK. In a moment, the new table, CARSALES, appears in a window.

6. Press F9 to begin editing, and add the following records.

Salesrep:	Atwater
January:	95,240.00
February:	112,350.00
March:	145,410.00
Salesrep:	Johnson
January:	103,700.00
February:	89,250.00
March:	121,305.00
Salesrep:	O'Niell
January:	121,500.00
February:	114,250.00
March:	97,310.00
Salesrep:	Williams
January:	146,200.00
February:	138,850.00
March:	179,990.00

10

Salesrep:	Averette
January:	122,800.00
February:	114,050.00
March:	163,990.00
Salesrep:	**O'Malley**
January:	86,600.00
February:	125,850.00
March:	144,050.00
Salesrep:	**Vasquez**
January:	96,500.00
February:	144,250.00
March:	161,300.00
Salesrep:	**Moore**
January:	68,900.00
February:	152,560.00
March:	114,020.00

7. When you are done adding the records, be sure to press F9 again to complete the data entry process and leave Edit mode.

Creating a Bar Graph Based on Multiple Fields

It's easy to create a graph that is based on more than one numeric field. You simply need to select more than one field for the Y axis in the Define Graph dialog box. To do so, hold down the Shift key and click on all desired field names to select them. The following example demonstrates this procedure. With the table still open as the active table, perform the following steps to create a bar graph based on multiple fields.

1. Press Ctrl+F7, or click the Quick Graph icon on the SpeedBar. This causes the Define Graph dialog box to appear.

2. Click the arrow in the drop-down list box, and choose Salesrep from the list of fields. When you do this, Salesrep appears in the upper-right side of the dialog box, under Field Used In X-Axis.

3. At the right side of the dialog box, click the Y-Value button to select it. Then click the arrow in the drop-down list box again to open the list box.

4. Hold down the Shift key and click all three fields, from January through March. They should now all be highlighted.

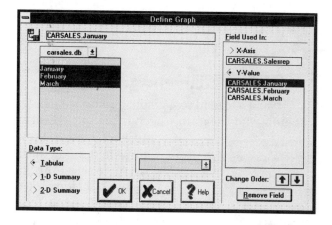

5. Click OK in the dialog box. In a moment, a new form appears, containing a graph of the car sales for each sales representative, as shown in Figure 10-5. Because you selected multiple fields for the Y-axis, the graph contains multiple bars for each of the months.

About the Form Design Mode

If you read Chapter 7, you know that when you are designing forms, you are in Design mode. Since graphs appear in Paradox forms, the same applies to graphs. When you want to make changes to the properties of a graph, you must switch to Design mode. Remember that

10

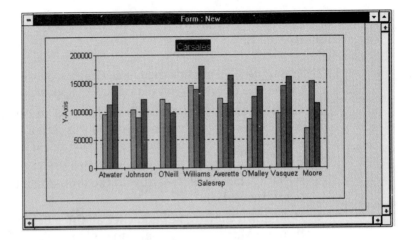

Graph based on
multiple fields
Figure 10-5.

 an easy way to switch between Design mode and viewing data is to use
the ⟨F8⟩ key, or to click the Design icon in the SpeedBar.

Adding a Legend to a Graph

To add a legend to a graph, you must be in Design mode. Press ⟨F8⟩
now, and the form will change from a display of the actual data (in the

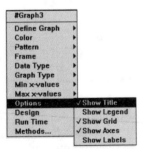

form of a graph) into a form design. Click
anywhere along the border that surrounds the
graph to select the entire graph, and then
right-click along the border to open the
properties menu. From this menu, click
Options. When you do so, another menu
appears with the five choices Show Title, Show
Legend, Show Grid, Show Axes, and Show
Labels.

Click Show Legend to turn on this option.
Then press ⟨F8⟩ or click the View Data icon to
switch back out of Design mode and into viewing data. The new graph
should now contain a legend, as shown in Figure 10-6.

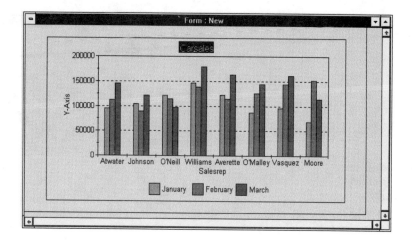

Creating an Area Graph

You can change the graph type to display an area graph—or, for that matter, to display any other type of graph—by switching to Design mode, selecting the entire graph, opening the properties menu, choosing Graph Type, and then choosing either 2D Area or 3D Area. You can see an example of an area graph if you perform the following steps:

1. With the current graph still displayed, press F8 to switch back into Design mode.

2. Click anywhere along the border that surrounds the graph to select the entire graph.

3. Right-click along the border to open the properties menu for the graph. Choose Graph Type to open the menu displaying the available graph types.

4. Choose 2D Area from this menu.

5. Press F8 or click the View Data icon to leave Design mode. In a moment, the graph reappears as a two-dimensional area graph, as shown in Figure 10-7.

10

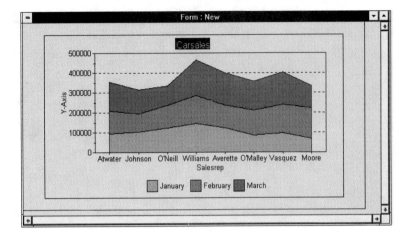

Area graph of
car sales
Figure 10-7.

Creating a Line Graph

You can display a line graph by switching to Design mode, selecting the
entire graph, opening the properties menu, choosing Graph Type, and
then choosing either 2D Line or 3D Line. You can see an example of a
line graph if you perform the following steps:

1. With the current graph still displayed, press F8 to switch back
   into Design mode.

2. Click anywhere along the border that surrounds the graph to select
   the entire graph.

3. Right-click along the border to open the properties menu for the
   graph. Choose Graph Type to open the menu displaying the
   available graph types.

4. Choose 2D Line from this menu.

5. Press F8 or click the View Data icon to leave Design mode. In a
   moment, the graph reappears as a two-dimensional line graph, as
   shown in Figure 10-8.

Working with Three-Dimensional Graphs

As noted earlier, three-dimensional (3D) graphs are variations of bar,
area, column, line, and pie graphs. You use the same techniques

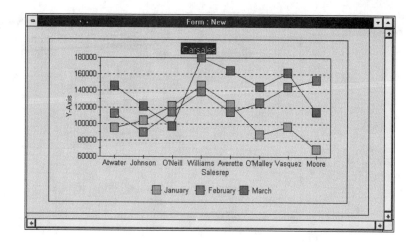

Line graph of
car sales
Figure 10-8.

described throughout this chapter to build these graphs; the only
difference is in the Graph Type choice that you make when you choose
Graph Type from the properties menu. Three-dimensional graphs are
preferred by many people, particularly for business presentations. The
added dimension provides visual interest that is hard to match with
two-dimensional graphs. If you haven't already experimented with
three-dimensional graphs, perform the following steps to try an
example now:

1. With the current graph still displayed, press F8 or click the View
   Data icon to switch back into Design mode.

2. Click anywhere along the border that surrounds the graph to select
   the entire graph.

3. Right-click to open the properties menu for the graph. Choose
   Graph Type to open the menu displaying the available graph types.

4. Choose 3D Rotated Bar from the menu.

5. Press F8 to leave Design mode. In a moment, the graph reappears
   as a three-dimensional rotated bar graph, as shown in Figure 10-9.

Working with Pie Charts

Because of their design, pie charts are a different type of graph. A pie
chart shows the relationship between a whole and its parts; you can

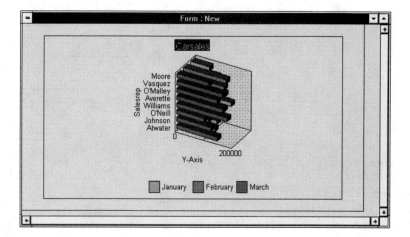

3D rotated bar
graph of car
sales
Figure 10-9.

plot only a single series of data (or, one set of values) in a pie chart. If
you select multiple sets of values, Paradox draws a different pie graph
for every set of values you select.

To work with a sample pie graph, first close the existing form (answer
No to the prompt that asks if you want to save the form). Then perform
the following steps:

1. Press Ctrl + F7, or click the Quick Graph icon on the SpeedBar. This
   causes the Define Graph dialog box to appear.

2. Click the arrow in the drop-down list box, and choose Salesrep
   from the list of fields. When you do this, Salesrep appears in the
   upper-right side of the dialog box, under Field Used In X-Axis.

3. At the right side of the dialog box, click the Y-Value button to
   select it. Then click the arrow in the drop-down list box again to
   open the list box.

4. Hold down the Shift key and click only the January and February
   fields to select them.

5. Click OK in the dialog box. In a moment, a new form appears,
   containing a graph of the car sales for each sales representative.

6. Press F8 or click the Design icon to switch to Design mode.

7. Click anywhere along the border that surrounds the graph to select
   the entire graph.

8. Right-click along the border to open the properties menu for the graph. Choose Graph Type to open the menu displaying the available graph types.

9. Choose 3D Pie from the menu.

10. Press ⎡F8⎤ or click the View Data icon to leave Design mode. In a moment, the graph reappears as a three-dimensional pie graph, as shown in Figure 10-10. Because you selected two fields for the Y axis, the graph contains two pies—one for each month.

Adding Text to a Chart

Since a chart appears in a Form window, you can add text anywhere you like, using the techniques that you used in Chapter 7 to add text to a custom form. To add text in a form, click on the Text tool in the SpeedBar. (If the SpeedBar is not visible, choose Properties/Desktop. Then click OK in the dialog box that appears, to redisplay the SpeedBar.) Next, click and drag in the Form Design window until the text frame that appears is as large as desired. Release the mouse button and start typing the text. You can resize the text frame at any time by first selecting the frame and then clicking and dragging on a corner handle.

3D pie graphs of car sales based on multiple fields
Figure 10-10.

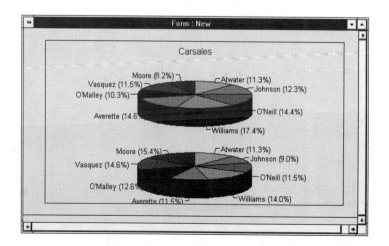

Quick Summary

Creating a Graph

With the desired table open in the active window, press Ctrl+F7. In the Define Graph dialog box that appears, select the desired fields to be used as the X and Y axes. Then click OK to create and display the graph. If desired, save the graph as you would save any other form, by choosing File/Save or File/Save As.

Printing a Graph

Create the graph (or load an existing form containing a graph and display it by pressing F8 or by clicking the View Data icon), and then choose File/Print.

Changing the Graph Type

With the graph visible in the Form Design window, click anywhere along the border surrounding the graph to select the entire graph. Right-click to open the properties menu, and choose Graph Type. From the menu that next appears, select the desired type of graph.

CHAPTER

11

USING THE RELATIONAL POWERS OF PARADOX

As you learned in Chapter 1, Paradox is a relational database manager. Its relational capabilities allow you to define relationships between two or more tables. This chapter describes two ways you can take advantage of the relational capabilities of Paradox.

In Paradox, you can draw relationships between tables either by using relational queries or by designing relational documents. The first half of this chapter describes how you can create relational queries. The second half of this chapter explains how to design relational documents such as forms or reports. In many cases, you can use either method to achieve the desired results. Some may find it easier to design relational forms and reports, as this method does not require the use of an ANSWER table. However, the creating of relational queries may be more familiar to Paradox for DOS users, because most relational work in Paradox for DOS is done through relational queries.

Using Queries to Draw Relationships

Chapter 6 introduced the use of queries and the concept of Query-by-Example. You can also use Query-by-Example to establish relationships between more than one table. By using example elements within Query Forms, you can link multiple tables by means of a common field that exists in each table.

The hands-on practice examples in this chapter make extensive use of the ABCSTAFF and HOURS tables from Chapters 3 and 4. If you did not already create those tables, you should do so now if you want to follow along with the examples.

Consider the ABCSTAFF and HOURS tables. The HOURS table contains records of the hours worked by each employee, and the client for whom (or assignment at which) the employee performed the work. However, the HOURS table does not contain the names of the employees. The ABCSTAFF table, on the other hand, contains the full name of each employee, but no record of the hours worked.

The payroll coordinator at ABC Temporaries now needs a report like the one shown in Figure 11-1. This report will be used by the payroll department to handle check requests when the payroll is processed.

This is a relational report because it draws its information from more than one table. The ABCSTAFF table contains the Last Name and First Name fields. The HOURS table contains the Assignment and Hours Worked fields. To produce a report based on these fields, you must design a query that retrieves data from both tables and links it into a single table. You can then use that table to produce the desired report.

The key to retrieving data from a relational database is to link records on some sort of matching field, a field that is common to both tables.

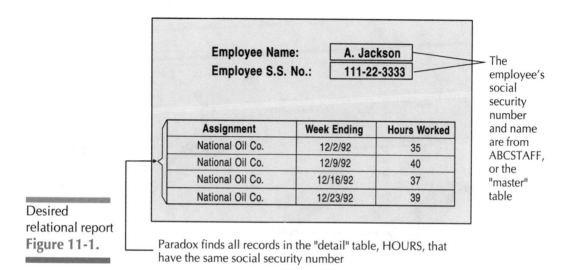

Employee Name: A. Jackson
Employee S.S. No.: 111-22-3333

The employee's social security number and name are from ABCSTAFF, or the "master" table

Assignment	Week Ending	Hours Worked
National Oil Co.	12/2/92	35
National Oil Co.	12/9/92	40
National Oil Co.	12/16/92	37
National Oil Co.	12/23/92	39

Desired relational report
Figure 11-1.

Paradox finds all records in the "detail" table, HOURS, that have the same social security number

The ABCSTAFF table contains, along with other information, the social security numbers and names of the employees. The HOURS table, on the other hand, contains the social security numbers, along with the hours worked by each employee for a given work week. Using two separate tables is a better solution than using a single table in this case, because a single table would require unnecessary duplication of information. If you had a single table with all of the fields present in these two tables, each time that you entered a record of the hours worked and the given week for an employee, you would need to duplicate the address, salary, hourly billing rate, and other information for that employee. To avoid such duplication, you can use two tables and link the tables together based on the contents of the common social security number field, as illustrated in Figure 11-2. With all relational databases, you can establish a link between common fields to match a particular record in one table with a corresponding record in another table.

Take ABC Temporaries' problem of the payroll again. If you needed to know how many hours Andrea Westman worked, you could look at the data from the two tables, as shown in Figure 11-3. You would first look at the listing from the ABCSTAFF table and find the social security number for Ms. Westman, which is 121-33-9876. You would then refer to the listing of the HOURS table and look for all of the records with a

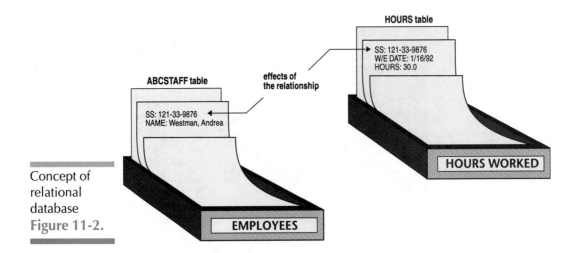

Concept of
relational
database
Figure 11-2.

matching social security number. You could use the Hours Worked
fields from these records to calculate the salary for Ms. Westman. You
could repeat the process of matching social security numbers between
the tables for every employee in the company.

It's critical to note that, without a field that contains matching data in
each of the tables, such a relational link is not possible. This is one
reason that the design of complex, relational databases is not a process
to be taken lightly. If an important field is not included in a table, you
may find it difficult or impossible to access multiple tables in the
desired manner. As Figure 11-3 illustrates, the Social Security field
enables you to access data simultaneously from both tables.

Querying from Two Tables

Normally, you query from two tables by performing the steps that
follow. (Do not try to do these now if you have never created a
relational query before; the hands-on practice section that follows this
one describes in detail how you perform such a query using the sample
tables you have created.)

To perform a relational query, first close any existing ANSWER table
and/or Query Form so you can start with a clean desktop. Choose the

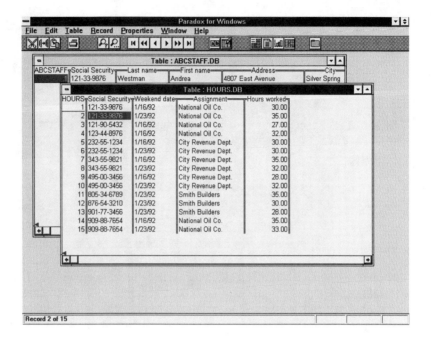

File/New/Query option. When the Select File dialog box appears, click the desired table to select it as the first table to be used in the query, and then click OK. When the Query Form appears, choose the fields for inclusion in the normal manner, by using the mouse or F6 to place check marks in the desired fields. You can also set any selection criteria that the records must meet by entering these criteria in the fields of the Query Form, as described in Chapter 6.

When the Query Form contains the desired check marks and criteria for the first table, choose Add Table from the Query menu or click the Add Table icon in the SpeedBar. In the Select File dialog box that then appears, click the next table you want to add to the Query Form and then click OK. Paradox places a query for the second table directly below the first, within the same query window. You can again choose the fields to be included in the answer and enter any desired selection criteria. Figure 11-4 shows a query window containing queries for two tables (ABCSTAFF and HOURS), with selected fields of Last Name and First Name from the ABCSTAFF table, and Weekend Date and Hours Worked from the HOURS table.

11

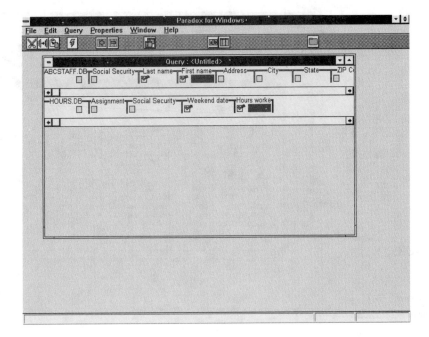

Partially filled-in query for two tables
Figure 11-4.

Finally, enter the example element that is used to link the tables that have the common field. To enter an example element, place the cursor in the common field, press the Example key (F5), and enter an example element, as shown in Figure 11-5.

An example element is not some arbitrary value that you must always use. Paradox is only concerned about what the examples represent—that is, the same value in two separate tables. (In Figure 11-5, the data entered as "identical" in both Social Security fields could have been entered as 12345, or as the word "nonsense.") You can enter any set of letters or numbers (but no spaces or punctuation marks) as an example element; what is important is that the example elements entered into the fields of the two tables are the same.

The example element appears highlighted as you enter it, which identifies it as an example element and not just criteria for the field. Once you've entered the example element in the first table, move the cursor to the common field in the second table, press the Example key

(F5) again, and enter the identical example element. In Figure 11-5, the Query Form includes the same example element in the Social Security fields of both the tables.

Performing the Query

Once you have entered the example elements, chosen the desired fields, and supplied any record selection criteria, you are ready to perform the query. Press F8, click the Run Query icon in the SpeedBar, or choose Run from the Query menu. In a moment, an answer based on the query will appear, as shown in Figure 11-6.

One important point to remember is that the order in which you supply the data does not matter. You could first fill in the example elements, then pick the fields to be included in the answer, and then provide any record selection criteria. Or you could perform all the necessary steps for one table, perform all the necessary steps for the second table, and then press F8 to process the query. Regardless of the

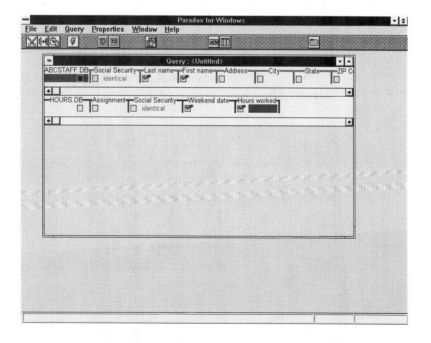

Filled-in query
for two tables
Figure 11-5.

11

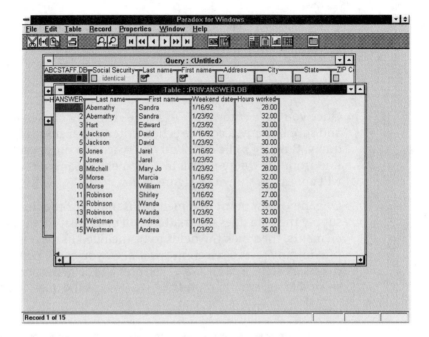

order, once you process the query, the answer appears. (Note, however, that the order of the fields in the query determines the order of the fields in the answer.) If you need a printed report at this point, the easiest method is to press Shift+F7 for a quick report.

Hands-On Practice: Querying from Two Tables

To get a list containing the employee's name, assignment, "week ending" data, and the number of hours worked with both tables linked through the common (Social Security) field, perform the following steps:

1. Choose the File/New/Query option.
2. When the Select File dialog box appears, click ABCSTAFF to highlight it, and then click OK.

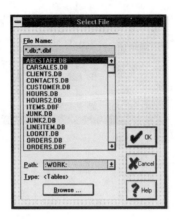

3. Use the mouse or the F6 key to place a check mark in the Last Name and First Name fields.

4. Click the Social Security field to place the cursor there, and press F5 to start an example element.

5. Enter **ABCD** as the example element.

6. Choose Add Table from the Query menu or click the Add Table icon in the SpeedBar. In a moment, the Select File dialog box again appears.

7. Click HOURS to highlight the table, and then click OK.

8. Use the mouse or the F6 key to place check marks in the Assignment, Weekend Date, and Hours Worked fields.

9. Click the Social Security field to place the cursor there, press F5 to enter an example element, and enter **ABCD** as the example element

10. Press F8 or click the Run Query icon on the SpeedBar. The result of the relational query should appear in an ANSWER table, as shown in Figure 11-7.

11

You can use selection criteria in either table to limit the records available in a relational query. As an example, perhaps you only want

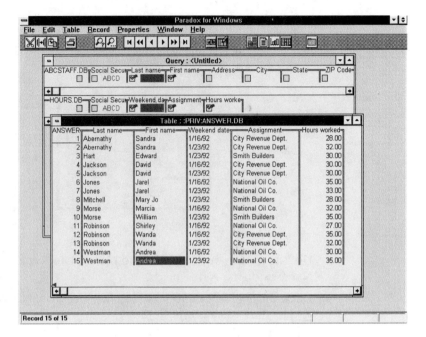

Results of first
practice query
Figure 11-7.

to see records for National Oil so that you can bill that particular client
for services rendered by the staff of ABC Temporaries. Click the query
window to make it the active window, and place the cursor in the
Assignment field of the HOURS table. Enter **National Oil Co.** as the
selection criteria. Press F8 or click the Run Query icon in the SpeedBar.
The ANSWER table will be rewritten to display only those employees
who put in time for National Oil, as shown in Figure 11-8.

Paradox allows you to add a selection criterion in the same query field
as the example element; just use a comma to separate the example
element and the selection criterion. As an example, perhaps you wish
to retrieve records using the fields you have already checked for
inclusion in the answer, but you only want to see records for Ms.
Andrea Westman. Click the query window to activate it and delete the
prior entry, National Oil Co., in the Assignment field of the HOURS
table (but leave the check mark in the field). In the Social Security field
of the HOURS table, click once just to the right of the existing example
element to place the insertion pointer there. Then add a comma after

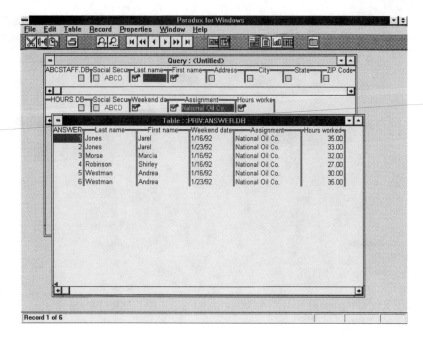

Query for
National Oil Co.
Figure 11-8.

the example element, and enter **121-33-9876**. Press [F8] or click the
Run Query icon in the SpeedBar to process the query. The results show
the records for Ms. Westman, as shown in Figure 11-9.

REMEMBER: If you often use the same query to link multiple tables,
save the query by choosing Save or Save As from the File menu.

11

Using Linked Tables with AND Selection Criteria

Paradox does not limit the way you use selection criteria: you have the
same flexibility as you do in queries performed on a single table. As an
example, perhaps you need a listing of employees who worked for the
City Revenue Department during the week ending 1/23/92. Perform the
following steps to accomplish this task:

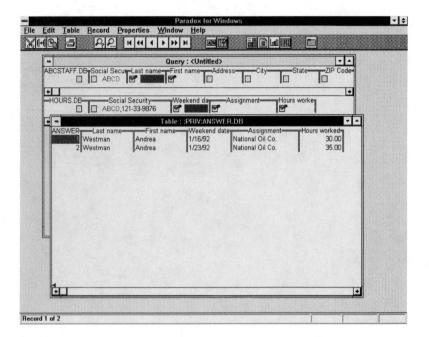

Relational
query for a
single name
Figure 11-9.

1. Click in the Social Security field in the HOURS table of the query, and remove the Social Security number and the comma with the ⌞Backspace⌟ key (but leave the example element in the Social Security field).

2. Click in the Weekend Date field of the query, and enter **1/23/92**.

3. Next, click in the Assignment field and type in **City Revenue Dept.**

 4. Press ⌞F8⌟ or click the Run Query icon on the SpeedBar to process the query. The results show the records for all employees who worked for the City Revenue Department *and* worked on the "week ending" date of 1/23/92, as shown in Figure 11-10.

The conditions do not need to be in the same table. For example, you might need a list of all employees assigned to National Oil who are earning more than $10.00 an hour. The fields you are using to limit the records, Salary and Assignment, are in two different tables. Perform the following steps to create the desired list:

1. Click the Salary field of the ABCSTAFF table in the query. In the Salary field, enter **> 10**.

2. Next, click the Assignment field of the HOURS table in the query. In the Assignment field, delete the prior entry for City Revenue Dept. and enter **National Oil Co.** as the condition. Then move the cursor to the Weekend Date field, and delete the prior entry in that field.

3. Press F8 or click the Run Query icon on the SpeedBar to process the query. Four records meet the two conditions, as shown in Figure 11-11.

Using Linked Tables with OR Selection Criteria

You can enter more criteria in the additional rows of the Query Forms to specify OR conditions, in which records are selected when one or another condition is met, but not necessarily both. As an example, perhaps you want to see all of the employees who are assigned to National Oil or to Smith Builders.

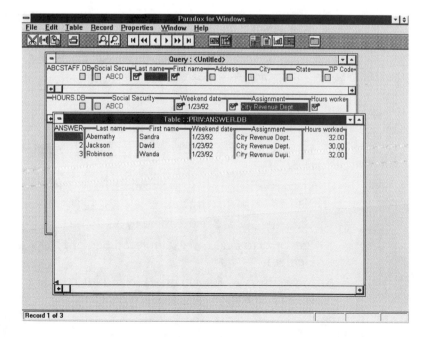

Relational query for a specific assignment and week ending date
Figure 11-10.

11

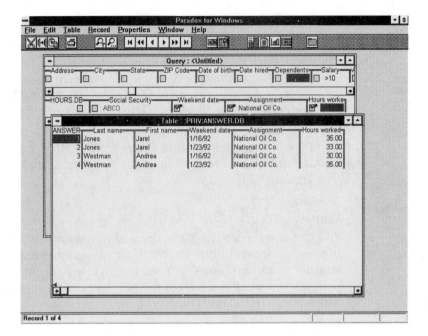

Query of linked
tables with
conditions in
separate tables
Figure 11-11.

First close the existing ANSWER table and the existing query. (Answer
No when asked if you want to save the query.) You need to use
something a little different for queries of multiple tables using OR
conditions. You must enter example elements that link either of the
conditions on each line of the Query Form. Perform the following steps
to try this:

1. Choose the File/New/Query option.

2. When the Select File dialog box appears, click ABCSTAFF, and then
   click OK.

3. Place check marks in the Social Security, Last Name, and First
   Name fields with the mouse or the F6 key.

4. Click the Social Security field to place the insertion pointer there.

5. Press F5 to begin an example, and enter **FIRST** as the example
   element.

6. Move the cursor down one line and into the Social Security
   column, and press F6 to add a check mark.

7. Press F5 to begin another example. Enter **SECOND** as the name for the second example.

8. Move the cursor over to the Last Name field, and press F6 to add a check mark in the field on the second row of the query form. Do the same for the First Name field.

9. Choose Add Table from the Query menu or click the Add Table icon on the SpeedBar. When the Select File dialog box appears, click HOURS, and then click OK.

10. Move the cursor to the Assignment field of the HOURS table, add a check mark with the mouse or with F6, and then enter **National Oil Co.** as the selection criteria.

11. Click the Social Security field of the HOURS table to place the insertion point there, and press F5 to begin the example element. Then enter **FIRST** as the matching example element for linking the tables.

12. Move the cursor to the Weekend Date and Hours Worked fields, pressing F6 to check them for inclusion in the ANSWER table.

13. Move the cursor back to the Assignment field, and down one line. Add a check mark with F6, and then enter **City Revenue Dept.** as the selection criteria for this row of the query.

14. Click the Social Security field of the second row to place the insertion point there. Press F5 to begin the example element, and enter **SECOND** as the matching example element for linking the tables.

15. Move the cursor over to the Weekend Date and Hours Worked fields of the second row, pressing F6 to include them in the ANSWER table. At this point, your query should resemble the example shown in Figure 11-12.

11

Before you process this query, take a moment to think about how it is structured. The first line of the Query Form for HOURS, which will select records that contain "National Oil Co." in the Assignment field, is linked to the ABCSTAFF table through the example element called FIRST. The second line of the Query Form for HOURS, which selects records with "City Revenue Dept." in the Assignment field, is linked to the ABCSTAFF table through the example element called SECOND. In the case of OR conditionals like this one, Paradox is performing two

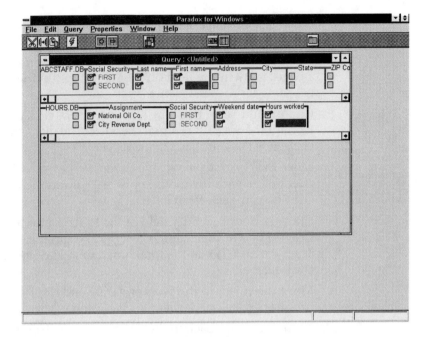

Filled-in query
forms for OR
conditionals
Figure 11-12.

separate queries at the same time: one to link records having "National
Oil Co." in a field, and the other to link records having "City Revenue
Dept." in the field. To see the results, press [F8] or click the Run Query
icon on the SpeedBar. In a moment, the ANSWER table will appear, as
shown in Figure 11-13.

Social Security	Last name	First name	Assignment	Weekend date	Hours worked
121-33-9876	Westman	Andrea	National Oil Co.	1/16/92	30.0
121-33-9876	Westman	Andrea	National Oil Co.	1/23/92	35.0
121-90-5432	Robinson	Shirley	National Oil Co.	1/16/92	27.0
123-44-8976	Morse	Marcia	National Oil Co.	1/16/92	32.0
232-55-1234	Jackson	David	City Revenue Dept.	1/16/92	30.0
232-55-1234	Jackson	David	City Revenue Dept.	1/23/92	30.0
343-55-9821	Robinson	Wanda	City Revenue Dept.	1/16/92	35.0
343-55-9821	Robinson	Wanda	City Revenue Dept.	1/23/92	32.0
495-00-3456	Abernathy	Sandra	City Revenue Dept.	1/16/92	28.0
495-00-3456	Abernathy	Sandra	City Revenue Dept.	1/23/92	32.0
909-88-7654	Jones	Jarel	National Oil Co.	1/16/92	35.0

Answer from
OR query based
on two tables
Figure 11-13.

Note that you can also use the OR operator in a field of a query to specify OR conditions. For example, you could enter "National Oil Co. OR Smith Builders" on a single line of a query in the Assignment field.

Querying More Than Two Tables

You can link as many tables as you need (up to the limits of open files that your operating system can handle at once) to obtain the answers you need while using Paradox. You can see an example of multiple linked tables by creating one more table, CLIENTS, that will contain the addresses of ABC Temporaries' clients.

Choose the File/New/Table option. When the Table Type dialog box appears, click OK to accept the default type of Paradox for Windows. In the Create Table dialog box, define the following fields:

Field Name	Field Type	Length
Client Name	Alphanumeric	25
Address	Alphanumeric	25
City	Alphanumeric	15
State	Alphanumeric	2
ZIP Code	Alphanumeric	5

After defining the structure, click Save As. In the Save As dialog box that appears, enter **CLIENTS** for a table name. Turn on the Display Table option in the dialog box, and then click OK. When the new table appears, press F9 to start editing, and add the three records shown here to the new table:

Client Name: **National Oil Co.**
Address: **1201 Germantown Road**
City: **Fairfax**
State: **VA**
ZIP Code: **20305**
Client Name: **City Revenue Dept.**
Address: **2000 Town Hall Square**
City: **Alexandria**
State: **VA**
ZIP Code: **22045**

11

Client Name: **Smith Builders**
Address: **2370 Rockville Pike**
City: **Rockville**
State: **MD**
ZIP Code: **30504**

When you are done, press F9 to complete the edits.

Perhaps you need a listing of assignments, the city of each assignment, the name of each employee, and "week ending" dates so you can track the validity of expense reports handed in by your staff for car mileage. The fields you need are in three different tables, so you need to fill in examples for three tables within a Query Form to get the answer you need.

Choose the File/New/Query option. When the Select File dialog box appears, click ABCSTAFF, and then click OK. When the Query Form appears, click the Social Security field to place the insertion point there, press F6 to add a check mark, and press F5 to begin an example. Enter **1234** as the example element. Then move the cursor to the Last Name field, and place a check mark with F6 to include this field in the answer.

 Choose Add Table from the Query menu or click the Add Table icon on the SpeedBar. When the Select File dialog box appears, click HOURS, and then click OK. When the Query Form for the HOURS table appears, click the Social Security field to place the insertion point there and press F5 to begin an example. Enter **1234** as the example element. Then move the cursor to the Weekend Date field and place a check mark in this field with F6 to include this field in the answer.

Click the Assignment field to place the insertion pointer there, and press F5 to begin the example element that will provide the link to the third table. Enter **5678** as the example element. Then choose Add Table from the Query menu or click the Add Table icon in the SpeedBar, click CLIENTS, and then click OK to display another Query Form. Click the Client Name field, press F5 to begin the example, and enter **5678** as the example element that tells Paradox to match the data found in the Assignment field of the HOURS table.

To complete the query, while the cursor is still in the Client Name field, first press F6 so that a check mark tells Paradox to include the name of the client field in the answer. Then move to the City field, and press

F6 again to add a check mark in this field. Press F8 or click the Run Query icon on the SpeedBar to process the query. The result, shown in Figure 11-14, includes the desired fields selected from the ABCSTAFF, HOURS, and CLIENTS tables.

One additional point can be noted from this example. The example element used to link the second and third tables was placed in two fields that had different field names. (The HOURS table stored the name of the client in a field called Assignment, while the CLIENTS table stored the names of the clients in a field called Client Name.) Unlike some relational database managers, Paradox does not require you to give fields identical field names before you can draw links between different tables. The only requirement is that the data contained in the linked fields can be matched. It would make no sense, for example, to try to draw a link between two fields containing dissimilar data, such as a phone number field and a date-of-birth field.

Don't close the table yet, as you will use it in the reporting example that follows.

Reporting Based on Relational Queries

Generating reports from a relational query is no different than generating reports from a nonrelational query. As with all reports, you have your choice of quick reports or custom reports. It's a simple matter

Social Security	Last name	Weekend date	Client name	City
121-33-9876	Westman	1/16/92	National Oil Co.	Fairfax
121-33-9876	Westman	1/23/92	National Oil Co.	Fairfax
121-90-5432	Robinson	1/16/92	National Oil Co.	Fairfax
123-44-8976	Morse	1/16/92	National Oil Co.	Fairfax
232-55-1234	Jackson	1/16/92	City Revenue Dept.	Alexandria
232-55-1234	Jackson	1/23/92	City Revenue Dept.	Alexandria
343-55-9821	Robinson	1/16/92	City Revenue Dept.	Alexandria
343-55-9821	Robinson	1/23/92	City Revenue Dept.	Alexandria
495-00-3456	Abernathy	1/16/92	City Revenue Dept.	Alexandria
495-00-3456	Abernathy	1/23/92	City Revenue Dept.	Alexandria
805-34-6789	Morse	1/23/92	Smith Builders	Rockville
876-54-3210	Hart	1/23/92	Smith Builders	Rockville
901-77-3456	Mitchell	1/23/92	Smith Builders	Rockville
909-88-7654	Jones	1/16/92	National Oil Co.	Fairfax

Table : D:\WINDOWS\ANSWER.DB

Results of query on three tables
Figure 11-14.

11

to create a quick report based on the relational results in an ANSWER table; once the ANSWER table is open in the active window, click the Quick Report icon on the SpeedBar (or press Shift+F7 to display the report, then click the Print icon or choose Report Print), and click OK in the Print File dialog box that appears to print the report. For example, if the ANSWER table from the last relational query were still active, you could do this to produce the report shown in Figure 11-15.

If you need a custom report, you can use the techniques outlined in Chapter 9 to design a report that uses the ANSWER table. To design a custom report based on an ANSWER table, choose the File/New/Report option. When the Data Model dialog box appears, choose ANSWER.DB from the File Name list box as the file to use for the report. Then design and save the report using the techniques outlined in Chapter 9, and run the report.

REMEMBER: If you are going to design custom reports that will be regularly used with the results of a particular query, you should save the query after designing it. This way whenever the report is needed, you can load the query and run it to generate an ANSWER table based on current data, and then load and run the report.

Before proceeding to the next section, close all open queries and ANSWER tables.

Designing Relational Documents

As mentioned at the start of the chapter, queries provide just one way to draw relationships between tables in Paradox. Another way is to design and use relational documents. In Paradox, relational documents are custom forms and reports that have been designed from the start to use multiple tables. The custom forms and reports that you designed in Chapters 7 and 9 made use of just one table at a time. However, you can use options in the Data Model dialog box (which appears when you begin designing a form or report) to base a form or report on multiple tables. This half of this chapter shows how you can specify multiple tables for use in a form or report, and how you can define the link, or relationship, between the tables.

Tuesday, September 8, 1992   ANSWER   Page 1

Social Security	Last Name	Weekend Date	Client Name	City
121-22-9876	Westman	1/16/92	National Oil Co.	Fairfax
121-22-9876	Westman	1/23/92	National Oil Co.	Fairfax
121-90-5432	Robinson	1/16/92	National Oil Co.	Fairfax
123-44-8976	Morse	1/16/92	National Oil Co.	Fairfax
232-55-1234	Jackson	1/16/92	City Revenue Dept.	Alexandria
232-55-1234	Jackson	1/23/92	City Revenue Dept.	Alexandria
343-55-9821	Robinson	1/16/92	City Revenue Dept.	Alexandria
343-55-9821	Robinson	1/23/92	City Revenue Dept.	Alexandria
495-00-3456	Abernathy	1/16/92	City Revenue Dept.	Alexandria
495-00-3456	Abernathy	1/23/92	City Revenue Dept.	Alexandria
805-34-6789	Morse	1/23/92	Smith Builders	Rockville
876-54-3210	Hart	1/23/92	Smith Builders	Rockville
901-77-3456	Mitchell	1/23/92	Smith Builders	Rockville
909-88-7654	Jones	1/16/92	National Oil Co.	Fairfax
909-88-7654	Jones	1/23/92	National Oil Co.	Fairfax

11

Quick Report based on relational ANSWER table **Figure 11-15.**

About Linking and Keys

In Paradox for Windows, whenever you create forms or reports that rely on multiple tables, the tables must be keyed, or indexed. Adding a key field or key fields (as described in Chapter 3) accomplishes three things in the area of linking tables:

✦ It establishes each record in the table as being unique

✦ It establishes a primary sort order for the table

✦ It ensures that there are no blank records in the table

When you design a document (a form, report, or mail merge) that relies on multiple tables, you are asking Paradox to evaluate a value in the table you are linking from, and to find all matching values in the table you are linking to. In a relational context, the table you are linking from is the master table, and the table you are linking to is the detail table. The detail table must be keyed, or indexed, on the field you will use to establish the link. An example of a link between the ABCSTAFF and the HOURS table (which you will create in the hands-on practice section that follows) is illustrated in Figure 11-16.

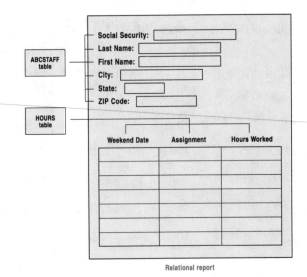

ABCSTAFF and
HOURS tables
linked in a
relational report
Figure 11-16.

Steps in Designing a Relational Document

The following paragraphs describe how to create your own relational forms or reports. If you've never created a relational document by using this technique, don't try to perform these steps now. The hands-on practice section that follows provides specific instructions that demonstrate this process. To create a relational document, you will perform these steps:

1. Choose New from the File menu. From the next menu to appear, choose which type of document you want to create (form, report, or mail merge). This brings up the Data Model dialog box, which is shown in Figure 11-17.

2. Add to the right side of the dialog box all the tables you need for the relationship. To add a table, click its name in the File Name list box, and then click the Add Table arrow (it's the right-pointing arrow in the dialog box). Alternately, you can double-click the table name in the File Name list box. Once you have placed all tables that are to be linked, you must create the needed links between the tables.

3. To create the link, click the master table and hold down the mouse button. When you do so, the cursor will change into the shape of a linking tool, as shown here.

4. While holding down the mouse button, drag to the detail table. As you do so, a solid line extends from the master table to the detail table.

5. Release the mouse. Paradox displays the Define Link dialog box shown in Figure 11-18.

6. In the Index list at the right side of the dialog box, double-click to select the desired key, or index, used in the detail table.

7. At the left side of the dialog box, double-click the desired field in the master table that will establish the link. Paradox draws a line

11

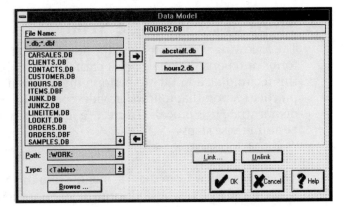

between the field and the index, indicating that the link has been
established, as shown in Figure 11-19.

8. Click OK to accept the link. The Define Link dialog box vanishes,
   revealing the Data Model dialog box underneath. This dialog box
   will display a line between the tables, indicating the presence of
   the link.

A Note About Automatic Links

If the fields that should be used to establish the link are obvious (such
as fields of identical types, with proper keys identified), Paradox will
create the link for you. You can click OK in the dialog box to accept the

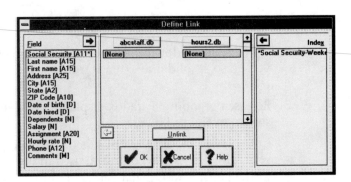

Define Link dialog box with link established **Figure 11-19.**

link, or click Unlink to remove the automatic link and manually create a link of your own choosing.

Modifying or Removing Existing Links

If you wish to change the method used to link tables, click the detail table in the Data Model dialog box, and click Link. This displays the Define Link dialog box. In this dialog box, click Unlink to remove the existing link. Then use the techniques described earlier to specify the link you want.

To remove an existing link, click the detail table in the Data Model dialog box, and than click Unlink.

Designing the Document

Once the desired link exists in the Data Model dialog box, click OK. In a moment, the Design Layout dialog box appears, as shown in Figure 11-20.

This dialog box should be familiar from Chapters 7 and 9. (You should read those chapters before attempting to create relational forms or reports. These basics of form and report design will not be covered again here.) Use the options in the Design Layout dialog box to establish the overall layout for your form or report, and then click OK to open a design window. Using the techniques outlined in Chapters 7 and 9, design the form or report as desired, and save it by choosing Save or Save As from the File menu.

11

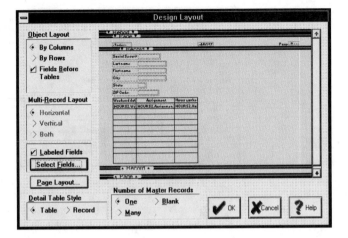

Hands-On Practice: Creating a Relational Report

This section demonstrates how you can use the techniques described in the previous section to create a relational report. The report uses the ABCSTAFF table as a master table, and the HOURS table as a detail table. One problem is that the HOURS table needs a key, since relational documents require the use of a key or index in the detail table. In this case, a key based on the Social Security field is needed. But, since more than one record in the HOURS table will normally have the same social security number, you need to create a key based on more than one field. A combination of social security and weekend date will suffice, since there should never be more than one record with the same social security number and the same week ending date. To satisfy this requirement, perform the following steps to restructure the HOURS table.

1. Choose the File/Utilities/Restructure option. When the Select File dialog box appears, click HOURS, and then click OK. This causes the Restructure Paradox for Windows Table dialog box to appear, as shown in Figure 11-21.

2. Click in the Field Roster area next to the Social Security field, drag the field up to the top of the table, and then release the mouse.

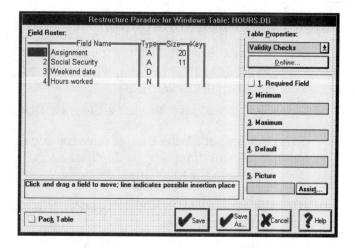

Restructure
Paradox for
Windows Table
dialog box
Figure 11-21.

This repositions the Social Security field so it is the first field in the table.

3. Now drag the Weekend Date field up until it is below the Social Security field, and then release the mouse. This repositions the Weekend Date field so it is the second field in the table. At this point, your table's structure should resemble the example shown in Figure 11-22, with the Social Security and Weekend Date fields as the first two fields in the table.

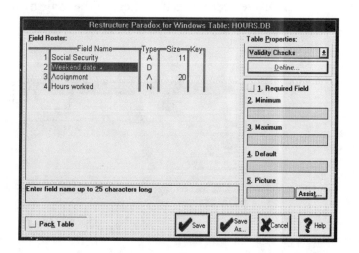

HOURS table
structure with
fields
repositioned
Figure 11-22.

11

4. Double-click the Key column beside the Social Security field to make this field a key field. (When you do so, an asterisk appears in the Key column, indicating the presence of a key field.)

5. Double-click the Key column beside the Weekend Date field to make this field a key field.

6. Click Save to save the changes to the HOURS table.

With the key added, the HOURS table is ready to support the use of relational forms or reports. To duplicate an example of a relational report, perform the following steps now:

1. Choose the File/New/Report option. In a moment, the Data Model Dialog box appears.

2. In the File Name list box, click ABCSTAFF. Then click the Add Table arrow (it's the right-pointing arrow in the dialog box).

3. In the File Name list box, click HOURS. Then click the Add Table arrow once again.

4. At the right side of the dialog box, click and hold down the mouse button on ABCSTAFF to identify it as the master table. While holding down the mouse button, drag to HOURS (the detail table) and release the mouse. Paradox now displays the Define Link dialog box, as shown in Figure 11-23.

Note that Paradox has defined the link automatically. Because both tables have a Social Security field of the same data type, and both fields

Define Link dialog box for ABCSTAFF and HOURS
Figure 11-23.

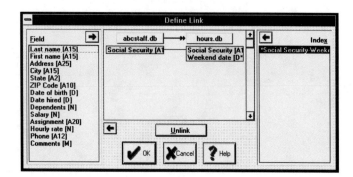

are used in keys, Paradox assumes that this is the proper field to use to establish the link.

5. Since Paradox has guessed correctly, click OK to accept the link. The Data Model dialog box reappears, with an arrow between ABCSTAFF and HOURS indicating the presence of the link.

6. Click OK. In a moment, the familiar Design Layout dialog box appears. For this example, you do not need all the fields in the master (ABCSTAFF) table, so use the Select Fields dialog box to remove the unnecessary fields now.

Note the presence of one option in the Design Layout dialog box that you have not seen in Chapter 7 or 9; there is a Fields Before Tables check box in the Object Layout portion of the dialog box. Paradox presents this option because you are designing a report that will display information from a master table and a detail table. When this option is turned on (which is the default), all fields of the current record in the master table appear before any fields in the detail table. If the option is turned off, detail records appear first. For this example, you may leave this option turned on.

7. Click the Select Fields button to bring up the Select Fields dialog box. Notice that in the dialog box (Figure 11-24), both tables are shown in the left side of the dialog box. The right side of the dialog box, under Selected Fields, shows a list of fields for the selected table on the left side of the dialog box. If you click

11

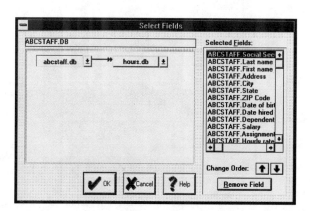

Select Fields dialog box with ABCSTAFF and HOURS tables
Figure 11-24.

ABCSTAFF, the list box shows the fields in the ABCSTAFF table. If you click HOURS, the list box shows the fields in the HOURS table.

8. If the fields for the ABCSTAFF table are not visible in the Selected Fields list box, click ABCSTAFF.DB now. In the Selected Fields list box, click Address, then click the Remove Field command button to remove the field from the list. Use the same technique to remove the Date of Birth, Date Hired, Dependents, Assignment, Salary, Hourly Rate, Phone, and Comments fields.

9. Since no fields in the HOURS table need to be removed for this example, click OK to close the Select Fields dialog box.

10. When the Design Layout dialog box appears, click OK. The new report appears in a Report Design window. You may want to click the window's Maximize button to see more of the report's design; if you do so, it will resemble the example shown in Figure 11-25.

In this case, no changes are needed to the default report. If you were designing a report for your own application, you could change the report as desired, using the techniques explained in Chapters 7 and 9.

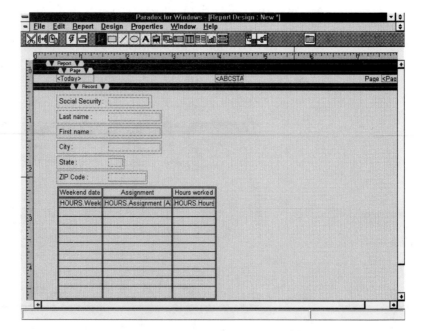

Relational
report within
Report Design
window
Figure 11-25.

Monday, September 21, 1992   ABCSTAFF   Page 1

Social Security: 121-33-9876

Last name: Westman

First name: Andrea

City: Silver Spring

State: MD

ZIP Code: 20910-0124

Weekend date	Assignment	Hours worked
1/16/92	National Oil Co.	30.0
1/23/92	National Oil Co.	35.0

Social Security: 121-90-5432

Last name: Robinson

First name: Shirley

City: Takoma Park

State: MD

ZIP Code: 20912

Weekend date	Assignment	Hours worked
1/16/92	National Oil Co.	27.0

Completed
relational report
Figure 11-26.

11. Save the report by choosing Save from the File menu. Call the
report RELATE1. You can try viewing a preview of the report by
clicking the View Data icon, by choosing Preview from the Report
menu, or by pressing [F8]. If you want a printed copy of the report,
click the Print icon in the SpeedBar, and click OK in the Print the
File dialog box that appears. The report that you view on screen (or
print) should resemble the example shown in Figure 11-26.

11

Quick Summary

Querying from Two Tables

Choose the File/New/Query option. In the Select File dialog box, choose the first table needed for the query. When the Query Form appears, check the fields to be included in the answer, and enter any desired criteria in the fields of the Query Form. When the first Query Form is filled out, choose Add Table from the Query menu, and, in the Select File dialog box that appears, choose the next table to add to the Query Form. Paradox places a query for the second table directly below the first within the same query window. You can again choose the fields to be included in the answer and enter any desired selection criteria. Press F8 or click the Run Query icon to process the query.

Using Linked Tables with AND Selection Criteria

Add as many conditions as necessary in the different fields of either of the Query Forms.

Using Linked Tables with OR Selection Criteria

In each Query Form, add additional lines for more criteria. Or, include the OR operator between multiple query criteria.

Generating Relational Reports Based on a Query

Build and process a query that performs the relational link. Then design (if necessary) and generate a report based on the ANSWER table provided by the relational query.

C H A P T E R

12

ADVANCED TOPICS

Once you have created tables to support your work, you will probably need to make changes to their design. No matter how much advance planning you do, you'll undoubtedly need to add fields or change existing fields. Fortunately, with Paradox no database design is cast in stone. You can readily add new fields or change the design of existing fields.

In addition to helping you manage the characteristics of your tables, Paradox lets you manage files by performing tasks that you would otherwise need to accomplish through the Windows File Manager or through DOS—tasks such as erasing, copying, or renaming tables. Paradox also makes it easier for you to manage objects in multiple directories, through the use of aliases and the File Browser. And you can share data between Paradox and other applications by exporting and importing data. This chapter covers all of these topics in detail.

Changing a Table's Structure

When you need to change the design of an existing table, you *restructure* the table. You can start the process of restructuring a table in any of the following ways:

✦ If the table is open and active (the window containing the table is the active window), choose the Table/Restructure option.

✦ If you are at the Paradox desktop but the table is not open, choose File/Utilities/Restructure. This causes a Select File dialog box to appear. Choose the desired table by name from the list box, and then click OK.

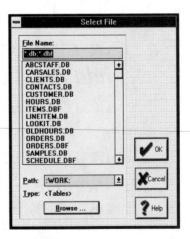

✦ If the table has been placed in the folder, open the Folder window, right-click the table's icon, and choose Restructure from the menu that appears.

Either of these methods causes the Restructure Table dialog box to appear, as shown in Figure 12-1.

TIP: If you want to change the name of a table, don't restructure it. Instead, choose the File/Utilities/Rename option.

Restructure
Table dialog box
Figure 12-1.

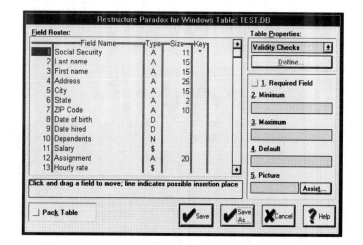

12

The Restructure Table dialog box is very similar to the Create Table dialog box that you used in Chapter 3 to create new tables. You can make the desired changes to the field names, field types, and sizes. (The paragraphs that follow provide more details on making changes to a table's structure.) When you are done making changes, click the Save or the Save As button. If you click Save, Paradox overwrites the old table structure with the modified structure. If you click Save As and enter a different filename in the dialog box that appears, Paradox writes the modified structure and the data in the old table to a new table, leaving the old table intact.

Think About Your Changes

Changes that you make to the structure of a table may, in some cases, cause problems with the existing data. For example, if you shorten the length of an alphanumeric field, existing data that is too long for the new field may be cut off. The following paragraphs describe data losses that may occur under certain circumstances when you change the design of your tables; they also provide techniques for specific types of table restructuring.

In some cases, a table restructuring operation causes the creation of a temporary *problems* table. Paradox stores records that are incompatible with the restructured table in the problems table. You can then examine the data in the problems table, and decide whether to make any changes necessary so that the data can be added to the original table. (You can move data from one table to another by choosing File/Utilities/Add; see "Using the Utilities" later in this chapter for further details.)

Adding Fields to a Table

To add a new field at the end of the table during the restructuring process, move the cursor to the last field in the existing structure and press the ⬇ key once. A new, blank field will appear. To add a new field between existing fields, move the cursor to the field where you want the new row to appear, and press the Ins key. A new, blank row will be inserted above the selected field.

Deleting Fields from a Table

To delete an existing field, move the cursor to the desired field and press Ctrl+Del. Since deleting fields as part of a table restructuring operation results in the loss of data (unless no data has been stored in the field), when you attempt to save the changes to the structure, Paradox displays a Restructure Warning dialog box warning you that data will be lost. You must then confirm the deletion by clicking Yes in the dialog box.

WARNING: If you delete a field that was used in custom forms or reports you have designed, the field object in the form or report loses its definition. The next time you open the form or report, you must either redefine the object or delete it.

Moving Fields

You can move a field to a new location within a table by clicking and dragging the field's number in the far left column of the Restructure Table dialog box. When you click at the field's number and hold down the mouse button, the entire field is highlighted with a double-line border. While holding down the mouse button, drag the field to the new position in the table, and then release the mouse button.

Editing a Field

To change a field's name, select the desired field (place the cursor in the field name box) and click it or press F2. Then make the desired changes using the standard editing keys. Or, you can select the desired

12

field and just begin typing a new field name; the new name will replace the old one.

WARNING: If you change a field name in an existing table and that field is used in a custom form or report, Paradox tries to handle the change automatically (updating the form or report for you) the next time you open the form or report. If you change more than one field name, Paradox may not be able to handle the change automatically, in which case you will have to redefine the fields in the form or report.

Shortening Alphanumeric Fields

If you shorten an alphanumeric field and there is existing data in that field of the table, you may lose data. When you restructure a table by shortening a field, Paradox displays a Restructure Warning dialog box when you try to save the table's changes. Choose the desired options in this dialog box (as explained next), and then click Yes to proceed with the restructuring operation, or click Cancel to cancel the operation.

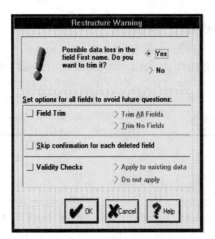

The Restructure Warning dialog box warns of possible data loss, and asks if you want to trim the existing data. In the Common Responses portion of the dialog box, you are presented with three options: Field Trim, Trim All Fields, or Trim No Fields. If you turn on the Field Trim option (the default), Paradox displays this same dialog box for each field you've shortened, and you must click Yes to proceed, in which case Paradox trims the contents of the fields to fit the new table. If you click Trim All Fields, Paradox trims the contents of all fields you have shortened in the structure as necessary to fit the new table. If you choose Trim No Fields and later confirm the restructuring process by clicking Yes in the dialog box, Paradox does not trim any data; instead, it moves any records with data that will not fit in the shortened fields into a *problems* table.

Converting a Non-Key Field to a Key Field

Since key fields must be the first fields in a table's structure (as explained in Chapter 3), if you convert a non-key field to a key field during a restructuring operation, the field must either be the first field in the structure or directly below existing key fields. (You can move fields around in a table's structure; to move a field, position the mouse pointer on the field's row number, click and hold down the left mouse button, and drag the field to its new location.)

Keep in mind that if you add keys to a table that previously had none, or had different keys, this may result in *key violations*. That is, there may be existing data that violates the rules established by the key. For example, if you restructure an existing table to add a key based on a combination of last name and first name, and there are two or more records with the same last and first names, the result will be a key violation. Only the first record that is unique (according to the specified key field or fields) will be retained; any that have duplicate keys will be discarded.

Changing Field Types

In theory, changing a field's type is a simple matter. In the Restructure Table dialog box, you simply move the cursor to the desired field type, press (Spacebar) to open the Field Types menu, and choose the new field type from the menu.

12

In practice, things may not be so simple. Paradox will change the field type as you dictate, but you may experience data loss, depending on the change you make. In some cases, Paradox can retain data even after a change in field types; in other cases, it cannot. Generally, Paradox retains the data if the change in field types is allowed and if the data makes sense in its new format. For example, if you changed a number field into an alphanumeric field, Paradox would retain the data; the existing numbers would simply appear as numeric characters in the new alphanumeric field. On the other hand, Paradox would not let you change a number field to a graphic field, because the change makes no sense.

A Note About Date Field Conversions   If you have dates stored in an alphanumeric field that you then change to a date field, Paradox retains the data if the dates were originally entered in an acceptable date format. Here are some examples of acceptable (and unacceptable) date formats:

Acceptable	Not Acceptable
4/30/52	April 30, 1952
12-Oct-94	October the 12th
7/22/1994	
15.09.92	The 15th of Sept., 1992

Saving the Restructured Table

When you are done changing the table's structure, you can click Save or Save As in the Restructure Table dialog box. Note the difference between the two options:

✦   Click Save if you wish to overwrite the old structure with the new structure. If there is a possibility of data loss due to changes in field lengths or types, Paradox displays a dialog box warning you of this fact.

✦   Click Save As if you wish to create a new table. Paradox displays a Save Table As dialog box:

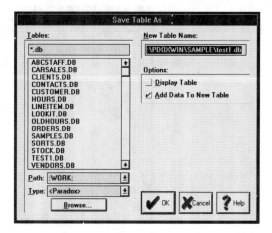

and you must enter a name for the new table, and then click OK. Also note the presence of the Add Data To New Table option in this dialog box. If this option is turned on (the default), Paradox copies as much data from the old table into the new one as is compatible with the new structure, while leaving the old table unchanged. If this option is turned off, Paradox copies the table's structure to the new table name, but leaves the table empty of any data.

Creating a New Table Based on an Existing Structure

When you are creating a new table, you can base its design on an existing table by clicking the Borrow button that appears in the Create Table dialog box. As detailed in Chapter 3, after you choose File/New/Table from the menu bar and accept the desired table type, the Create Paradox for Windows Table dialog box appears, as shown in Figure 12-2.

Click the Borrow button in the lower-left corner of the dialog box, and a Borrow Table Structure dialog box appears. This dialog box contains a list box of the other tables in your working directory.

12

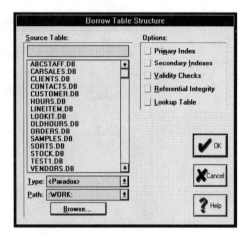

Click the desired table (or use the Browse button to find a table in a different directory or drive). Once you have selected the desired table and turned on any of the options at the right side of the dialog box, click OK. When you do so, the structure for the table you just selected appears in the Create Table dialog box. You can proceed to make any desired changes to the table's structure, and then save the new table under the filename of your choice by clicking Save As in the dialog box.

You can turn on any of the options on the right side of the Borrow Table Structure dialog box, if you want any of these properties from the

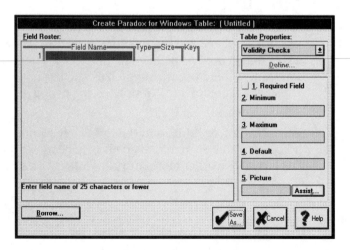

Create Table
dialog box
Figure 12-2.

"borrowed" table to apply to the new table you are creating. If you check the Primary Index option, any primary index or key fields in the borrowed table are made key fields in the new table. If you check the Validity Checks option, any validity checks in the borrowed table are also established in the new table. The other options (Lookup Table, Secondary Indexes, and Referential Integrity) are beyond the scope of this book. Suffice it to say that these are advanced options that you can apply to Paradox tables. If you check these options in the dialog box, any of these qualities from the borrowed table will also be applied to the new table.

Using the Utilities

The File/Utilities menu lets you perform a number of file management tasks from within Paradox. You can copy, delete, and rename tables, and you can add data (in an existing table) to another table. You can also import and export data between Paradox and other software.

Moving Records Between Tables

You can copy records from one table to another using File/Utilities/Add. (Certain rules govern tables when you add data from one to another; see the paragraphs that follow these steps for more details.) You can add records from one table to another by performing the following steps:

1. Choose the File/Utilities/Add option. You will see the Table Add dialog box, as shown in Figure 12-3.

12

2. In the Add Records From Source Table text box, enter the name of the table that contains the records you want to add. (You can click in the text box and type the name, or pick a table by name from the list box at the left side of the dialog box.)

3. In the To the Target Table text box, enter the name of the table you want the records added to. Again, you can click in the text box and type the name, or click in the text box to place the cursor there and then pick a table by name from the list box at the left side of the dialog box. You can also search other directories and/or drives by clicking the Browse button to bring up the File Browser.

4. Choose the options that you want in the Options area of the dialog box. (These options are explained in the paragraphs that follow.)

5. Click Add. The records from the source table are added to the target table.

Some rules apply to the moving of records between tables. Obviously, the two tables must have compatible field types in the same order, although Paradox does not require the fields to have the same names. The following additional rules apply:

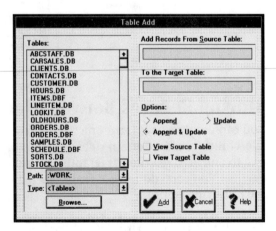

Table Add
dialog box
Figure 12-3.

✦ You can add alphanumeric fields of any length to other alphanumeric fields of any length. (If an alphanumeric field in the source table is added to a shorter alphanumeric field in the target table, Paradox trims any values that won't fit.)

✦ You can add any kind of number field in the source table (number, short number, or currency) to any kind of number field in the target table.

✦ You can only add date, memo, formatted memo, graphic, OLE, and binary fields to other fields of the same type. For example, you can only add a graphic field in the source table to a graphic field in the target table.

✦ You *cannot* move records between different types of tables. For example, you cannot move records from a Paradox for Windows type table into a dBASE type table. (You can, however, get around this limitation by copying a table to a new table with a different extension; choose File/Utilities/Copy, and when you enter the target filename, use .DBF for dBASE-type tables or .DB for Paradox-type tables.)

✦ The target table can have more fields than the source table. In such cases, you must make sure that first fields of the target table match the fields of the source table (the fields must be compatible types, as just described, and in matching order.)

NOTE: If the target table is a keyed table, any records in the source table that violate the key (in other words, that have the same key value as existing records in the target table) will not be added to the target table.

The Options in the Table Add Dialog Box

You can use the options in the Table Add dialog box (refer to Figure 12-3) to add records to the target table, update records in the target table, or both.

12

✦ Turn on the Append option if you want to add records from the source table to the target table. If the target table is not keyed,

Paradox adds the records to the end of the table. If the target table is keyed, Paradox inserts the new records at the proper position in the table, based on the key values.

✦ Turn on the Update option if you want to update existing records. If the target table isn't keyed, records from the source table overwrite matching records from the target table. (Records from the source table that don't match any records in the target table are not added.) If the target table is keyed, records from the source table overwrite matching records in the target table, and the original records in the target table are moved to a temporary table named CHANGED.

✦ Turn on the Append & Update option if you want to add new records and update existing records (following the rules noted previously).

✦ Turn on the View Source Table and/or View Target Table options as desired, if you want to see either table open in a window after the operation is complete.

Copying Tables

You can copy tables by choosing File/Utilities/Copy and filling in the desired options in the dialog box that appears. This is the recommended way to make copies of Paradox tables. You should *not* use the Windows File Manager or the DOS COPY command to make copies of tables, because you may not copy all related files of the table. If you let Paradox copy your tables, it copies all related files automatically. You can make copies of tables by performing the following steps:

1. Choose File/Utilities/Copy. This brings up the Copy dialog box, as shown in Figure 12-4.

2. In the Source File text box, enter the name of the table that you want to copy. (You can click in the text box and type the name, or click in the text box and pick a table by name from the list box at the left side of the dialog box.)

3. In the Destination File text box, enter the name for the new table.

NOTE: You *must* include an extension for the copied table name. If you include a .DB extension, Paradox creates a copy of the table using the Paradox for Windows file format. If you include an extension of .DBF, Paradox creates a copy of the table using the dBASE-type file format. This is true regardless of the file format type used by the source table.

4. Click Copy to perform the copy operation.

Renaming Tables

You can rename tables by choosing File/Utilities/Rename and filling in the desired options in the dialog box that appears. This is the recommended way to rename Paradox tables. You should *not* use the Windows File Manager or the DOS RENAME command to rename tables, because you may not rename all related files of the table. If you let Paradox rename your tables, it renames all related files automatically.

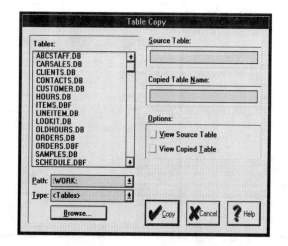

Table Copy
dialog box
Figure 12-4.

12

NOTE: A table must be closed before you can rename it. If a table is open and you attempt to rename it, Paradox displays a "File Is Busy" error dialog box.

You can rename a table by performing the following steps:

1. Choose File/Utilities/Rename. This causes the Rename dialog box to appear, as shown in Figure 12-5.

2. In the Source File text box, enter the name of the table that you want to rename. (You can click in the text box and type the name, or click in the text box and then pick a table by name from the list box at the left side of the dialog box.)

3. In the Destination File text box, enter the new name for the table.

4. Click Rename to rename the table.

NOTE: Keep in mind that custom forms or reports you've created may refer to your existing tables. If you rename a table to which you referred in a custom form or report, the next time you open the form or report it won't be able to locate the table. You will have to redesign the form or report to refer to the table by its new name.

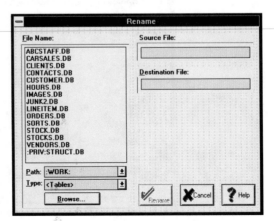

Rename dialog box

Figure 12-5.

Deleting Tables

You can delete tables or other files by choosing File/Utilities/Delete. When you do so, the Delete dialog box appears, as shown in Figure 12-6.

Enter the name of the desired table in the text box, or choose a table by name from the list box at the left side of the dialog box. Then click Delete to delete the table. Paradox displays another dialog box to ensure that deleting the table is what you want to do; click Yes in the second dialog box, and the table will be deleted from the disk.

NOTE: A table must be closed before you can delete it. If a table is open and you attempt to delete it, Paradox will display a "File Is Busy" error dialog box.

Make absolutely sure that you want to delete a table before confirming the deletion. Once you delete a table, you cannot recover it without special DOS techniques that are beyond the scope of this book.

Emptying Tables

The File/Utilities menu choice in Paradox has an Empty option, which you can use to empty a table—that is, remove all its records. To empty a

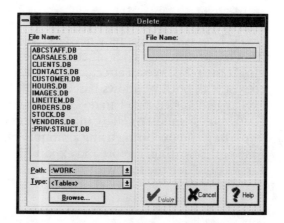

Delete dialog
box
Figure 12-6.

12

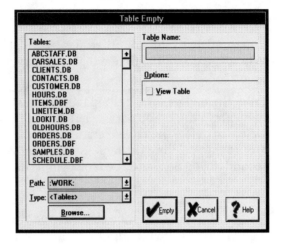

Table Empty
dialog box
Figure 12-7.

table, choose File/Utilities/Empty. (If the table is open in the active window, you can choose the Table/Empty option to accomplish the same task.) When you choose File/Utilities/Empty, the Table Empty dialog box appears, as shown in Figure 12-7.

Enter the name of the table you wish to empty in the text box, or choose a table by name from the list box. Then click Empty to empty the table of all records.

Exporting and Importing Data

No PC is an island. You may need to use other programs along with Paradox, or others in your office may use popular programs like Quattro Pro, Lotus 1-2-3, WordPerfect, or Excel. Paradox can comfortably coexist with both Windows-based and DOS-based software; you can exchange data between Paradox and other programs by choosing the File/Utilities/Import or File/Utilities/Export option. Paradox supports importing and exporting using a number of different formats. At the time of this writing, import and export file formats supported by Paradox include the following:

Lotus 1-2-3, version 1.A
Lotus 1-2-3, version 2.*x*
Excel
Quattro (DOS), version 1.*x*
Quattro Pro (DOS)
Quattro Pro (Windows)
ASCII, Delimited text
ASCII, Fixed Length text

If you want to use data from a Paradox table in your DOS-based word processor, you can use the ASCII Fixed Length choice to create a file that nearly all word processors can use. See your word processor's manual for details on how to insert the text file into a document.

NOTE: Because dBASE is one of the two native file formats used by Paradox for Windows, there are no specific menu or dialog box options for importing or exporting files to dBASE format. Paradox reads dBASE files unchanged, and you can copy a Paradox table (that uses the native Paradox for Windows file type) to a dBASE file format by choosing the File/Utilities/Copy option and entering a filename with a .DBF extension in the Copied Table Name text box of the dialog box that appears. See "A Note About dBASE Files" later in this chapter for additional details.

This list may not be all inclusive; it is possible that successive versions of Paradox for Windows will support additional file formats. If you need a format that is not on this list, check your Paradox documentation to see if that file format is supported.

TIP: If you are using another software package that is not supported, check that software's documentation to see if you can use a common "intermediate" format to exchange data. As an example, if your spreadsheet's files cannot be directly read by Paradox, but your spreadsheet can export files in Lotus 1-2-3 format, you could save a spreadsheet in Lotus 1-2-3 format, and then import it into a Paradox table.

12

If you are exporting data, you may want to perform a query first to select the desired information. Then export the ANSWER table using File/Utilities/ Export. This way you can export only the necessary data.

There are certain rules for exporting and importing data. You can export data to a new file, but you cannot export data into an existing file. And with the exception of delimited ASCII files, you can import data only into new tables; you cannot import data into an existing table. (If you want to put data from another program into an existing table, you can get around this limitation by importing the data into a new table, and then moving the data from the new table into the existing table with File/Utilities/Add.)

Exporting Data

To export a table, choose the File/Utilities/Export option. When you do so, the Table Export dialog box appears, as shown in Figure 12-8.

Click the table you want to export in the list box of table names. Then click the desired file format in the Export File Type list box to select it, and click OK. The next dialog box to appear varies, depending on which file type you selected.

Table Export
dialog box
Figure 12-8.

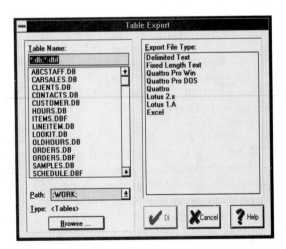

Exporting a Table as a Spreadsheet

If you choose to export the table to any of the spreadsheets supported by Paradox, you next see the Spreadsheet Export dialog box.

In the Table Name text box is the name of the Paradox table that you chose to export. In the New File Name text box is the name for the exported file. By default, this name will be the same as the name of the table, with an appropriate extension that matches the type of spreadsheet file you are creating. The Make Row Headers From Field Names option (which is turned on by default) causes the field names to appear in the first row of the spreadsheet as row headers. If you do not want this to happen, click the option to turn it off. When you are done making selections in this dialog box, click OK to have Paradox create the spreadsheet file.

Exporting Tables as Delimited Text Files

If you choose to export the table as a Delimited text file, you next see the Delimited ASCII Export dialog box.

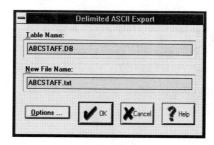

12

In the Table Name text box is the name of the Paradox table that you chose to export. In the New File Name text box is the name for the exported file. By default, this name will be the same as the name of the table, with an extension of .TXT. If you click the Options button in the dialog box, a Text Options dialog box appears.

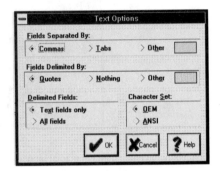

In this dialog box, you can choose whether fields in the exported file are to be separated by commas, tabs, or another character that you specify. You can also choose whether fields are to be delimited by commas, tabs, or another character that you specify. You can choose whether only text fields are to be delimited, or whether all fields are to be delimited. And you can specify which character set should be used; the default is OEM, which causes the exported file to use the character set normally used by Paradox. If you choose ANSI, the characters used match the ANSI (American National Standards Institute) standard character set. Unless you specifically know that you want an exported file using the ANSI character set, you should leave this option set at its default setting of OEM. When you are done making selections in the dialog box, click OK to have Paradox create the delimited ASCII file.

Exporting Tables as ASCII Fixed Length Files

If you choose to export the table as a Fixed Length text file, you next see the Fixed Length ASCII Export dialog box.

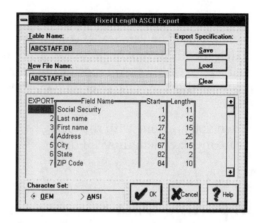

In the Table Name text box is the name of the Paradox table that you chose to export. In the New File Name text box is the name for the exported file. By default, this name is the same as the name of the table, with an extension of .TXT.

The lower portion of the dialog box contains a representation of the table's structure. You can edit this structure if desired; you can change the names of the fields, the starting position in the text file (it's the value under the Start column), and the length of each column. Note that if you change the length and a column's length is too short to hold the data that's in a record, Paradox trims the record to fit when it exports the data to the ASCII file.

The Save, Load, and Clear buttons are used to save the specifications you use (for exporting a file) to a separate file; to load specifications for file export from a previously saved file; or to clear the dialog box of any previously changed export specifications. These options are not discussed at length here due to their advanced nature. In a nutshell, you may find them useful if you regularly export and import files. After editing a structure as desired, you can use the Save button to save the specifications you use when exporting the file. See your Paradox documentation for more information on the use of the Load, Save, and Clear buttons.

At the bottom of the dialog box are options for choosing the desired character set used in the text file. You can choose OEM or ANSI. The

12

default is OEM, which causes the exported file to use the character set normally used by Paradox. If you choose ANSI, the characters used match the ANSI (American National Standards Institute) standard character set. Unless you specifically know that you want an exported file using the ANSI character set, you should leave this option set to OEM.

When you are done with the dialog box, click OK to have Paradox create the fixed-length ASCII file.

Importing Data

To import a table, choose the File/Utilities/Import option. When you do so, the File Import dialog box appears, as shown in Figure 12-9.

You can enter the filename of the file you want to import in the File Name text box. (Be sure to include the proper extension; in many cases, doing so will help Paradox automatically identify the type of file it is importing.) Or, you can click the desired filename in the list box of filenames. Use the Type drop-down list box at the bottom of the dialog box to pick a file type to import; when you do this, all files matching that type appear in the list box.

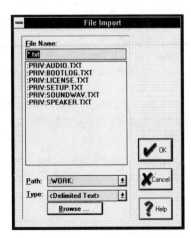

File Import dialog box
Figure 12-9.

Once you have entered the desired filename, click OK. The next dialog box to appear varies, depending on which file type you selected.

Importing a Spreadsheet

If you choose to import a spreadsheet file, you next see the Spreadsheet Import dialog box.

In the File Name text box is the name of the spreadsheet file that you chose to import. In the New Table Name text box is the name for the new table. (By default, this is the same name as the spreadsheet, but without the spreadsheet's extension.) Beneath the New Table Name text box are options for the type of table you prefer; Paradox is the default, but you can also turn on the dBASE option to make the imported table a dBASE-type table.

In the From Cell and To Cell text boxes, you can enter a spreadsheet range to import the data from; the From Cell represents the upper-left corner of the range, and the To Cell represents the lower-right corner of the range. Or, you can enter a named range in the Named Ranges text box. (If you are unfamiliar with these terms, see your spreadsheet documentation for a detailed explanation of cells and spreadsheet ranges.)

The Get Field Names From First Row option (which is turned on by default) causes the names in the first row of the spreadsheet to be used as field names in the new table. If you do not want this to happen, click

12

the option to turn it off. When you are done with the dialog box, click OK to have Paradox import the spreadsheet into a new table.

Importing a Delimited Text File

If you choose to import a Delimited text file, you next see the Delimited ASCII Import dialog box.

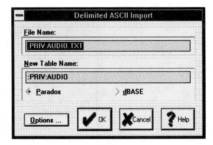

In the File Name text box is the name of the text file that you chose to import. In the New Table Name text box is the name for the new table. Beneath the New Table Name text box are options for the type of table you prefer; Paradox is the default, but you can also turn on the dBASE option to make the imported table a dBASE-type table.

If you click on the Options button in the dialog box, a Text Options dialog box opens.

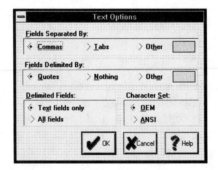

In the Fields Separated By portion of the dialog box, you can choose whether the fields in the text file are separated by commas, tabs, or some other character (commas is the default). In the Fields Delimited By portion of the dialog box, you can choose whether the fields in the text file are delimited by quotes, nothing, or some other character. In the Delimited Fields portion of the dialog box, you can choose Text Fields Only (in which case the delimiters you specified appear only around text fields) or All Fields (in which case the delimiters you specify appear around all fields). You can also select the desired character set used by the ASCII text file: OEM (the Paradox default) or ANSI (American National Standards Institute character set). If you are not sure which character set to use, leave the option set at the Paradox default of OEM.

When you are done with the options, click OK in the dialog box to have Paradox import the file and create a new table based on that file.

Importing a Fixed Length Text File

If you choose to import a Fixed Length text file, you next see the Fixed Length ASCII Import dialog box.

In the File Name text box is the name of the text file that you chose to import. In the New Table Name text box is the name for the new table. Beneath the New Table Name text box are options for the type of table you prefer; Paradox is the default, but you can also turn on the dBASE option to make the imported table a dBASE-type table.

The lower portion of the dialog box contains a representation of the table's structure. You can edit this structure if desired; you can change the names of the fields, the field type, the starting position in the text

12

file (it's the value under the Start column), and the Length of each column. Note that if you change the length and a column's length is too short to hold the data that's in a record, Paradox trims the record to fit when it imports the data into the Paradox table.

The Save, Load, and Clear buttons are used to save the specifications you use for exporting a file to a separate file; to load specifications for file export from a previously saved file; or to clear the dialog box of any previously changed export specifications. These options are not discussed at length here due to their advanced nature. In a nutshell, you may find them useful if you regularly export and import files. After editing a structure as desired, you can use the Save button to save the specifications you use when exporting the file. See your Paradox documentation for more information on the use of the Save, Load, and Clear buttons.

At the bottom of the dialog box are options for choosing the desired character set used in the text file. Again, you can also select the desired character set used by the ASCII text file: OEM (the Paradox default) or ANSI (American National Standards Institute character set). If you are not sure which character set to use, leave the option set at the Paradox default of OEM.

When you are done with the options, click OK in the dialog box to have Paradox import the file and create a new table based on that file.

A Note About dBASE Files

Because dBASE is one of the two native file formats used by Paradox for Windows, there are no specific menu or dialog box options for importing or exporting files to dBASE format. Paradox reads dBASE files in their native format, whether they are dBASE III PLUS or dBASE IV files. To open a dBASE file in Paradox, use the same File/Open option that you use to open any Paradox table. Paradox automatically works with the file in its native format, and any changes you make to the file are saved in the dBASE file format.

If you need to copy a Paradox-type table to a dBASE file format so it can be used by dBASE or another program that reads dBASE files, choose the File/Utilities/Copy option. When the Table Copy dialog box appears, enter a filename of your choosing in the Copied Table Name text box, making sure to include a .DBF extension. This extension tells Paradox to copy the file in dBASE file format. Paradox normally creates a dBASE III PLUS file, unless the table structure contains a field type that is unique to dBASE IV, such as the floating number field.

Hands-On Practice: Moving from Paradox to Quattro Pro

To provide an example of file export and import techniques, this portion of the chapter demonstrates how to import and export Quattro Pro worksheets using Paradox. If you make use of Quattro Pro or a compatible spreadsheet, you may want to consider duplicating the examples, using your copy of Quattro Pro.

Exporting a Paradox table to a Quattro Pro worksheet is a simple matter. You can try it by performing the following steps.

1. Choose File/Utilities/Export.
2. When the Table Export dialog box appears, click HOURS.DB.
3. In the Export File Type dialog box, click Quattro Pro Win (if you are using Quattro Pro for Windows), or click Quattro Pro DOS (if you are using Quattro Pro for DOS). (If you are using another spreadsheet such as Lotus 1-2-3 or Excel, click the name that corresponds to your spreadsheet.)
4. Click OK. In a moment, the Spreadsheet Export dialog box appears.
5. See the note that follows, and then click OK to create the spreadsheet file.

NOTE: In the New File Name portion of the Spreadsheet Export dialog box, you can, if desired, enter a drive and path name for the file you are creating. This may save time, as you can use this method to store the file in your spreadsheet's working directory. As an example, if spreadsheet files were stored on drive C in a subdirectory named QPRO and you wanted to name the worksheet file HOURS, you could enter C:\QPRO\HOURS in response to Paradox's request for a filename.

12

Once you have stored or copied the Quattro Pro file onto the appropriate disk or subdirectory, you can load Quattro Pro in the usual manner and get into the Quattro Pro worksheet. If you are using Quattro Pro for DOS, use / File Retrieve to display the directory of Quattro Pro files. In Quattro Pro for Windows, use the File/Open menu option. From the directory or dialog box that appears, highlight the desired file (in this case, HOURS.WQ1 for Quattro Pro for DOS or HOURS.WB1 for Quattro Pro for Windows) and press [Enter]. The spreadsheet is loaded, and appears similar to the example shown in Figure 12-10.

Hands-On Practice: Moving from Quattro Pro to Paradox

As an example of a spreadsheet that can be imported into Paradox, consider the spreadsheet shown in Figure 12-11. The sample spreadsheet is typical of a Quattro Pro spreadsheet in that certain fields (columns, in the spreadsheet) contain headings in the form of labels, numeric data, and formulas that result in the display of numeric data.

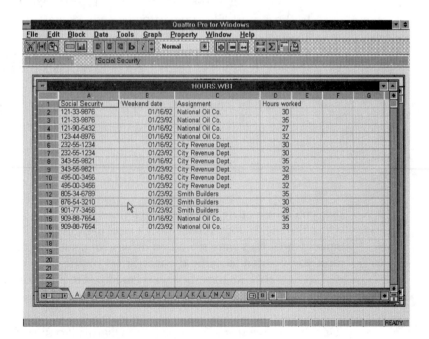

The HOURS Table in the Quattro Pro worksheet
Figure 12-10.

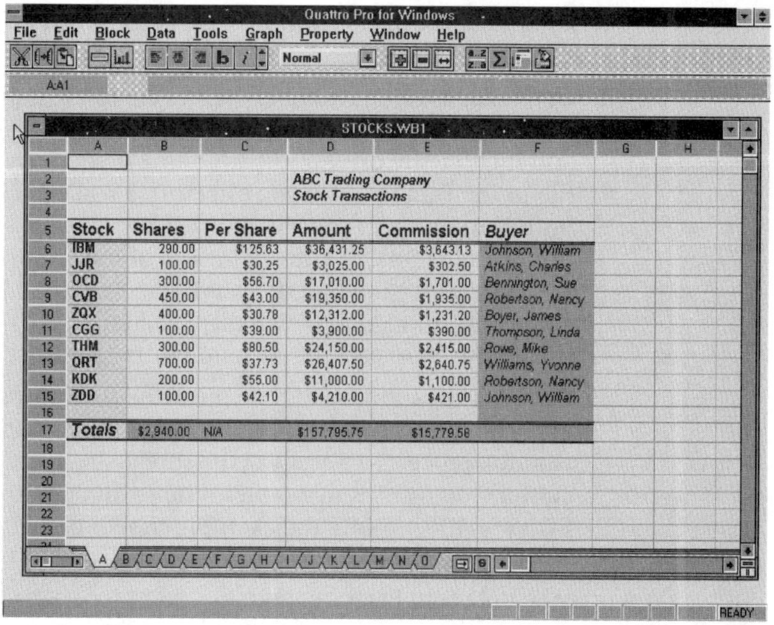

Sample Quattro
Pro spreadsheet
Figure 12-11.

In the example, the figures in columns B and C are actual values, but the figures in columns D and E are calculated from formulas entered in those columns. Columns A and F contain labels, or text entries. The totals and averages at the bottom of the spreadsheet are also based on formulas stored in cells at the bottom of the spreadsheet. When Paradox converts the spreadsheet to a Paradox table, the necessary calculations stored in the spreadsheet formulas are performed for the existing data within the spreadsheet. The Paradox table that results from the conversion does not contain Quattro Pro formulas. Instead, the Paradox table contains the numbers that appear as a result of those formulas.

Since Paradox can deal with multiple versions of Quattro Pro, you do not need to prepare the Quattro Pro spreadsheet file in any special way. (This is equally true of files created by various versions of Lotus 1-2-3.) To make the file easier to locate, you may want to copy the file from your Quattro Pro data disk or Quattro Pro subdirectory into the PDOXWIN\SAMPLE subdirectory. Perform the following steps to import a spreadsheet file:

12

1. Choose File/Utilities/Import. This causes the File Import dialog box to appear.

2. In the File Name text box, type the complete name of your spreadsheet file. (Include the extension used by your spreadsheet, and include the drive and path name if you have not copied the file to the Paradox working directory.) You can click on the Browse button to bring up the File Browser if you want to search another drive or directory. If you are unsure of the spelling for the filename, you can enter an asterisk and a period followed by the extension, and Paradox will display all files with that extension; then, you can pick a file by name from the list box.

3. Click OK. In a moment, the Spreadsheet Import dialog box appears. In this case, the default options will suffice, so click OK. Paradox proceeds to analyze the spreadsheet, and converts its contents to records in a table. When you open the new table in Paradox, it resembles the example shown in Figure 12-12.

Once the data is in Paradox, you may want to make changes to some records or to the structure of the table to take better advantage of the

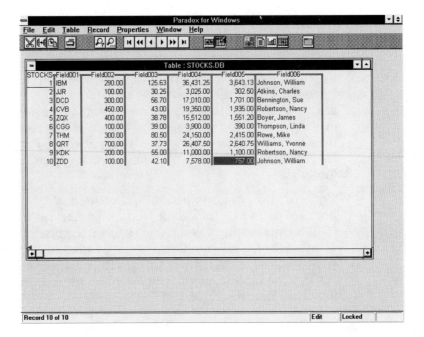

Stocks
spreadsheet
imported into
Paradox table
Figure 12-12.

capabilities of Paradox. By default, Paradox uses any labels in the first row of the imported spreadsheet as field names. If cells in those rows are blank, Paradox substitutes the default field names Field-1, Field-2, Field-3, and so on. You can modify the structure of the table if desired, changing any field names to ones you may prefer.

You may also want to delete certain records from the Paradox database. Any rows in the spreadsheet that contained other descriptive text for the columns will appear as unwanted records in the Paradox table. You can easily delete these records by getting into Edit Mode by pressing ⌷F9⌷, and then pressing the ⌷Ctrl⌷+⌷Del⌷ key combination while the cursor is at an unwanted record to delete the record.

Helpful Hints When Importing Spreadsheet Files

You can save some cleanup work with the Paradox database by doing some preparation work within the spreadsheet before leaving your spreadsheet. As an example, any spreadsheet macros may clutter your table, appearing as fields of text. Headers entered as labels above the columns of spreadsheet data can present the same problem if they were not entered into the first row of the spreadsheet. You may want to specify a range of data that contains only the information you need while in the spreadsheet, and export that range of data to a separate spreadsheet file. Then import that spreadsheet file into Paradox and add the necessary field names to the table by restructuring it.

In Quattro Pro or Lotus 1-2-3, you can export a range of a spreadsheet as a separate spreadsheet file by using the File Xtract command. Simply get into your spreadsheet in the usual manner and choose the File Xtract command. Select Formulas from the next menu or dialog box to appear, and then enter a name for the new spreadsheet. Finally, place the cursor at the start of the range of cells to be stored in the new spreadsheet, press the period key to anchor the range, and move the cursor to the end of the range of cells; then press ⌷Enter⌷. The new spreadsheet will be created, and you can then use that spreadsheet within Paradox.

One major advantage of performing this type of preparation before you leave the spreadsheet environment is that if you transfer columns of numbers that do not contain any headings to Paradox, they will be

12

imported into the new database as numeric fields. Then you won't need to modify the table structure to change text fields to numeric fields to obtain proper totals.

Protecting Tables

To ensure security, Paradox lets you protect your tables from unauthorized access. Perhaps you are storing salary records, medical histories, or something else that contains sensitive information, and you do not want any savvy computer user to be able to browse through your files at will. Paradox lets you protect your files against unauthorized use with passwords.

NOTE: You should write down the passwords that you assign to tables in a secure but safe place. If you assign a password to a table and later forget the password, *there is no way to access that table without the password*. Also, it might be a wise idea to store an unprotected copy of the table in a safe place, such as on a floppy disk in a locked file cabinet.

To protect a table from unauthorized access, choose the File/Utilities/Restructure option. This causes the Select A File dialog box to appear. Click the desired table by name in the list box, and then click OK. In a moment, the Table Restructure dialog box appears.

Click the drop-down list box under Table Properties, and choose Password Security from the list. Then click the Define button. In a moment, the Password Security dialog box appears.

In the Master Password text box, type the desired password. Press `Tab` or click the Verify Master Password text box to move the cursor there, and type the password again. (Paradox makes you type the password twice to ensure that you have typed it correctly.)

TIP: Passwords are case sensitive.

You may notice the presence of an Auxiliary Passwords button, used to enter auxiliary passwords for specific types of protection, such as data entry rights, update rights, and rights for specific fields of a table. If you are not using Paradox on a network, you can omit the addition of any auxiliary passwords. With the master password entered, click OK in the dialog box. Then click Save in the Restructure Table dialog box to save the table with its password assigned.

Once you have protected a table with a password, any attempt during a given session in Paradox to use the working directory containing that table will result in the appearance of the Enter Password(s) dialog box.

At this point, you must enter the password before Paradox will allow you to gain access to the table.

Changing or Removing a Password

Remember to close an open table before you try to remove its password.

To change a password, or to remove password protection from a table, choose the File/Utilities/Restructure option. When the Select File dialog box appears, click the desired table by name in the list box, and then click OK. (If you are opening the table for the first time during this session with Paradox, you are asked for the password before you can

12

restructure the table.) In a moment, the Table Restructure dialog box appears.

Click the drop-down list box under Table Properties, and choose Password Security from the list. Then click the Modify button in the dialog box. In a moment, the Password Security dialog box appears. Because an existing password is in effect for the table, the Password Security dialog box now contains Change and Delete buttons.

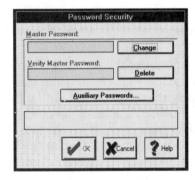

To change an existing password, click Change, and then enter the new password in the Master Password and Verify Master Password text boxes. Then click OK. To remove password protection from the table, click the Delete button to delete the existing password; then click OK. Finally, click Save in the Restructure Table dialog box to save the changes and close the dialog box.

NOTE: You cannot delete the password for a table that is currently open. If you try to do so, Paradox displays a "File Is Busy" error dialog box. Close the table first, then use the procedure outlined to delete the password.

Working with Aliases

Throughout this book, you have been using the default working directory to store the example tables, forms, and reports that you have created. However, as you use Paradox for your own database management tasks, you will probably create additional directories for the storage of the various files you create under Paradox. To help you work with Paradox objects that may be stored in many different directories, Paradox lets you use *aliases*. And Paradox lets you define aliases by using an Alias Manager dialog box, which you can open by choosing the File/Aliases option.

An *alias* is nothing more than an abbreviation for a directory path. You can use an alias to refer to objects in a directory, without typing the full drive and path name. As an example, if your hard disk had a directory named C:\PDOXWIN\ACCOUNTS, you could assign the alias of :FINANCE: to the directory. (You do not need to surround an alias name with colons; Paradox does this automatically.) From then on, you could open files in that directory by referring to it as :FINANCE:, instead of as C:\PDOXWIN\ACCOUNTS. You can select aliases from any of the dialog boxes that appear when you open files (such as the Open Table dialog box).

Before you can use an alias, you must define it. To define an alias, perform the following steps:

1. Select the File/Aliases option. This causes the Alias Manager dialog box to appear, as shown in Figure 12-13.
2. Click the New button to add a new alias. The insertion point will appear in the Database Alias text box.
3. Type a name for the alias. Leave the entry in the Driver Type text box set to the default of STANDARD; this assumes the use of Paradox and dBASE-type tables.
4. Tab down to the Path box, and enter the directory path to which the alias will be assigned. You can include drive identifiers.

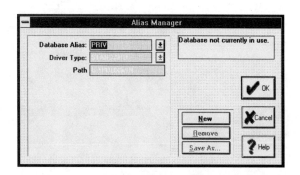

12

Alias Manager
dialog box
Figure 12-13.

5. Click the Keep New button to define the new alias.

6. If you want the alias to last only for the current session in Paradox, click OK. If you want the alias to be a permanent addition to your Paradox configuration, click the Save As button. Then click OK in the next dialog box. (This causes the changes to be saved to Paradox's configuration file, ODAPI.CFG.)

Once you have assigned an alias, that alias automatically appears as one of the possible choices in the Path drop-down list box that is a part of all open file dialog boxes within Paradox. When opening a file, just click on the alias by name, and the appropriate objects in the subdirectory assigned to that alias will appear in the list box.

Using the File Browser

Paradox dialog boxes that ask for the name of a file (such as the Open File dialog box) usually contain a Browse button. When you click the Browse button, the File Browser appears. The File Browser is an aid you can use to search various drives and/or directories for specific files. Figure 12-14 shows the File Browser (yours will look different, depending on the contents of your working directory).

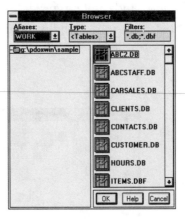

File Browser

Figure 12-14.

With the File Browser, you can easily choose a single file. Click the desired directory at the left side of the Browser window, and icons representing the files in that directory will appear at the right side of the window. Click the icon representing the file you want, and then click OK. Paradox enters the file name in the filename text box that you were in before you brought up the File Browser.

You can also easily change drives or directories. To do so, click the arrow in the drop-down list box under Aliases to open the drop-down list box. When you do so, the list box displays all drives on your system.

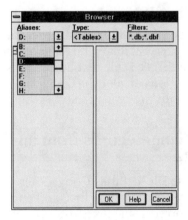

Use the scroll bars, if necessary, to view the available drives. Click on the desired disk drive, and all directories for that drive appear on the left side of the File Browser window. Click the desired directory on the left side of the Browser window, and icons representing the files in that directory will appear at the right side of the window. You can then click the icon representing the file you want, and click OK to close the File Browser window.

12

Quick Summary

Restructuring a Table

Choose File/Utilities/Restructure. In the Select File dialog box that appears, choose the desired table, and then click OK. In the Restructure Table dialog box that appears, make the desired changes to the table's structure. When you are done, click Save or Save As to save the modified table.

Adding Records in One Table to Another

Choose File/Utilities/Add. Enter the name of the source table in the Source Table text box, and enter the name of the target table in the Target Table text box. Choose the options that you want in the Options area of the dialog box, and then click Add to add the records to the target table.

Copying Records from an Existing Table to a New Table

Choose File/Utilities/Copy. Enter the name of the source table in the Source Table text box, and enter the name of the new table in the Copied Table text box. Turn on the View Source Table and/or View Copied Table options as desired, and then click Copy to copy the records to the target table.

Renaming a Table

Choose File/Utilities/Rename. Enter the name for the existing table in the Table text box, and enter the new name for the table in the New Name text box. Then click Rename to rename the table.

Deleting a Table

Choose File/Utilities/Delete. Enter the name of the table to be deleted in the Table Name text box, or choose a table by name from the list box on the left side of the dialog box. Then click Delete to delete the table.

Quick Summary *(continued)*

Emptying a Table

Choose File/Utilities/Empty. Enter the name of the table you wish to empty in the Table name text box, or choose a table by name from the list box. Then click Empty to empty the table of all records.

Exporting a Table

Choose File/Utilities/Export. When the Table Export dialog box appears, click the table to be exported in the list box of table names. Next, click the desired file format in the Export File Type list box to select it, and then click OK. In the next dialog box, select the appropriate options, and then click OK to export the file.

Importing a Table

Choose File/Utilities/Import. When the File Import dialog box appears, enter the filename of the file to be imported, including the extension. Next, click the desired file format in the Type list box to select it, and then click OK. In the next dialog box, select the appropriate options, and then click OK to import the file.

Protecting a Table from Unauthorized Access

Choose File/Utilities/Restructure. In the Select File dialog box that appears, click the desired table by name in the list box, and then click OK. In the Table Restructure dialog box that appears, click the drop-down list box under Table Properties, and choose Password Security from the list. This causes the Password Security dialog box to appear. In the Master Password text box, type the desired password. Press Tab or click the Verify Master Password text box to move the cursor there, and type the password again. (Paradox makes you type the password twice to ensure that it has been typed correctly.)

12

CHAPTER

PARADOX WINDOWS PARADOX WINDOWS PARADOX WINDOWS PARADOX WINDOWS PARADOX WINDOWS PARADOX WINDOWS

13

NETWORKING WITH PARADOX

This chapter provides information that you will find useful if you intend to use Paradox for Windows on a network. The chapter includes an overview of local area networks, requirements for using Paradox on a network, instructions for using Paradox on a network, and general hints for effective network use.

Because of the complexity of local area networks, this chapter is written at a slightly higher level than most other chapters in this book. It is assumed that you are already familiar with the use of

Paradox, the use of Windows, basic DOS commands (including the use of DOS subdirectories), and the network commands for the particular network on which Paradox is installed. Refer to the appropriate manuals for network operation if you have any questions regarding the use of your network's operating system commands.

Paradox and Networks

A *local area network*, or LAN, is a system of computer communication that links together a number of personal computers, usually within a single building, so that various computer users can easily transfer information back and forth. In its minimal configuration, a local area network consists of two PCs connected by some type of cable that allows the transfer of information between the two machines. A local area network allows users to share printers, modems, hard disks, and other devices that may be attached to computers on the network. Local area network users can also share files (such as Paradox tables) and other commonly used software. Figure 13-1 shows how computers can be linked together using a local area network. There are other network wiring designs, but the ones illustrated here are by far the most common. A bus network uses a cable which terminates on both ends, and computers are attached at various points along the cable. A token-ring network uses a cable which, with its connectors and adapters, forms a closed loop. Computers are attached at various points along the loop.

A local area network lets users share printers, modems, hard disks and software.

There are differing designs for local area networks, but all LANs are made up of the same basic components: the computers and the physical cable that links them together. PC-based networks can be classified into two overall types: server-based, and peer-to-peer. A *server-based* network is made up of a combination of servers and workstations. *Servers* are computers that provide devices that all network users can take advantage of. Most servers are one of three types: *file servers*, which provide shared hard disks; *print servers*, which provide shared printers; and *communications servers*, which provide shared modems. Servers can simultaneously provide more than one of these functions. For example, a single server may have a hard disk and a printer attached, in which case it is both a file server and a print server.

Workstations are computers attached to the network that do not normally provide shared resources for other users. Workstations are

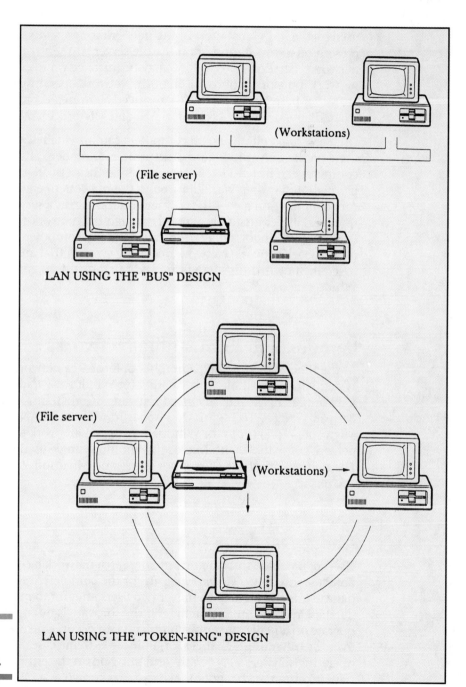

(Workstations)

(File server)

LAN USING THE "BUS" DESIGN

(File server)

(Workstations) →

LAN USING THE "TOKEN-RING" DESIGN

Local area
networks
Figure 13-1.

13

used by the individual users of the network to run software that may be present on a workstation or on the file server. On server-based networks, Paradox for Windows may be installed on file servers of a network, on workstations, or on both. Network operating systems that are server-based include Novell Advanced Netware, 3Com 3Plus/3Plus Open, Banyan VINES, AT&T StarLAN, and Microsoft LAN Manager.

On a *peer-to-peer* network, all computers can provide resources for other users on the network. A hard disk, printer, or modem attached to any computer can be used by all other users on the network (assuming permission has been granted through the network operating software). Any computer on a peer-to-peer network can act as a server of shared resources, if permission is granted through the network software. Paradox for Windows may be installed on any computer on a peer-to-peer network. Network operating systems that are peer-to-peer based include Artisoft's LANtastic and Microsoft Workgroups for Windows.

Paradox and Compatible Networks

In order for a network to run Paradox for Windows, it must use DOS 3.1 or higher and Mircrosoft Windows 3.0 or higher.

At the time of this writing, a number of local area network operating systems are compatible with Paradox for Windows. Paradox can run on networks using Novell Advanced Netware, 3Com 3Plus/3Plus Open, Banyan VINES, AT&T StarLAN, LANtastic, Microsoft LAN Manager, or Microsoft Workgroups for Windows. Also, any network that is 100 percent compatible with Microsoft Windows can be used with Paradox. The network must use DOS 3.1 or above and Microsoft Windows 3.0 or above.

About Database Integrity

Users of database software on any local area network face the issue of database integrity. *Database integrity*, or the completeness of the database, is threatened whenever two users attempt to modify the same database record at the same time. If the software is not designed to operate on a network, serious problems can occur. One user may write over the other user's changes, or, in more extreme cases, the network operating software may "crash" and bring down the entire network. In network lingo, such a potential disaster is known as a *collision*.

To prevent such problems, Paradox performs automatic table and record locking, and also lets users specifically lock files when desired. *Table locking* is when a table in use by one user is restricted or made unavailable to other users on the network. *Record locking* is the same type of safeguard applied to an individual record within a file. Paradox will automatically perform the most advantageous type of locking on any table that you use. In addition to the locking that Paradox sets up automatically, you can use the File/Multiuser/Set Locks option to designate tables as locked or as available.

Requirements for Network Use

To run Paradox on a network, you need certain minimum hardware configurations in your file servers or workstations. The computers can be any 100 percent IBM–compatible computers, with any combination of disk drives. They must be equipped with a minimum of 4 megabytes of RAM and with DOS 3.1 or above (or with DOS 3.2 or above, if you are using the IBM Token Ring network).

A Note About Installation

See your network documentation for specific hardware requirements for computers attached to your type of network.

The actual installation process won't be described in this book, as it varies greatly depending on what type of network you are using and whether you are installing Paradox for Windows on a server or a workstation. For specific instructions regarding installation of Paradox on your particular network, consult Chapter 15 of the *Getting Started* manual that comes with your Paradox documentation. The remainder of this chapter assumes that your network administrator has already installed Paradox on your network for your use. If you are faced with the task of installing Paradox for Windows on a network, you should read Chapter 15 of the manual.

About the User Count

If you try to start Paradox on a network and are denied access to the program, one likely reason is that the user count has been exceeded. The *user count* is the total number of persons authorized to use Paradox on the network at any given time. The user count for your network is the sum total of all counts authorized by the licensing agreement for

13

each copy of Paradox installed on the network. (Whenever you start Paradox, the title screen displays both the authorized user count and the number of users currently using Paradox.) If all the counts available are in use, you must wait for someone who is currently using Paradox on the network to quit using Paradox before you can use the program. To avoid this kind of problem on a long-term basis, you may wish to purchase additional copies of Paradox. On server-based networks, one sure way around this problem is to install a copy of Paradox on your workstation's local hard disk. That way, you will always have access to the program, although no one else on the network will be able to use your copy of Paradox.

NOTE: If a user exits Paradox improperly (such as by simply turning off the computer without first exiting from Paradox), Paradox does not make that user count available to anyone else on the network. To restore the user count, that user must log back onto the network from the same workstation (although Paradox does not need to be restarted).

Using Paradox on a Network

The built-in sophistication of Paradox for Windows lets you use it on a network much as you would use it on a computer not attached to a network. As mentioned, Paradox automatically locks tables when necessary, preventing other users from having full access to them. To share tables with other users, you needn't take any special precautions, other than storing the tables in a shared directory on the network. As you use Paradox on the network, certain operations that you perform will cause Paradox to place limitations, in the form of locks, on what other users can do with the data that you are using at that moment. This prevents damage to a table when two or more users are working with the same data. As an example, if you restructure a table, Paradox automatically places a "write lock" on that table, so no other user can try to add or edit data while you are changing the table's structure.

And if another user is editing a table, Paradox will not let you restructure that table until that user finishes with the table. If a table that you want to use is restricted in some way by a lock, Paradox displays a message in the status bar telling you that the table has been locked.

Paradox also places automatic locks on records as you edit them. When you edit a value in a particular record, you may notice the word "Locked" in the status bar. Paradox automatically locks the record you are editing to prevent two users from attempting to edit the same record at the same time. As soon as you leave Edit mode or move the cursor off the record, Paradox unlocks the record.

Placing Explicit Table Locks

While Paradox does an excellent job of placing locks automatically, at times you may prefer to lock a table manually to ensure that you can access it when you need to. As an example, suppose you have a request to restructure a table as soon as possible. However, you are on your way out the door to lunch and habit tells you that it is difficult or impossible to get full control over that shared table in the busy hours following lunch. You may decide to place a lock on the table now, so that you can restructure it when you return from lunch. To place an explicit lock on a table, choose the File/Multiuser/Set Locks option. When you do so, the Table Locks dialog box appears, as shown in Figure 13-2.

Either enter the table name in the Table Name text box or pick the desired table from the list box. Then choose the type of lock you want by clicking the desired option; your choices are No Lock, Open Lock,

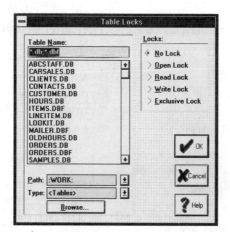

Table Locks
dialog box
Figure 13-2.

13

Read Lock, Write Lock, or Exclusive Lock. Finally, click OK to set the lock (or to clear a previous lock, if you selected No Lock). Table 13-1 shows the rights of network users depending on the type of lock you place.

NOTE: You can obtain an exclusive lock only if no other users are currently using the table in any way (this includes using any queries, forms, or reports that access the table).

Record Locking on Demand

You can lock a single record, allowing other users to modify other records while preventing anyone else from modifying the selected record. Paradox automatically locks a record whenever you are in Edit mode and you begin to change the record. You can also lock a record

No Lock	Places no lock on the table, and removes any locks you placed previously.
Open Lock	Allows you to open the table. This type of lock prevents another user from placing an exclusive lock on the table, which would then deny you access.
Read Lock	Ensures that you can read from the table. No other user can place a kind of lock that would prevent you from reading the table. Other users can place a write lock on the table, which would prevent you from writing to it.
Write Lock	Ensures that you can read and write to the table. Other users will be able to read it, but will be unable to write to the table.
Exclusive Lock	Ensures that you have complete access to the table. Prevents other users from using it in any way.

Network Users'
Rights Under
Table Locking
Table 13-1.

explicitly by placing the cursor anywhere in the record and pressing
[F5]. (You can unlock a locked record with [Shift]+[F5]) When you press
[F5] or begin editing a record while in Edit mode, the status line at the
bottom of the window indicates that the record has been locked. Other
users will be able to view the record, but will not be able to modify or
delete the record until you unlock it by pressing [Shift]+[F5], by leaving
Edit mode, or by moving the cursor away from the record.

NOTE: You can also use the Record/Lock option to lock a record,
and the Record/Unlock option to unlock a record.

TIP: All explicit locks—or locks that you place on a table or a record
manually—are automatically released when you exit Paradox, so
there is no need to remember to unlock tables before exiting the
program.

Who Has the Lock?

On a busy network, you may see a "Table locked" error message while
trying to gain exclusive access to a particular table. To find out who is
responsible for tying up the table in this kind of situation, use the
File/Multiuser/Display Locks option, choose the name of the table you
want to use in the Select File dialog box that appears, and click OK.
Paradox displays a table containing the names of the users who have
placed locks on the table. Unfortunately, Paradox cannot kick those
users off the network for you; you'll have to solve that sort of problem
on your own.

Setting Your Private Directory

When operating on a network, you need a place to store the temporary
tables that Paradox creates (such as ANSWER tables). Such a directory is
referred to as your *private directory*. You would not want to store
temporary tables in a shared directory, because other Paradox users
could then overwrite your temporary tables. If you do not specify a

13

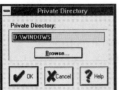

private directory by name, Paradox automatically stores your temporary tables in a private directory it creates on your local hard disk. You can specify a different location for your private directory by choosing Private Directory from the File menu. When you do so, the Private Directory dialog box appears.

Enter the desired directory name and then click OK; the change in private directory will take effect.

NOTE: If you are on a server-based network and your workstation does not have a local hard disk, Borland recommends that you use the network home directory on the file server as the private directory. You cannot use a floppy drive as a private directory.

Viewing Users

Sometimes it is helpful to see who else is using Paradox in a network environment. You can see a list of other users on the network by choosing the File/Multiuser/Who option. When you do so, Paradox displays the Current Users dialog box.

When you are done with this list, click OK to put it away.

You can also see your network user name from within Paradox by choosing the File/Multiuser/User Name option. When you do so, the Network User Name dialog box appears.

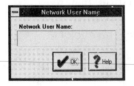

When you are done, click OK to put away the dialog box. Note that if you are not connected to a network, no user name is displayed.

Changing the Retry Period

If another table or a record within a table is locked by another user and you try to make use of that table or record, Paradox by default makes just one attempt to open the table or record for editing and immediately reports that the object is already locked by another user. You can specify a *retry period*, which is a time (measured in seconds) between attempts at accessing the table or record. Once you specify a retry time (other than zero), Paradox continuously attempts to gain control of a locked table or record, waiting the specified amount of time between tries.

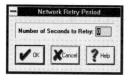

To specify a retry period, choose the File/Multiuser/Set Retry option. When you do so, the Network Retry Period dialog box appears, as you can see here.

Enter the number of seconds that you want Paradox to wait between retries. If you enter 0 (the default), Paradox will not perform any retries.

Changing the Network Refresh Rate

Whenever you are working with shared tables, your screen image may not necessarily reflect the most up-to-date data at a given instant. It is possible that you will view a table and someone will modify a record two seconds after you have opened the table in a window on your screen. Until your screen is "refreshed" (updated) with the most current

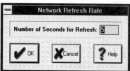

information in the table, you will be looking at slightly outdated data. You can change the interval of time at which Paradox automatically refreshes your screen by choosing the File/System Settings/Auto Refresh option. When you do so, the Network Refresh Rate dialog box appears.

In the Number of Seconds for Refresh text box, enter a value for the refresh time. Then click OK to apply the value.

A Note About File Management Tasks on a Network

When network users of Paradox perform file management tasks such as copying tables and restructuring tables, Paradox automatically places locks on the tables. If you are in that situation, keep the following points in mind:

✦ When you copy a table, Paradox automatically places a lock on both the source table and the copied table. Other users cannot change the data in or the structure of the source table until you are finished with

13

the copy operation. Also, if another user has a lock on a table, you cannot make a copy of that table until the other user removes the lock.

✦ When you use the File/Table Utilities/Add option to add records from one table to another, Paradox automatically places a lock on the target table. Other users cannot change the data or the structure of the source table, and they will not be able to perform any operation that requires a lock on the target table. Also, if another user has placed a lock on the source or the target table, you must wait until the lock is removed before you can add records.

✦ When you restructure a table, Paradox automatically places a lock on it. Other users cannot change the table's data or structure until you are finished with the restructuring operation.

✦ You cannot delete a table if any other network users have that table open. Until the table has been closed by any and all users, any attempt to delete it will result in a "File is Busy" error dialog.

General Network Hints

You should keep in mind certain points to make the most effective use of Paradox on a network. In any multiuser environment, large numbers of files tend to clutter the working space on the file servers. To hold such clutter to a minimum, heavy users who don't need to share table access should be provided with individual subdirectories on each file server, or on local hard disks if available. If users are going to create smaller files that will not be used by other networks users, encourage them to store such files at their workstations rather than on the file server. This will leave the server more available for its intended purpose, of providing shared files. Back up all tables and associated objects regularly, using floppy disks or a tape backup. And create and thoroughly test new tables, forms, and reports at a workstation before placing the files in shared space on the file server. A multiuser environment is not the best place to finalize the design of a working system.

Remember to regularly back up tables and associated objects.

Quick Summary

Placing a Lock on a Table

Choose the File/Multiuser/Set Locks option. In the Table Locks dialog box that appears, enter the table name or pick the desired table from the list box. Next, choose the type of lock desired by clicking the desired option and then clicking OK. (Remember, the options are No Lock, Open Lock, Read Lock, Write Lock, and Exclusive Lock.)

Listing Locks Placed on Tables

Choose the File/Multiuser/Display Locks option. Then choose the name of the table you are attempting to use in the dialog box that appears. Paradox will display a table containing the names of the users who have placed locks on the table.

Specifying a Retry Period

Choose the File/Multiuser/Set Retry option. When the Network Retry Period dialog box appears, enter the number of seconds that you want Paradox to wait between retries, and then click OK. If you enter 0 (the default), Paradox will not perform any retries.

Changing the Network Refresh Rate

Choose the File/System Settings/Auto Refresh option. When the Network Refresh Rate dialog box appears, enter a value (in seconds) for the refresh time, and then click OK.

Listing Users on the Network

Choose the File/Multiuser/Who option. The Current Users dialog box that appears will contain the names of all network users.

Displaying Your Network User Name

Choose the File/Multiuser/User Name option to display the Network User Name dialog box.

13

CHAPTER

14

CUSTOMIZING PARADOX

You can customize certain aspects of Paradox's behavior. You can view and change certain system settings, including your printer's setup. In addition, you can change some properties of your desktop, such as the background used and the appearance of the SpeedBar. Finally, you can change the international settings through Windows. This chapter covers these topics.

Changing Your Printer Setup

You can gain direct access to Windows' printer setup facilities through the Printer Setup option in the File menu. You can choose from among different printers you have already installed under Windows, and you can select different printer settings such as portrait or landscape mode. You can also choose different paper trays, if this feature is supported by your printer.

NOTE: The Printer Setup option on the File menu lets you choose from a list of printers that have already been installed under Windows. However, you cannot use this menu option to install a printer. Refer to your Windows documentation for directions on how to install new printers under Windows.

Choosing Printer Setup from the File menu brings up the Printer Setup dialog box, as shown here.

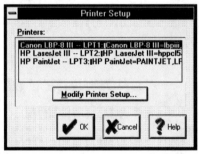

The Printers list box contains the names of all the printers you selected when you installed Windows.

To change printers, click the desired printer in the list box to select it, and then click OK. The newly selected printer will be used until you again change the printer through the Printer Setup dialog box.

REMEMBER: While the Printer Setup option in Paradox's File menu lets you change printers, the control of the printer is actually under Microsoft Windows. Most other Windows applications also contain a Printer Setup option, so if you later choose Printer Setup from the File menu of another Windows application and change printers, that choice will be in effect for Paradox as well.

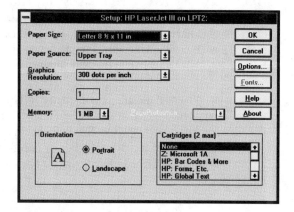

To modify the printer setup, click the Modify Printer Setup button in
the Printer Setup dialog box. This brings up a setup dialog box for the
selected printer. The appearance of this dialog box varies depending on
the printer you have specified. Figure 14-1 shows the printer setup
dialog box for the Hewlett-Packard LaserJet III.

Since there are literally hundreds of printers on the market, it is
impossible to explain all the possible setup dialog box settings in this
book. Each printer's dialog box will contain options that apply to that
particular printer. Some of the more common options that appear in
printer setup dialog boxes are described in the following paragraphs.
The dialog box for your printer may have other options; refer to your
printer documentation for an explanation of any options that are not
covered here.

Paper Size   This list box lets you choose from among various paper
sizes. U.S. sizes of 8.5 by 11 inch (letter) and 8.5 by 14 inch (legal) are
often included among the choices, as are the European sizes A4 (210 by
297 mm) and B5 (182 by 257 mm). Some printers offer an Envelope
choice within the Paper Size list box, which you can choose when
printing on envelopes.

Paper Source   Many laser printers have more than one paper tray; on
such printers, you can choose from among the different trays using the
Paper Source list box.

Graphics Resolution   You can usually choose different printing resolutions, measured in dots per inch (dpi). Many laser printers offer choices of 300 by 300 dpi, 150 by 150 dpi, or 75 by 75 dpi. The higher settings, when available, produce finer, higher-quality images, but take longer to print than the lower-resolution settings.

Copies   When available, this setting tells Windows how many uncollated copies to print whenever a software application (like Paradox) sends a print job to the printer. When you want sets of collated copies, choose the number of copies from the dialog box that appears when you choose File/Print or click the Print icon within Paradox.

Orientation   This setting lets you choose between *normal*— or portrait—orientation, and *sideways*— or landscape—orientation.

NOTE: If you are using a laser printer equipped with slots for font cartridges, you can usually select these from a list box that appears somewhere in the printer setup dialog box. (You can refer to your printer's documentation to determine the fonts that can be used with your particular laser printer.)

Changing the Desktop Properties

You can use the Desktop option on the properties menu to change the title of the window containing Paradox, and you can assign a graphic bitmap file to be used as the background. You can also change the appearance of the SpeedBar; Paradox lets you define a fixed or a floating SpeedBar, and a single-row or double-row SpeedBar.

To change the desktop properties, choose Desktop from the properties menu. When you do so, the Desktop Properties dialog box appears, as shown in Figure 14-2.

In the Title text box, you can type another title to appear on the desktop title bar. The default is Paradox for Windows. In the Background Bitmap text box, you can type the name of a bitmap file, or you can click the Find command button to open a Select a File dialog box and see a list of bitmap files. Once you select a bitmap and click OK in the dialog box, the bitmap image appears as the background within

Desktop
Properties
dialog box
Figure 14-2.

Paradox. As an example, Figure 14-3 shows the chessboard bitmap
provided with Windows Paintbrush used as a background bitmap in
Paradox. (Figure 14-3 also shows a floating SpeedBar at the left side;
floating SpeedBars are explained next.)

In the SpeedBar portion of the Desktop Properties dialog box, you can
choose the type of SpeedBar you want. Paradox lets you specify whether
the SpeedBar will be fixed (attached to the top of the screen), or
floating. If you choose floating by turning on the Floating option, you
can drag the SpeedBar anywhere on the screen. With the Floating
option turned on, you can also choose the options 1 Column, 2
Columns, 1 Row, or 2 Rows. In Figure 14-3, the SpeedBar is of the
floating 2-column variety.

Changing International Settings Through Windows

The default date, number, and currency settings used by Paradox are
actually controlled by Windows. It is worth knowing how to change
these settings, because they are often used in Paradox forms and
reports. To change the international settings, first go to the Windows
Program Manager. Then double-click the Control Panel icon in the
Main window to open the Control Panel. At this point, double-click the
International icon in the Control Panel window. This brings up the
International dialog box, which is shown in Figure 14-4.

14

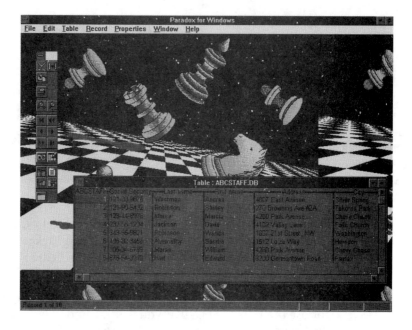

Paradox using
CHESS.BMP
bitmap file and
floating
2-column
SpeedBar
Figure 14-3.

Select the desired options in the dialog box, using the same selection
techniques you would use to select any options in Windows dialog

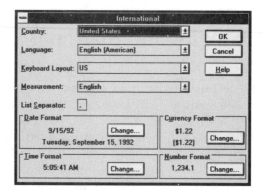

International
dialog box
Figure 14-4.

boxes. The specific uses for these options are detailed in the following paragraphs.

Country   Choose a desired country in the Country drop-down list box. When you do, Windows sets the Date, Time, Currency, and Number format boxes in the dialog box to reflect the standards used by that country. For example, if you select Germany from the Country list box, the Date setting will change to *DD/MM/YY*, the Time setting will change to 24-hour format, and the currency format will change to Deutschemarks.

Language   Use the Language drop-down list box to control the language that Paradox (and your other Windows-based applications) will use when sorting tables. (Many Windows applications, including Paradox, apply different sorting rules to punctuation, depending on the language selected.)

Keyboard Layout   Use the Keyboard Layout drop-down list box to select the keyboard layout used by Windows. Under Windows, each available keyboard layout offers characters for each country's language; see your Windows manual for further details.

Measurement   In the Measurement drop-down list box, choose either English or Metric as the preferred system of measurement. If you choose Metric, the rulers in the form design and report design windows show measurements in centimeters. If you choose English, the rulers show measurements in inches.

List Separator   The List Separator text box defines the character used to separate items within a list. To change the symbol, click within the box, delete the old symbol, and type a new one.

Date Format   The Date Format area of the International dialog box displays both the short date format (right underneath the words "Date Format") and the long date format (directly underneath the short format) used in Windows to display dates. You can change the date format by clicking the Change button under Date Format and then choosing the desired date format options in the International-Date Format dialog box that appears next.

14

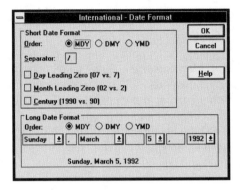

Under both Short Date Format and Long Date Format, you can choose MDY (month-day-year), DMY (day-month-year), or YMD (year-month-day). You can also change the symbol used as the separator in the date format by typing the desired symbol into the Separator text box, and you can specify the number of digits used for each part of the date by clicking the desired check boxes. Under Long Date Format, you can display the date as a combination of words and numbers. Choose the desired options in the list boxes, and then click OK.

Time Format   The Time Format area of the International dialog box displays the format used to display times in Windows. You can change the time format by clicking the Change command button under Time Format, and then choosing the desired time format options in the International-Time Format dialog box that appears next.

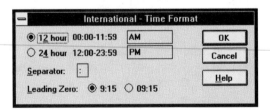

In the International Time Format dialog box, you can choose either the 12-hour or 24-hour time format, and you can change the symbol used as the separator within the time format by typing the desired symbol into the Separator text box. You can change whether leading zeros are used by turning on or off the Leading Zero option.

Currency Format   The Currency Format area of the International
dialog box displays the format used to display currency values in
Windows. You can change the currency format by clicking the Change
button under Currency Format, and then choosing the desired currency
format options in the International-Currency Format dialog box that
appears.

In the International Currency Format dialog box, you can change the
symbol used for currency, the placement of the currency symbol, the style
used to display negative values, and the number of digits used to the right
of the decimal point.

Number Format   The Number Format area of the dialog box displays
the format used to display numeric values in Windows. You can change
the number format by clicking the Change button under Number
Format, and then choosing the desired number format options in the
International-Number Format dialog box that appears.

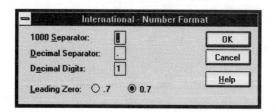

In the International Number Format dialog box, you can change the
separators used for thousands, the character used for the decimal point,
and the number of digits used to the right of the decimal point. You
can determine whether leading zeros are used by turning on or off the
Leading Zero option.

Select the desired options, and then click OK in the dialog box to make
the changes take effect.

NOTE: Paradox for Windows reads the international settings from the Windows environment when the program (Paradox) is first loaded. If you are running Paradox and you make changes to the international settings through the Windows Control Panel, you must completely exit Paradox and restart the program before the changes will take effect.

A Final Note About the Configuration Utility

Advanced Paradox users and application developers who program using Object PAL (Paradox for Windows' programming language) can change advanced settings used by Paradox through the Configuration Utility. The Configuration Utility is a stand-alone Windows program with its own icon contained in the same program group as the Paradox icon. You can start the Configuration Utility by double-clicking the Configuration Utility icon within in the Paradox program group. The use of the Configuration Utility is beyond the scope of this text; however, you can find out more about the utility by referring to the "Configuring Paradox" chapter in the *Getting Started* manual provided with your Paradox documentation.

Quick Summary

Selecting a Different Printer

Choose File/Printer Setup to open the Printer Setup dialog box. Click the desired printer in the Printers list to select it, then click OK.

Changing Your Printer Setup

Choose File/Printer Setup to open the Printer Setup dialog box. Click the desired printer in the Printers list to select it, then click Modify Printer Setup. In a moment, the Printer Setup dialog box for your particular printer appears. Choose the desired options in the dialog box, then click OK.

Changing the Desktop Properties

Choose Properties/Desktop from the menu bar to display the Desktop Properties dialog box. Choose the desired options, such as Title, Background Bitmap, and Type of SpeedBar, then click OK.

Changing the International Settings
Used by Paradox

From the Windows Program Manager, open the Main group (if it is not already open) and double-click the Control Panel icon. When the Control Panel window opens, double-click the International icon to open the International dialog box. Use the options within the dialog box to choose the desired country, language, keyboard layout, measurement, and date, number, time, and currency formats. Then click OK to accept the changes.

A P P E N D I X

INSTALLATION

This appendix provides instructions for installing Paradox on a single-user system. For network installation of Paradox, refer to Chapter 15, "Networking Paradox," in the Getting Started manual included with your Paradox documentation.

Before installing Paradox, check the contents of your Paradox package to ensure you have all of the documentation and disks readily available. You should also have the correct hardware (an IBM-compatible computer with 80286 or better processor and at least 4 megabytes of RAM, a hard disk with at least 12 megabytes of free disk space (20 megabytes is recommended), and EGA or higher monitor). A mouse is not required, but is highly recommended. Also, Microsoft Windows (3.0 or higher) must already be installed on your system.

TIP: Before installing the software, it is wise to make a complete backup copy of your program disks. If you do not know how to back up disks, refer to your Windows or DOS documentation for directions.

During the installation process, you need to have the following information available:

✦ The serial number of your copy of Paradox (it is printed on disk #1).

The Paradox files take up 12 megabytes of disk space. Be sure to allow yourself adequate additional space for storing the tables, forms, and reports you create.

✦ The drive (or directory) from where you are installing Paradox. Assuming you are installing from a floppy drive, this will usually be drive A or B.

✦ The directory name where you want the Paradox system files installed. (By default, Paradox puts these files in C:\PDOXWIN.)

✦ The directory name where you want the ODAPI files installed. ODAPI, or Open Database Architecture Programming Interface files, make up the program that lets Paradox share tables with other Borland Windows products. (By default, Paradox puts these files in C:\WINDOWS\SYSTEM.)

To install Paradox, perform the following steps:

1. Start Windows in the usual manner. (Generally, you type **win** at the DOS prompt.)

2. Insert the Paradox program disk 1 in your floppy-disk drive. (If you have more than one drive, you can use any floppy drive that matches the size disks you are using.)

3. From the Windows Program Manager, choose Run from the File menu. This causes the Run dialog box to appear, as shown here:

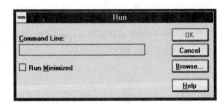

4. In the Command Line text box, type **a:\install** if the floppy disk is in drive A, or **b:\install** if it is in drive B. Then click OK. In a moment, the Paradox for Windows Installation dialog box appears, as shown here:

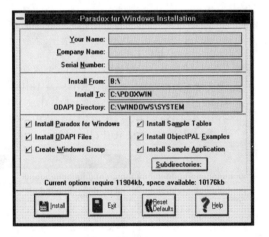

NOTE: If there is not enough disk space on drive C, but there is sufficient disk space on another hard disk drive, change the drive onto which Paradox installs the program. For example, instead of installing the program in C:\PDOXWIN, you could specify D:\PDOXWIN or E:\PDOXWIN in the Install To text box. The installation will create this directory if it does not already exist on the specified hard disk. You can also click the Subdirectories button in the dialog box to change the subdirectories where the sample tables, sample application, and Object PAL examples are stored.

5. Enter the requested information in the text boxes. You can move from box to box by pressing the (Tab) key or by clicking in the desired box with the mouse. Only the Name, Company Name, and

Serial Number boxes must be filled in. Leave the default values in the remaining boxes, and Paradox will use the default choices for installing the program.

TIP: If you are short on disk space, you can click the appropriate check boxes to turn off the options for installing the sample tables, the Object PAL examples, and the sample application. The exercises in this book do not make use of any of these options; however, the exercises provided in the Paradox documentation do make use of these options.

6. To start the installation process, click the Install command button in the Paradox for Windows Installation dialog box. From time to time, Paradox will display a dialog box requesting another disk. When this occurs, insert the requested disk in the floppy drive you have been using, and click OK.

Be sure to read the README file that appears on your screen at the end of the installation process.

Once the installation process is complete, Paradox will automatically open the Windows Notepad containing a README file. This file contains recent information about Paradox that is not included in the printed documentation. You should read this file, and then exit from the Windows Notepad.

If you accepted the default options during installation (including the creation of a Windows program group), a new program group named Paradox for Windows will be added to your Windows desktop. You can start Paradox by opening that program group and double-clicking the Paradox for Windows icon that it contains.

APPENDIX

B

A GUIDE TO WINDOWS

As noted in the beginning of this text, this book assumes that you have a basic working knowledge of Windows. If you do not, this appendix provides a basic primer on the use of Windows.

Why Windows?

In 1981, Microsoft released the first version of MS-DOS, an operating system designed for use with the IBM Personal Computer (which was introduced at the same time). The MS-DOS operating system provided a base upon which users could run *applications*— programs like word processors, spreadsheets, and database managers. Besides running applications, MS-DOS provided needed file management functions for common tasks like copying and deleting files and formatting floppy disks.

MS-DOS served its purpose, but also had its drawbacks. Chief among them included a degree of "user-unfriendliness" due to its somewhat cryptic command structure. Users of MS-DOS had to know how to type specific commands for copying files, erasing files, formatting disks, and so on. To run programs, you had to know exactly what command to type. And the popularity of hard disks complicated matters; with a hard disk, you needed to know an additional series of cryptic commands for navigating among subdirectories.

Windows makes computer use easier by replacing complex DOS commands with mouse actions on pictures of objects.

To make using a computer easier, Microsoft developed a graphical environment known as Windows. The ideas behind the Windows environment had been seen before, most notably in Apple Computer's Macintosh line of personal computers, and earlier in a series of custom workstations developed by Xerox Corp. at that company's Palo Alto Research Center. The basic idea behind a graphical environment like Windows is to make computer use easier by replacing a hard-to-remember series of commands with visual objects that you can manipulate on a screen. For example, instead of typing a command to copy a file from the hard disk to a floppy disk (as is required under MS-DOS), in Windows you can accomplish this task by pointing with a mouse to a picture of the file, and dragging the picture over to another picture of a floppy disk drive.

While Windows has been around for some time, early versions suffered from significant limitations. As a result, Windows did not gain popularity until the release of Version 3.0 in 1990. Because of the ease of use offered by this version and its update, version 3.1 (released in 1992), millions of computer users have adopted Windows as an operating environment of choice. If you are new to Windows, this appendix will help you get more out of Windows in a short period of time.

B

A Note About Hardware

Windows requires a fully IBM-compatible computer with an 80286 or better processor and a hard disk drive. While Windows requires just 2 megabytes of memory and any type of graphics monitor, Paradox for Windows requires a minimum of 4 megabytes of memory and an EGA, VGA, or better monitor.

Windows does not require a mouse, but the use of one is highly recommended. Also, there are some operations in Paradox for Windows that you cannot accomplish without a mouse. For this reason, this text assumes that you are using a mouse with Windows.

About the Mouse

There are three basic operations you perform with the mouse. These are pointing, clicking, and selecting (also called dragging). The mouse controls the location of a special cursor, called the *mouse pointer*. Depending on where you are on the screen while using a given software package, the mouse pointer can take on different shapes. However, when you are selecting items in Windows, it usually assumes the shape of an arrow pointing upwards and to the left.

✦ *Pointing* refers to positioning the mouse pointer directly on an object. To do so, simply roll the mouse in the direction of the object. As you do so, the mouse pointer will move in the same direction on the screen.

✦ *Clicking* refers to pressing the left mouse button *once*. By pointing to different items and clicking them, you can select the item.

✦ *Right-clicking* refers to pressing the right mouse button once. Some software packages, including Windows applications made by Borland, make regular use of the right mouse button for various functions.

TIP: You can swap the functions of the left and right mouse buttons by opening the Control Panel, double-clicking the mouse icon, and turning on the Swap Left/Right buttons option in the dialog box which appears.

✦ *Double-clicking* refers to pressing the left mouse button twice in rapid succession.

✦ *Dragging* refers to pressing and holding down the left mouse button while moving the mouse. This is commonly done to select a range of data or text in all Windows applications.

 TIP: When manipulating a mouse, a surface with a small amount of friction seems to work better than very smooth desks. Commercial pads are available if the top of your desk is too smooth to obtain good results.

Starting Windows

To start Windows, at the MS-DOS prompt (usually C:\>), type **WIN** and press .

In a moment, the Windows desktop appears on your screen, which resembles the one shown in Figure B-1. (Your actual screen is sure to differ somewhat, because Windows lets you place different objects at any location on the screen.) If you don't see the Windows desktop, but instead see the message bad command or filename, you need to add the directory containing Windows to the PATH statement in your computer's AUTOEXEC.BAT file. Refer to your DOS manual for details on adding or editing the AUTOEXEC.BAT file on your computer.

 NOTE: If others have been using the copy of Windows installed on your computer, the desktop may be customized and you may not see the desktop completely open in a window. If this is the case, look for a small figure ("icon") labeled "Program Manager" somewhere on the screen, and double-click on this image with the mouse to open the Windows desktop. If you don't see the icon, press Ctrl+Esc, and choose Program Manager from the list which next appears on your screen.

The Windows desktop is provided by an important part of Windows called the Program Manager. (Notice that the title bar of the Windows desktop reads "Program Manager.") The Program Manager organizes your different applications into groups. For example, Paradox for Windows is normally installed into its own group, and you may have other groups if you have other Windows applications installed on your machine. The default installation of Windows also provides some groups. A Main group contains applications used to configure and customize the Windows environment; an Accessories group contains some simple Windows applications; a Startup group (in Windows version 3.1) contains any programs that you want to load each time Windows is started; and a Games group contains the well-known Solitaire program, and a program called Minesweeper (in Windows 3.1), or Reversi (in earlier versions of Windows).

As its name implies, the Microsoft Windows environment makes extensive use of windows, or rectangular areas, on the screen. Each program that you use resides in its own window. Hence, you could have Paradox for Windows running in one window, while a word processor like Windows Write runs in another. This ability to run numerous applications at the same time is known as *multitasking.*

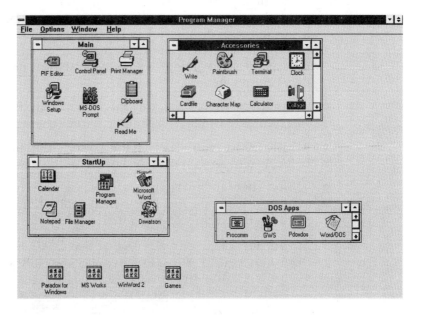

Typical
Windows
desktop
Figure B-1.

TIP: Another excellent way to learn about Windows is to run the Windows tutorial. To run the tutorial, get into the Program Manager, press Alt+H to open the Help menu, and choose Windows Tutorial. Note that the tutorial requires the use of a mouse.

Parts of a Window

To use Windows effectively, you need to be familiar with a number of items commonly seen throughout the Windows desktop. These elements are described briefly here. See Figure B-2 to find out where they appear on your screen.

✦ **Title bar** The title bar forms most of the top border of any window, and it displays the name of the window.

✦ **Menu bar** The menu bar contains menu choices that you can use to access different commands and options of an application.

✦ **Control menu** The Control menu icon appears in the upper-left corner of any window. When you click on it, you pull the Control menu down from the icon. You can use it to control the appearance of a window, as detailed under "Using the Control Menu" later in this appendix. Each Windows application has its own Control menu, and each window that is open inside an application has its own Control menu.

✦ **Maximize button** Clicking this button with the mouse "maximizes" a window, expanding it to fill the screen.

✦ **Minimize button** Clicking this button "minimizes" a window, reducing it to an icon near the bottom of the screen.

✦ **Icons** These are small, pictorial representations of items in Windows. Icons are used to represent applications, files, or other windows that have been minimized.

✦ **Scroll bars** These are bars located at the right and bottom edges of a window. Only when the contents of a window cannot fit completely within the window do scroll bars appear. The scroll bar at the right edge of a window is known as the vertical scroll bar, and the scroll bar at the bottom edge of the window is known as the horizontal scroll bar.

B

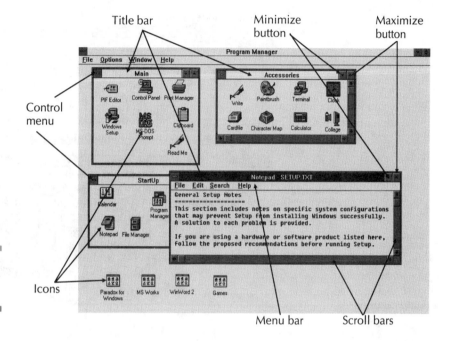

Parts of a
window
Figure B-2.

Window Types

There are three types of Windows used within Microsoft Windows;
group windows, application windows, and document windows. *Group
windows* are windows that contain the contents of program groups.
When you install Paradox for Windows, the program automatically
creates a Paradox for Windows program group. Double-clicking on the
program group icon causes it to open into a group window. In Figure
B-3, the windows titled "Main" and "Accessories" are group windows.

Application windows are windows that contain an application that is
running, such as Paradox for Windows. *Document windows* are windows
that contain documents created by a particular application. Because
they are dependent on the application, document windows always exist
inside of an application window. (Note that some software vendors use
the terms "object windows" or "child windows" to refer to document
windows, and the term "parent windows" to refer to application
windows.) In Figure B-3, an application window contains Paradox for

Group windows

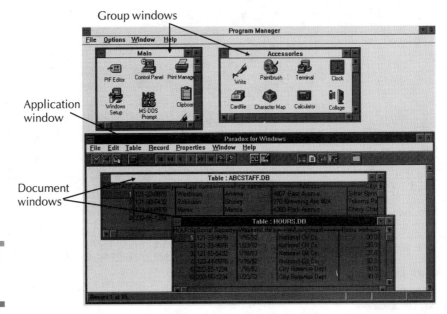

Application
window

Document
windows

Different types
of windows
Figure B-3.

Windows. Two tables have been opened inside of Paradox for
Windows; each of these resides within its own document window.

Working with Icons

As shown in Figure B-1, the Windows desktop typically contains icons
that represent different applications, documents, or groups within
Windows. To examine and use these groups, applications, and
documents, you must first expand the icon into an open window. To
do this with the mouse, simply double-click on the icon. Keyboard
users must use different techniques, depending on where the icon is
located:

✦ If the icon is within a group window, use the cursor keys to
highlight the desired icon, and press (Enter).

✦ If the icon is an application on the Windows desktop, press (Alt)+(Esc)
repeatedly until the icon is selected; then press (Enter).

✦ If the icon is a document icon or a group icon, press ⌈Ctrl⌉+⌈F6⌉ repeatedly until the desired icon is selected; then press ⌈Enter⌉.

Working with Menus

You can open menus and choose menu options in Windows in a number of ways. The most common method involves *clicking* and *dragging* with the mouse. That is, you click on the menu name and hold down the left mouse button (this opens the menu), drag down until the desired menu option is highlighted, and then release the mouse. You can also click on the menu name to open the menu, then click the desired menu option.

You can also use ⌈Alt⌉-key combinations from the keyboard to open menus. Press ⌈Alt⌉ plus the underlined letter of the menu name to open the menu. Then, use the cursor keys to highlight the desired menu option and press ⌈Enter⌉, or press the underlined letter of the desired menu option and press ⌈Enter⌉. As an example, in any Windows application you can press ⌈Alt⌉+⌈F⌉ to open a File menu.

Once the menu is open, you can press ⌈P⌉ to select the Print option of the menu. Note that the letter "P" of the Print option is underlined in the illustration.

If you want to close a menu without choosing a command, you can click anywhere outside of the menu, or you can press the ⌈Esc⌉ key.

Working with Windows

To make the best use of Windows, you should know how to easily move between windows and control the appearance and size of windows.

Moving Between Windows

When you have numerous application windows open on your Windows desktop, you can select the desired window by clicking anywhere within it. From the keyboard, you can move between different applications by repeatedly pressing [Alt]+[Esc]. If you have multiple document windows open in a single application (such as multiple tables open in Paradox, or multiple documents open in your word processor), you can move between them from the keyboard by opening the Window menu with [Alt]+[W] and choosing the desired window by name from the menu.

TIP: In Windows, you can also use [Alt]+[Tab] to switch between the current application, and the one most recently used.

Moving Windows

As on a conventional desktop, on the Windows desktop you can move different objects in various windows to wherever you want them on the screen. Mouse users can move a window by clicking and dragging its title bar to the desired location. If you're using the keyboard to move an application window, press [Alt]+[Spacebar] to open the Control menu for that application and choose Move. To move a document window, press [Alt]+[-] to open the Control menu for that document window, and choose Move. Finally, use the cursor keys to position the window at the desired location, and then press [Enter].

Sizing Windows

Besides moving windows on the Windows desktop, you can change the size of windows. You might want to do this to fit more windows on the screen, or else to view a single window in greater detail. To size a window with the mouse, place the mouse pointer over any edge of the window until the pointer changes into a double-headed arrow. Then click and drag the window border until the window is of the desired size. Note that if you drag from the window's corner, you change the size both horizontally and vertically, while if you drag from any side, you will change the size only in one direction (horizontally or vertically, depending on which side you are dragging).

To size an application window using the keyboard, press [Alt]+[Spacebar] to open the Control menu for that application, and choose Size from the menu. To size a document window, press Alt+- to open the Control menu for that document window, and choose Size from the menu. Finally, use the cursor keys to readjust the window to the desired size, and then press Enter.

Maximizing and Minimizing Windows

Maximizing and minimizing are two special ways of changing the size of a window. To maximize a window (enlarge it to the fullest size possible), click on the Maximize button (it's in the upper-right corner of the window). From the keyboard, for application windows, press Alt+Spacebar and choose Maximize from the Control menu. For document or group windows, press Alt+- and choose Maximize from the Control menu.

To minimize a window (reduce it to an icon), click on the Minimize button (in the upper-right corner of the window, to the left of the Maximize button). From the keyboard, for application windows, press Alt+Spacebar and choose Minimize from the Control menu. For document or group windows, press Alt+- and choose Minimize from the Control menu.

When you restore a window, it assumes the size it had been before you maximized or minimized it. To restore a window that has been minimized, double-click on its icon. From the keyboard, if the icon is on the Windows desktop, press Alt+Spacebar and choose Restore from the Control menu. If the icon is a document icon or a program group icon, press Alt+- and choose Restore from the Control menu.

Scrolling the Contents of a Window

Another advantage of the use of a mouse is that this way you can use the scroll bars to scroll the contents of a window. As mentioned, the vertical scroll bar is located at the right edge of a window and the horizontal scroll bar is located at the bottom of the window. Clicking on the up-arrow and down-arrow buttons at the top and bottom of the vertical scroll bar scrolls the view within the window upward or downward relative to the window's contents, respectively. Clicking on the left-arrow and right-arrow buttons at the left and right ends of the horizontal scroll bar scrolls the view within the window to the left and right relative to the window's contents, respectively. And you can cause a relative movement within a window by dragging the scroll box (the rectangular boxes located within both scroll bars) to a desired location. For example, if you drag the vertical scroll box halfway down the vertical scroll bar and release the mouse button, you will scroll halfway down within the contents of the window. You can also click above and below (or to the left or right) of the scroll box to move within the window.

Using the Control Menu

As mentioned, every window has a Control menu that lets you move, size, or close windows from the keyboard. You can open the Control menu for an application with the mouse, or by clicking the Control menu box in the window's upper-left corner, or by pressing Alt+Spacebar. To open the Control menu for a document or for a group window, click the Control menu box in the window's upper-left corner, or press Alt+–. Figure B-4 shows an example of a Control menu.

The functions provided by the Control menu are summarized in Table B-1.

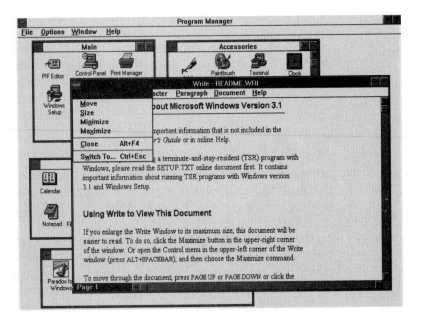

Control menu
Figure B-4.

Restore	Restores a window to the size it had prior to the last minimize or maximize operation
Move	Enables you to move a window with the cursor keys
Size	Enables you to size a window with the cursor keys
Minimize	Reduces a window in size to an icon
Maximize	Enlarges a window in size to the maximum size possible
Close	Closes a window
Switch To	Lets you switch to another application by displaying the Task list
Next	Chooses the next open window within an application

Functions of the
Control Menu
Table B-2.

Depending on the application you are using, some Control menus may not include the Switch To or Next options. Also, some Control menus may have other options; for example, the Document Control menu of many high-end Windows word processors has a Split option, which lets you split a word processing document into two windows.

Working with Dialog Boxes

As you open menus in Windows, you may notice that some menu options are followed by an ellipsis (...). When you choose these options, you see a dialog box asking for more information. As an example, Figure B-5 shows the dialog box that appears when you choose Print

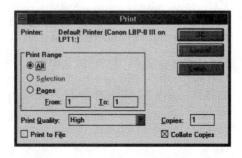

Print dialog
box from
Windows Write
Figure B-5.

from the File menu in Windows Write. (Your dialog box may differ, depending on what type of printer you are using.)

Dialog boxes contain the default settings relating to a chosen command, and they provide an easy way for you to modify those default settings. You can choose OK (by clicking on the OK button or by pressing (Enter)) to accept the default settings, or you can change any of the settings. While different dialog boxes contain different available options, all dialog boxes provide some or all of the following common elements:

✦ **Text box** Text boxes are rectangles that accept text that is typed in response to a prompt—for example, a prompt for a filename or for a numeric value of some type. Note that text boxes are sometimes combined with list boxes (described next), to form combination boxes. In combination boxes, you can either choose your selection from the list box or type your selection in the text box.

✦ **List box** List boxes contain lists of available choices, such as filenames or styles of fonts. Some list boxes are of the drop-down variety; these initially show just one choice. Other list boxes display all possible choices, along with a scroll bar to view the choices. To see additional choices in a drop-down list box, click on the down arrow, or (Tab) to the list and press (Alt) plus the down-arrow key.

✦ **Check box** Check boxes are squares that contain an "X" to indicate when the option is turned on. If the option is off, the check box is empty. You can turn on (or off) a check box by clicking it.

✦ **Command button** Command buttons appear as rectangular buttons with rounded edges. You use them to implement commands or other actions, or to display an additional dialog box. Most dialog boxes contain command buttons labeled OK and Cancel (or Close), which you use to confirm or cancel an action. If a command button name is followed by an ellipsis, choosing that button brings up another dialog box.

✦ **Option button** Option buttons are rounded buttons that you can turn on or off. The button is filled in if the option is turned on, and is blank if the option is turned off.

Moving Within a Dialog Box

In most cases, it is easiest to navigate within a dialog box by using your mouse rather than the keyboard. With the mouse, you can click on any of the desired dialog box options. To turn on (or off) option buttons or check boxes, click on the desired button or box. To open a drop-down list box, click on the arrow at its right edge.

TIP: Double-clicking a dialog box option is the equivalent of selecting the desired option and choosing OK from the dialog box.

From the keyboard, you can move around in a dialog box by pressing Tab or Shift + Tab , or by pressing Alt plus the underlined letter in the option name. Note that you can always choose the OK and Cancel buttons by pressing Enter (for OK), or by pressing Esc (for Cancel). To open a list box from the keyboard, move to the list box using Tab or Shift + Tab , and then press Alt plus the down-arrow key. (The up-arrow and down-arrow keys can be used to move within the list box, once it is open.) To select an option button or a check box, press Alt plus the underlined letter in the option name.

Switching Between Applications

When you have more than one application running under Windows, you'll probably want to switch between applications. There are a number of ways that you can do this:

✦ You can press Alt + Esc repeatedly. Each time that you press Alt + Esc , you switch to the next Windows application in succession (in the order in which they were originally opened). Note that Alt + Shift + Esc also switches between applications in the reverse order.

✦ You can press Ctrl + Esc to bring up the Windows Task List, shown here.

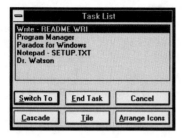

The Task List shows all applications running under Windows. Click the desired application by name in the Task List then click Switch To to switch to that application. (You can also double-click the application name in the Task List; this is equivalent to selecting the application and clicking the Switch To button.)

✦ If the desired application is visible in a window, you can click anywhere in that window to switch to that application.

Using Windows Help

Windows provides its own help facility, which you can use to get help on various Windows topics. You can get Windows-specific help by opening the Help menu in the Program Manager. In addition, you can obtain help that's specific to the Windows application you are working with by pressing F1 while in that application or by choosing Help from the application's own menu bar.

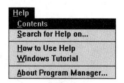

The Program Manager's Help menu offers the choices shown here.

✦ **Contents**   Opens table-of-contents window that displays the available help topics

✦ **Search For Help On**   Opens dialog box where you can type a subject name and then click the Show Topics button to see help topics related to that subject

✦ **How To Use Help**   Opens a window that explains how to use the help system

✦ **Windows Tutorial**   Starts the Windows tutorial

B

♦ **About Program Manager** Opens a window with memory statistics and copyright information

To obtain specific help with the Windows help facility, open the Help menu and choose How To Use Help. When you do so, the Contents screen shown in Figure B-6 appears. You can view more of the contents of the window by clicking the Maximize button in the help window.

You can use the scroll bar to view the full contents of the window. To view any of the help topics, click the underlined topic that you wish to view. From anywhere in the help facility, you can return to this Contents screen by clicking the Contents command button in the upper-left corner of the help screen. When you are done with the help facility, you can close the window by double-clicking its Control menu or pressing [Ctrl]+[F4].

In Windows help, and within the help facilities of many Windows applications, there is a button bar with buttons you can use to gain quick access to particular topics. In the case of Windows help, the

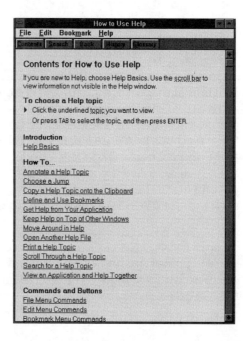

Contents for
How To Use
Help screen
Figure B-6.

button bar contains five buttons labeled Contents, Search, Back, History, and Glossary. The use of these buttons is detailed in the table that follows.

Button	Function
Contents	Displays the help contents window for the current application
Search	Lists all words you can use to search for topics in the application's help facility. By typing or selecting one of these words, you can search for and go to a specific topic
Back	Displays the last topic viewed. Each click of the button moves you back one topic at a time in the order in which you viewed the topics
History	Displays the last 40 topics viewed in the help session. The most recent topic viewed is listed first. To review a topic, double-click it
Glossary	Opens another window showing a glossary of terms. To view a definition of a term, click the desired term

Exiting Windows

There are a number of methods of exiting Windows. You can open the Program Manager's File menu and choose Exit; if the Program Manager is the active window, you can press [Alt]+[F4]; finally, you can double-click the Program Manager's Control menu icon. Using any of these methods brings up a dialog box that contains two choices, OK and Cancel. Choose OK to exit Windows. If you have any applications open, you are asked if you want to save any changes you have made to documents in those applications. Once you have responded to any of such prompts, Windows returns you to the DOS prompt.

WARNING: Never turn off your computer without first closing all applications and exiting Windows. If you turn off your computer while Windows is running and applications are open, you may lose data.

B

Using the Print Manager

All Windows applications with printing capabilities, including Paradox for Windows, normally make use of the Windows Print Manager. The Print Manager is the portion of Windows that manages all requests for printing. (It is possible to substitute a third-party program for the Print Manager; if you are using a third-party program instead of the Windows Print Manager, the text of this section may not apply to your system.) The Print Manager handles print requests in the background, enabling you to send different Windows documents to the printer while you keep working. As you send documents to the printer, the Print Manager stores them in a print queue. The *print queue* is a list of files waiting to be sent to the printer.

Once you have sent a file to the printer from your application, the Print Manager appears as an icon at the bottom of the Windows desktop. You can open the Print Manager by double-clicking the icon; alternately you can press Ctrl+Esc to bring up the Windows Task List, and choose Print Manager from the Task List. Either way, the Print Manager appears, as shown in Figure B-7.

Most of the window consists of the print queue, which is the list of all documents sent to the Print Manager. Above the print queue, at the top of the window, are Pause, Resume, and Delete command buttons for controlling printing, as explained in a moment. Also at the top of the

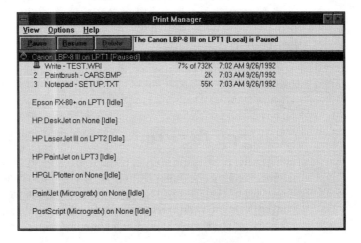

Print Manager
window
Figure B-7.

window are three menus: View, Options, and Help. You use the View menu to change the way information is displayed by the Print Manager, you use the Options menu to change various options for the Print Manager, and you use the Help menu to display the Print Manager's help facility (the menu choices are covered in more detail shortly).

Pausing and Resuming Printing

There will probably be times you need to halt printing temporarily, such as when the printer suddenly needs paper, a new ink cartridge, or a new ribbon. You can use the Pause and Resume buttons to halt and resume printing. To pause a print job, click the print job to select it (if it is not already selected), and then click Pause. To resume printing, click the print job that is paused, and then click Resume.

Removing a Job from the Queue

If you decide to cancel a print job, you can remove it from the print queue. To do so, click the desired job to select it, and then click the Delete button.

 NOTE: If your printer is connected to a local area network, the network operating system software may ignore requests to cancel a print job. See your network software documentation for details on how print requests are handled.

Changing the Print Order

By default, print jobs are sent to the printer in the order in which they are received by the Print Manager. If you like, however, you can change the order of the files in the print queue. To do so, click and drag a filename in the queue to the new location. (Files at the top of the list are printed first, and files at the bottom of the list are printed last.)

B

Closing the Print Manager

To close the Print Manager, click the Print Manager window's Control menu to open it, and choose Close; or press [Alt]+[F4] while the Print Manager window is the active window.

NOTE: Closing the Print Manager deletes all jobs still in the print queue. If you want to remove the Print Manager from the screen but continue printing, instead minimize the Print Manager by clicking its Minimize button.

About the Print Manager Menu Options

The various menu options available in the Print Manager are briefly summarized in the tables that follow. For more details, refer to your Windows documentation.

View Menu Commands

The first menu option on the Print Manager is View.

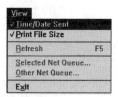

The View options are described here.

Time/Date Sent	Specifies whether print queue should display the time and date that files are sent to the printer.
Print File Size	Specifies whether print queue should display sizes of files that are sent to the printer.
Refresh	Updates the list of files sent to the network printer you are using. On a local area network, Print Manager periodically updates the status of network printers. The Refresh command immediately updates the status for all files that have been sent to the printer.

Selected Net Queue	Displays a list of all files in the queue of a network printer you are connected to.
Other Net Queue	Displays a list of all files in the queue of a network printer you are not connected to.
Exit	Leaves Print Manager.

Options Menu Commands

The Print Manager's Options pull-down menu looks like this:

Each of the menu items is described here.

Low Priority	Assigns a lower priority to printing, causing more of your computer's processor time to be used for running applications. Choosing this option causes Print Manager to run slower, but may speed up your applications.
Medium Priority	Assigns a medium priority to printing. This causes your computer's processor time to be shared as equally as possible between Print Manager and any other Windows applications that are running.
High Priority	Assigns a higher priority to printing, causing more of your computer's processor time to be used for printing files. Choosing this option speeds up Print Manager, but may slow down your other applications.

Alert Always	Always displays a message if a situation occurs that requires your attention during printing (as an example, you are using a sheet-fed printer and you need to insert a new sheet of paper). The message appears even if Print Manager is not currently active.
Flash If Inactive	Causes the Print Manager title bar or icon to flash when Print Manager is inactive and has a message.
Ignore If Inactive	Ignores messages if the Print Manager window is inactive or has been reduced to an icon.
Network Settings	Controls interaction between Print Manager and a network printer. Use this option to specify whether you want Print Manager to ignore the status of network print queues, or whether you want to bypass Print Manager when printing to a network printer.
Network Connections	Connects and disconnects from network printers.
Printer Setup	Lets you install printers, and selects printing options.

Help Menu Commands

If you select Help from the menu, you will see the following pull-down menu:

The following table describes the Help menu commands.

Contents	Opens a table-of-contents window that shows the available help topics.
Search For Help On	Opens dialog box where you can type a subject name and then click Show Topics button to see help topics related to that subject.

| How To Use Help | Opens a window that explains how to use the Help system. |
| About Print Manager | Opens a window with memory statistics and copyright information. |

Overview of Windows Applications

Much of the benefit behind Windows comes from its ability to simultaneously work with many programs. To get you started, Windows provides some simple applications which you may wish to use along with your application software. They won't be explained in great detail here, as the purpose of this book is to cover the use of Paradox for Windows. But they are mentioned briefly, purely for your reference. To load any of these programs, double-click the desired icon in the Accessories group window on your Windows desktop. Alternatively, from the keyboard, press Ctrl+Esc to open the Windows Task List, choose Accessories to switch to the Accessories group, use the cursor keys to highlight the desired icon, and then press Enter.

The Clock displays the time based upon your system's internal clock. You can display either an analog or a digital style clock, which fills an entire window. As with any other window, you can change the size of the clock window to suit your needs. To change the style of display, open the Clock's Settings menu by pressing Alt+S or by clicking Settings in the menu bar, and choose Analog or Digital as desired. If the clock displays an incorrect time, you need to use the DOS TIME command or your system's own configuration utility to set the computer's time.

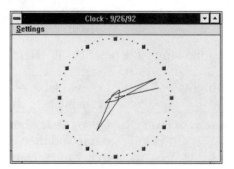

The Calculator provides a desktop calculator with memory. Mouse users can click on any of the calculator keys to enter values or perform operations. From the keyboard, you can use the numbers along the top row of the keyboard, or you can press the [Num Lock] key and then use the numeric keypad on the right side of the keyboard. The plus and minus keys are for addition and subtraction, and the asterisk and slash keys are for multiplication and division. To clear the Calculator, press [Esc]. Note that you can also switch from the standard calculator to a more complex scientific calculator (which is described in greater detail in your Windows documentation) by choosing Scientific from the Calculator's View menu.

The Calendar offers a complete appointment scheduling calendar. You can display a monthly calendar or a daily appointment calendar, and you can enter dates into the 21st century. The Calendar program provides its own set of commands from its menu bar; for more details on its operation, see your Windows documentation.

The Cardfile lets you create a file of cards, similar in appearance to 3 × 5 file cards. You can track any data you would otherwise track in a conventional 3 × 5 file card system by means of this simple, straightforward filing system. The Cardfile provides options for editing, printing, and searching for cards. And you can use Save and Open options in the File menu to save different sets of cards to different disk files.

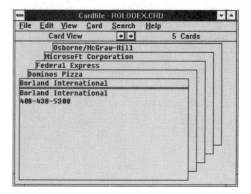

The Notepad provides a simple word processor, with block move and block copy capabilities (also called "cut and paste"), and simple search capabilities. You can save text that you type in the Notepad to a file using the Save option on the File menu, and you can print the contents of the Notepad by choosing Print from the Notepad's File menu. The Notepad stores text as a normal ASCII file, so virtually all other word processors can import text that is created in the Notepad. Note that files created in the Notepad are limited in size to approximately three pages of single-spaced text.

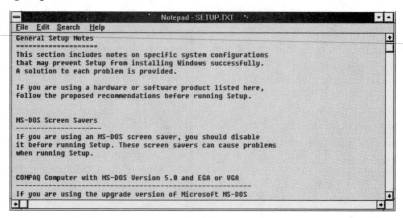

The Terminal program is a communications software package that lets you log onto bulletin boards or on-line services. The Terminal program offers features for capturing files sent from a remote system. Your system must, of course, have a modem to use this option. See your Windows documentation for full details of the program.

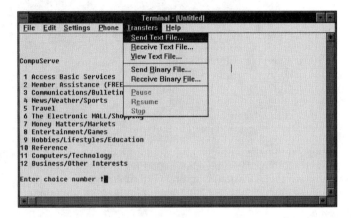

In addition to these programs, Windows provides two fairly comprehensive applications packages, Write (Figure B-8) and

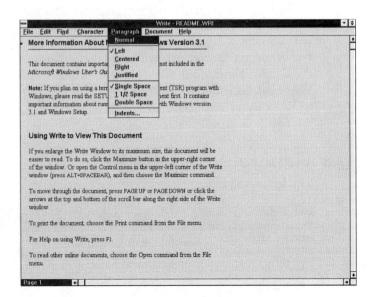

Windows Write
Figure B-8.

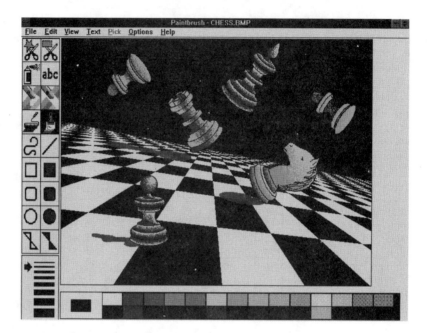

Windows
Paintbrush
Figure B-9.

Paintbrush (Figure B-9). Write is a word processor with considerably more power than the Notepad. You can use Write to create text in a variety of formats and type styles. Paintbrush is a drawing program that you can use to draw illustrations and diagrams. You can save the art that you create to a file and/or print it, and you can also copy it into the Windows Clipboard, and later copy it from the Clipboard into a Write document. Your Windows User's Guide (provided with your Windows documentation) provides separate chapters describing the use of Write and Paintbrush.

General Windows Keys

The following table lists keys commonly used in Windows:

Key	Purpose
F1	Displays a help window
Ctrl + Esc	Brings up the Task List
Alt + Esc	Switches to the next application

Key	Purpose
Alt + Shift + Esc	Switches to previous application
Alt + Tab	Switches to the next or previous application; hold down Alt while repeatedly pressing Tab
Prt Sc	Copies screen image to the Windows Clipboard
Alt + Prt Sc	Copies the active window image to the Windows Clipboard
Alt + Spacebar	Opens the Control menu for an application window
Alt + –	Opens the Control menu for a document window
Alt + F 4	Quits an application or closes a window
Ctrl + F 4	Closes a document window or an active group window
Alt + Enter	Switches a DOS application running in a window between windowed size and full-screen size

INDEX

E

F

U

V

W

X

Y

Function Key Actions That Work with Both Tables and Forms

Key	Action
F1	Help
F2	Field view
Shift+F2	Memo view
Ctrl+F2	Go to next field, stay in field view
F3	Super back tab (moves backwards from one area to another in a dialog box, or between tables or regions in a multitable form)
F4	Super tab (moves from one area to another in a dialog box, or between tables or regions in a multitable form)
F5	Lock record
Shift+F5	Commit record
F6	Inspect properties of selected object (same as right-click)
Shift+F6	Inspect properties of multiple selected objects (same as Shift+right-click)
F10	Menu
F11	Previous record
Shift+F11	Previous set of records
Ctrl+F11	First record
F12	Next record
Shift+F12	Next set of records
Ctrl+F12	Last record

Function Key Actions for Forms

Key	Action
Shift+F3	Page back
Shift+F4	Page forward
Ctrl+F5	Post/keep locked
F7	Table mode
F8	Design/view data toggle
F9	Enter/exit Edit mode*

*When you press F9 while in the Form Design window, Paradox opens the form in Edit mode. This is equivalent to pressing F8 (View Data) followed by F9 (Edit Data).

Function Key Actions in Queries

Key	Action
F1	Help
F2	Field view
Ctrl+F2	Next field, stay in field view
F3	Up image
F4	Down image
F5	Start example element
F6	Check mark
Shift+F6	Cycle through possible check mark types
F8	Run query
F10	Menu
F11	Copy example
F12	Paste example

Function Key Actions for Tables

Key	Action
Ctrl+F5	Post/keep record
F7	Quick form
Shift+F7	Quick report
Ctrl+F7	Quick graph
F9	Enter/exit Edit mode

Edit Menu Shortcuts

Key Combination	Menu Command
Alt+Backspace	Edit / Undo
Shift+Del	Edit / Cut
Ctrl+Ins	Edit / Copy
Shift+Ins	Edit / Paste
Del	Edit / Delete

Numeric Keypad Combinations

This table shows the operations Paradox performs when you use the keys on the numeric keypad. You must ensure that `Num Lock` is off whenever you use the `Alt` key along with a keypad key.

Key Combination	Non-Field View	Field View
`Pg Up`	Up one set of records	Up one set of records
`Ctrl`+`Pg Up`	Left one screen	Left one screen
`Pg Dn`	Down one set of records	Down one set of records
`Ctrl`+`Pg Dn`	Right one screen	Right one screen
`Home`	First field of record	Beginning of field
`Shift`+`Home`	Select to first field of record*	Select to beginning of field
`Ctrl`+`Home`	First field of first record	First field of first record
`Alt`+`Home`	First field of record	First field of record
`End`	Last field of record	End of field
`Shift`+`End`	Select to last field of record*	Select to end of field
`Ctrl`+`End`	Last field of last record	Last field of last record
`Alt`+`End`	Last field of record	Last field of record
`←`	Left one field	Left one character
`Shift`+`←`	Select left one field*	Select left one line within field
`Ctrl`+`←`		Left one word
`Alt`+`←`	Left one field	Left one field
`→`	Right one field	Right one character
`Shift`+`→`	Select right one field*	Select right one line within field
`Ctrl`+`→`		Right one word
`Alt`+`→`	Right one field	Right one field
`↑`	Up one field	Up one line within field
`Shift`+`↑`	Select up one field*	Select up one line within field
`Alt`+`↑`	Up one field	Up one field
`↓`	Down one field	Down one line within field
`Shift`+`↓`	Select down one field*	Select down one line within field
`Alt`+`↓`	Down one field	Down one field
`Ins`	Insert record	Insert record
`Shift`+`Ins`	Paste	Paste
`Ctrl`+`Ins`	Copy	Copy
`Del`	Delete selected text	Delete selected text
`Shift`+`Del`	Cut	Cut
`Ctrl`+`Del`	Delete record	Delete record
`Backspace`	Delete character to left	Delete character to left
`Ctrl`+`Backspace`	Delete word to left	Delete word to left
`Alt`+`Backspace`	Undo record edit	Undo record edit
`Esc`	Undo field edit	Undo field edit
`Tab`	Commit value, move to next field	Commit value, move to next field
`Shift`+`Tab`	Commit value, move to previous field	Commit value, move to previous field
`Enter`	Commit value, move to next field	Commit value, move to next field

* You can only select multiple fields in tables, not in forms.